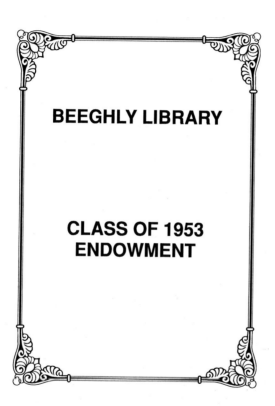

The Radical Enlightenments of Benjamin Franklin

———

New Studies in American Intellectual and Cultural History
DOROTHY ROSS and KENNETH CMIEL,
Series Editors

The

R A D I C A L

E N L I G H T E N M E N T S

of

Benjamin Franklin

Douglas Anderson

THE JOHNS HOPKINS UNIVERSITY PRESS

BALTIMORE & LONDON

© 1997 The Johns Hopkins University Press

All rights reserved. Published 1997

Printed in the United States of America
on acid-free paper

06 05 04 03 02 01 00 99 98 97   5 4 3 2 1

The Johns Hopkins University Press
2715 North Charles Street
Baltimore, Maryland 21218-4319
The Johns Hopkins Press Ltd., London

*Library of Congress Cataloging-in-Publication Data
will be found at the end of this book.*

A catalog record for this book is available from
the British Library.

ISBN 0-8018-5445-8

FRONTISPIECE. This portrait of Benjamin Franklin has been attributed to
the early American artist Robert Feke by Lawrence Park and Henry Wilder
Foote, who trace the painting to Feke's 1746 Philadelphia visit, when Franklin
was forty years old. It is the earliest known portrait of Franklin and represents
him as he would have appeared when he was engaged in the intellectual, political, and literary activities that reflect his complex sense of vocation. In 1746,
Franklin had just begun his electrical experiments and was on the point of drafting his controversial pamphlet *Plain Truth* the following year. Reproduced by
permission of Harvard University.

For David Levin

All the things we are pleased to say "are" really are in process of becoming, as a result of movement and change and of blending one with another. We are wrong to speak of them as "being" for none of them ever is; they are always becoming. In this matter let us take it that, with the exception of Parmenides, the whole series of philosophers agree . . . and among the poets the greatest masters in both kinds, Epicharmus in comedy, Homer in tragedy. When Homer speaks of "Oceanus, source of the gods, and mother Tethys," he means that all things are the offspring of a flowing stream of change.

PLATO, *Theaetetus*

CONTENTS

PREFACE

The scope and the nature of this book have changed repeatedly over the course of its composition, in response to a growing awareness on my part of the complexity of Franklin's early career: both the extent and the subtlety of his engagement with the intellectual and political disciplines of the eighteenth century. Nearly sixty years ago, Carl Van Doren began his superb biography of Franklin by apologizing for the bulky nature of his attempt to fit all the facets of Franklin's career into a single book. Even so, Van Doren writes, he cut his account to the bone. My own excisions are even more drastic, resulting at last in the decision to explore the implications of the extraordinary conjunction of influences that made Franklin's brief residence in London, from Christmas Eve 1724 through July 1726, so formative a time in his life.

In these months, Franklin earned the nickname that, almost prophetically, foretells so much of his mature interests and activities. His fellow apprentices and journeymen at Watt's Printing House named him the "Water-American" in recognition of the strength he derived (as they thought) from his peculiarly spare diet. An interest in bodily mechanics had, in fact, already spurred the young Franklin to study books on swimming and to become a master teacher of that skill. In *Some Thoughts concerning Education,* John Locke notes the special status accorded swimming in the educational practices of the Romans, who ranked it with literacy as a necessary skill for the well-prepared imperial citizen.[1] A titled

English gentleman, accordingly, sought out Franklin as a swimming instructor for his sons, who were "about to set out on their Travels." The elements of nature observed a republican indifference to the privileges of class.

Franklin's subsequent experiments with electricity were, in a similar way, studies of "fluid" movement, the most dramatic evidence of which involved the circulation of powerful electric discharges in the atmosphere. In his later diplomatic correspondence, Franklin comes to recognize a geographical order to the Mississippi watershed, suggesting that the coastal colonies would in time become a single, vast, commercial community in a transatlantic, Anglo-American empire. In the service of that visionary empire, he crossed the ocean six times in the last years of his life, finally becoming in some respects the sailor he had wanted to be as a boy in Boston, when he had distinguished himself among his peers in the construction of wharves and the handling of boats.

But a nickname is the least of Franklin's crucial acquisitions in his first visit to London. The dramatic expansion of his youthful ambitions during those nineteen months is the clearest indication we have that the metamorphosis he tentatively began as a contributor to his brother's small Boston newspaper accelerated rapidly in these stimulating surroundings and took unforeseen directions. Norman Fiering notes in connection with his study of Jonathan Edwards that the period from 1649 to 1759, spanning key work of Descartes and Adam Smith, "may have been the most fruitful epoch of psychological investigation in the history of the West," shaping a new moral philosophy rooted in an empirical study of man.[2] Franklin lived in London in the midst of this fascination with moral and spiritual empiricism. He began to see himself as a moralist and philosopher, a citizen of the liberal public sphere that Jürgen Habermas associates, in its purest form, with the intellectual life of London between the Glorious Revolution and the emergence of the skeptical psychology of David Hume.[3]

Science and political economy engaged young Franklin's interest as he gradually familiarized himself with what was arguably the economic and scientific capital of Europe. Poetry, which his father had once ridiculed him for writing, reasserted its claim on his attention, especially the great Augustan verse of the day, with its inclusive intellectual and spiritual aspirations. Between his return to America in 1726, as Thomas Denham's aspiring merchant clerk, and his second voyage to England in 1757, as a colonial agent for the Pennsylvania Assembly, Franklin secured his fortune as a businessman and completed the expansive processes of self-education that were to form the basis of the diplomatic and political achievements of the last thirty-three years of his life.

My attention here focuses on the implications of Franklin's transatlantic education—the reading and the writing that prepared him to exploit the resources of London at an especially fertile time in that city's intellectual life and apply them to the increasingly partisan political and religious communities of British North America. Franklin's early career as an artisan, a businessman, a journalist, and a politician embodies in remarkably complete fashion the modes of cultural transmission by which the language and the ideas associated with English opposition to an English political establishment gained currency in American intellectual circles. J.G.A. Pocock observes that London was the "vortex" where critics of Whig oligarchy in the early eighteenth century learned to articulate their hostility to authority, where "their consciousnesses were expanded and transformed" by the city's restlessly diverse print culture.[4] Drawn as he was to that vortex, both by inclination and accident, Franklin offers a singularly concrete instance of how a gifted reader might incorporate such an experience and shape it to meet the contingencies of a colonial setting.

This complex process involves more than the movement of books in a transatlantic literary marketplace. The steadily expanding catalogues of the Library Company of Philadelphia during the first years of its existence are one important index of the state of cultural exchange between Europe and British North America in the opening decades of the eighteenth century. Franklin's book sale advertisements are another. I present an extract of Franklin's early cataloguing and advertising activity in a brief appendix to these chapters, in order to suggest what such documents can disclose. But the subtle, assimilative work of readers is the single most vital link in the transatlantic chain of transmission, which came to form what Bernard Bailyn identifies, in his influential study, as *The Ideological Origins of the American Revolution*. And it is as a reader in a library that Franklin first invites us to consider him at the outset of his extraordinary career.

This presentation of himself as an engaged and reflective reader is so conspicuous a feature of the *Autobiography*—and so consistent with the surviving records of his early life—as to make all the more remarkable our modern tendency to associate Franklin almost exclusively with the values of the workplace.[5] Leisure was at least as critical to Franklin's development as industry or thrift, but it was a leisure fully occupied with sorting through the rich intellectual resources that the printing profession was increasingly making available to the literate world. Those resources were neither coherent nor systematically organized by a collecting intelligence. Franklin's first "libraries," it is important to recall, were booksellers' shops in Boston or London, where the full disorder of cultural life was reflected on shelves arranged (as Franklin's own contemporary catalogues suggest) not by subject, author, or content but by volume size. This was an education mediated by no religious or ideological authorities other than the principles and inclinations of the student. Franklin chose his reading as independently as he shaped his diet, with the result that his literary practice came to reflect what Michael Kammen terms the invertebrate pluralism of colonial culture.[6]

In its methodological freedom, this is a radical education. Gordon Wood cautions students of the colonial imagination not to associate radicalism in the Anglo-American eighteenth century with a "beseiged, underground ideology."[7] Wood's reminder has a special pertinence to Franklin's early career. Monarchical and republican sympathies coexisted in the culture as a whole, and within particular individuals conservative and radical ideas mingled with exhilarating disregard for consistency or purity. In his own account of the "radical criticisms of the Whig order" in the early eighteenth century, Pocock approvingly quotes Macaulay's assessment of the intellectual disorder of these decades: "During many years, a generation of Whigs, whom Sidney would have spurned as slaves, continued to wage deadly war with a generation of Tories whom Jeffreys would have hanged for republicans."[8] The student who turns—as Franklin did—to John Trenchard and Thomas Gordon for stirring language in defense of the cause of civil and religious liberty will discover that *Cato's Letters* begin their assault on the English establishment very much in the spirit of disgruntled financial conservatives, enraged over the South Sea stock crisis and the "Murtherers of our Credit" who had jeopardized the sacred "Security of Property."[9]

The intellect was proving to be a remarkably invertebrate and pluralistic entity in the years that Benjamin Franklin undertook his self-education in the "Republic of Letters." Among colonial writers and thinkers, Franklin is the first to sense the imaginative possibilities of this rich intellectual climate, to find formal means of making the apparent disorder and multiplicity of his culture subservient to larger moral and political ends. He was, as he might have put it himself, gifted both at detecting and at proposing "designs." These are the twin activities that, he suggests, first occupied him in the Junto's informal reading room in 1731, when he jotted down the "plot" of his own grand narrative of history. The chapters of this book follow the development of that narrative as it emerges from Franklin's earliest work, steadily securing him, by 1757, a degree of eminence among his fellow colonists that he was able to draw upon throughout the diplomatic challenges of the last third of his life.

By necessity, I devote a great deal of attention to writing other than Franklin's that had a direct and lasting impact on his conduct of life, first in Boston, then in London, and after he returned to America. Much of this work will be familiar to students of Franklin's life, but my purpose in revisiting his reading in Locke, Shaftesbury, and Mandeville (among others) is to reestablish the close connection that Franklin insisted upon with individual sentences as much as with influential ideas. A printer is by necessity a meticulous reader, word by word and line by line. Franklin disciplined his own writing by applying this compositor's scrutiny to the words of his stylistic and intellectual models. Other writers treated in these pages—Thomas à Kempis, William Lilly, John Ray, Sir William Petty—are less familiar figures to the modern reader, but their prominence for Franklin both invites and rewards the same compositor's attentiveness.

Franklin's self-education did not abruptly stop, of course, in 1726. So many books circulated through Franklin's Philadelphia print shop that he had occasionally to run advertisements in the *Pennsylvania Gazette* to determine who owned some book in his possession or who had borrowed a prized volume of his own. It is more than simply expedient, however, to remember Poor Richard's maxim of 1738: Read much, but not many books.[10] Intellectual curiosity should be selective as well as energetic, intense as much as encyclopedic. Lord Shaftesbury's *Soliloquy; or, Advice to an Author* instructed Franklin on the distinction between being well read and reading many authors. The surviving records of Franklin's life indicate that a sensible basis for treating his intellectual and literary development would be a reconstruction of the educational significance of the months in London and the impact of those months on the years in which Franklin established his reputation and authority.

In studying Franklin's literary development, I have been guided by a few principles, in addition to simple affection and respect for my subject. The first of these is that Franklin is in no sense our contemporary. This statement may seem to be purely a matter of fact, but Franklin is often called to account as a precursor for variously identified deficiencies of our own day: expedient materialism, pragmatic guile, the manipulation of image over substance, metaphysical shallowness, imperialistic politics.[11] A little study very quickly discloses that, in fact, Franklin is much less materialistic, guileful, or secular than modern commentators often take him to be. He is really no one's contemporary, as William Blake would astutely perceive when he associated Franklin with the apocalyptic mythology of his own revolutionary (and conservative) verse. Blending elements of the fifteenth-century spiritual discipline of Thomas à Kempis with the journalistic energy of Daniel Defoe, the urbane reason of Lord Shaftesbury with the scientific initiative of Thomas Edison, Franklin places exceptional demands on the historical imagination of his readers—demands that are inevitably slighted by writers who emphasize only one set of interests or one facet of a complex temperament.

A second guiding principle in these pages recognizes that the biographical, historical, and textual scholarship on Franklin have greatly outstripped literary criticism in their contributions to an understanding and appreciation of Franklin's accomplishments. The *Autobiography* has engrossed the attention of literary critics and literary historians, even to the point of serving as the filter through which much of Franklin's earlier work is to be seen and sifted. *A Dissertation on Liberty and Necessity, Pleasure and Pain,* which Franklin wrote in London when he was nineteen, becomes a discredited and discreditable document because the sixty-five-year-old autobiographer suggests that we dismiss it. The "Articles of Belief and Acts of Religion" becomes less important than the project for achieving moral perfection because the latter is examined at length in the admittedly fragmentary *Autobiography,* which mentions the former only in passing. There are distinguished exceptions to this rule of inverted perception in Franklin studies, but by and large critical ingenuity has focused on the *Autobiography* alone, assuming (as Mitchell Breitwieser does) that the bulk of Franklin's output is perfectly lucid and requires very little explication.[12] In fact, it has the charged lucidity of a fully saturated laboratory solution, requiring only the slightest application of critical terms to precipitate the rich configuration of ideas that it contains.

No other writer in Franklin's time had so complete and extensive an experience of what Alvin Kernan describes as the implications of living in a print culture. Not even Samuel Johnson's Grub Street education could match Franklin's thorough professional acquaintance with the technology and the business of printing and publishing, with the emerging authority of the common reader as well as the common speaker, for whom access to the press was infinitely more available than access to the forums of power in an "oral" politics.[13] Robert Ferguson comes closest to a full appreciation for this dimension of Franklin's example when he identifies him as the "master of accommodation" in the literature of the Founders—an advocate of communities of agreement distinguished by Franklin's wide-ranging humanity and his politic use of humor.[14]

But Ferguson is much too willing to see these strategies of consensus purely as strategies of control and to identify Franklin's primary motive as a pragmatic fear of discord, driven by social and secular understanding rather than by religious belief. Franklin began his life with a systematic inquiry into the grounds for religious belief and a repeated affirmation of the metaphysical certainties indicated in physical nature. He was more closely and cordially associated than any of the major political figures of the revolutionary period with the tumultuous forces of the Great Awakening, admiring rather than fearing George Whitefield's ability to energize the hearts and spirits of his listeners. The challenge of how the human character as an agent of good might best be set in motion is the first problem in dynamics to which Franklin addressed himself in life, and it is a problem with both metaphysical and physical dimensions. Government, understood as either a collective or an individual enterprise, does not exist without some sustained social motion to "govern," to steer, to direct. With this examination of the fundamental energies of life, Franklin begins his course.

The chapters that follow reflect the eclectic nature of Franklin's early career in their mixture of chronological and thematic emphases. The first two chapters draw their titles from Franklin's private religious liturgy of 1728 and focus on the literary evolution of his theology of works between the letters of "Silence Dogood" (1722) and his impassioned defense of the heterodox Irish clergyman Samuel Hemphill in 1735. The last two chapters have a similar degree of historical particularity, emphasizing the work of Franklin's last full decade in America. This period begins with his advocacy of the Pennsylvania militia association in the 1747 pamphlet *Plain Truth* and closes with the unusually rich rhetorical texture of his last two almanacs for 1757 and 1758. But the chapters consider this critical decade through a careful examination of Franklin's seminal, and controversial, 1751 essay "Observations Concerning the Increase of Mankind."

The two middle chapters range more widely over the full thirty-year span with which I am concerned. Chapter 3 places the twenty-five-year production of *Poor Richard's Almanac* in the context of early eighteenth-century moral and educational psychology. Chapter 4 examines broad intellectual continuities uniting Franklin's 1726 journal of his return voyage to Philadelphia with the successive editions of his *Experiments and Observations on Electricity*, first published in 1751. All six chapters weave into this portrait of the first half of Franklin's public life a detailed account of how his reading illuminates the rhetorical ambitions of his writing.

I choose to describe the development of Franklin's rhetorical ambitions as radical enlightenments partly in response to the same perception that influenced Henry May to observe that Franklin's relationship to the intellectual currents of the eighteenth century could not readily be categorized in any of May's four broad strains of the American "Enlightenment."[15] If anything, Franklin combines elements of all four of May's groups: the Moderate, the Skeptic, the Revolutionary, and the Didactic mingle in his temperament. It is my contention that they do so virtually from the beginning of Franklin's career, in ways that illuminate the remarkable stature that he was able to earn among his contemporaries twenty years before the outbreak of the Revolutionary War.

This feature of Franklin's mind can prove bewildering to modern readers who are predisposed to see him through Max Weber's lens as an apologist for capitalism and empire. Even a critic sympathetic to radical ideas like Michael Warner, who recognizes Franklin's extraordinary freedom from economic or cultural prejudice, finds it difficult to credit the subversive implications that he finds in Franklin's work. Surely Franklin cannot really mean to argue against the motives of capitalism or in favor of cultural relativism in America![16] My hope is that this book will make Franklin's radical intentions much clearer to the modern reader, more moving and more useful to the pluralistic republic that Franklin envisioned.

ABBREVIATIONS

CMM   Anthony Ashley Cooper, Third Earl of Shaftesbury, *Charact-eristics of Men, Manners, Opinions, Times.* 3 vols. London, 1714.

Fable   Bernard Mandeville, *The Fable of the Bees.* 2 vols. Edited by F. B. Kaye. Oxford: Clarendon, 1924.

Writings *Benjamin Franklin: Writings.* New York: Library of America, 1987.

Papers   *The Papers of Benjamin Franklin.* 30 vols. Edited by Leonard W. Labaree, William B. Willcox, et al. New Haven: Yale University Press, 1959.

Spectator *The Spectator.* 8 vols. London, 1897.

NOTE: Irregularities in spelling, capitalization, and punctuation, as well as the use of emphatic italics, occurring in quoted passages reflect eighteenth-century printing practices.

The Radical Enlightenments of Benjamin Franklin

INTRODUCTION

In 1793, William Blake dramatized a central political and conceptual transformation of eighteenth-century life when the hero of his visionary poem "America: A Prophecy" shatters the "heavy iron chain" of Albion's authority. Orc, the spirit of revolution, rises from the ocean to proclaim the end of empire:

Solemn heave the Atlantic waves between the gloomy nations,
Swelling, belching from its deeps, red clouds & raging Fires.
Albion is sick! America faints! enrag'd the Zenith grew.
As human blood shooting its veins all round the orbed heaven,
Red rose the clouds from the Atlantic in vast wheels of blood,
And in the red clouds rose a Wonder o'er the Atlantic sea,
Intense! naked! a Human fire fierce glowing, as the wedge
Of iron heated in the furnace: his terrible limbs were fire,
With myriads of cloudy terrors, banners dark, & towers
Surrounded: heat but not light went thro' the murky atmosphere.

The King of England looking westward trembles at the vision.[1]

The newborn "Wonder" appears as a colossal atmospheric projection of the human circulation, glowing like a comet in the night sky, casting "beams of blood" on the "temple" of English power, and announcing its doom in a line Blake drew directly from the last plates of *The Marriage of*

Heaven and Hell: "For Empire is no more, and now the Lion & Wolf shall cease."[2] The thunderous voice with which Orc pronounces this sentence arouses Albion's Angel to a celestial combat calmly witnessed by some of America's revolutionary heroes, whose names Blake weaves into his rolling fourteeners: "Washington, Franklin, Paine and Warren, Allen, Gates, and Lee."

The drama of the poem begins with a similar group of representative Americans witnessing the arrogant display of Albion's Guardian Prince, but it is primarily Franklin's scientific prominence, rather than the political and military achievements of his contemporaries, that incites Blake's imagination in the marvelous "Spectre" of Orc. The atmosphere of the vision is hot, murky, electrically charged, and though Orc's prophecy is of dawn, "a fresher morning," his words and his presence are a lightning stroke, crushing "That stony law" of the old commandments and replacing it with an affirmative faith in the sacredness of the common:

> For every thing that lives is holy, life delights in life;
> Because the soul of sweet delight can never be defil'd.
> Fires inwrap the earthly globe, yet man is not consum'd.[3]

The fiery Old Testament trial of Shadrach, Meshach, and Abednego influenced Blake in this last image, along with the foretold fires of the biblical apocalypse whose judgmental fury Blake repudiates. But the figure of Benjamin Franklin, unconsumed by atmospheric electrical fire on the banks of the Schuylkill, is the most striking contemporary analogue for Orc's hopeful picture of human triumph. Of the revolutionary heroes whom Blake cites in his poem, it is Franklin who best understands and best represents this fertile relationship between a new science and a new politics, who dramatizes most fully and effectively the destruction of a stony law in the religious imagination, and who enacts across the full range of his work the delight of life in life. Blake's lines are in many respects a figurative representation of the achievements of Benjamin Franklin—achievements that Franklin himself understood to be as much metaphorical as political or scientific. They were, in other words, a writer's achievements.

In a lifetime essentially coterminous with the eighteenth century, Franklin's interests and experience embraced the full scope of intellectual investigation in his day: religion, economics, science, politics. More than any other single figure in Anglo-American culture, he addressed himself to all four of these broad areas of thought, making significant written contributions in all of them, in a prose style (and through forms or vehicles) calculated to reflect the central preoccupation of his contemporaries with motion and change, the forces finally embodied so explosively in William Blake's Orc. To an extraordinary degree, in fact, Franklin was able to turn his attention in life first to matters of religion, then to economics, science, and politics, in ever-widening orbits of complexity, settling with himself first the private issues of belief and the material necessities of existence before turning outward to a study of the natural world and its human communities.

That he was able to proceed with any success at all along such a systematic path was due in large measure to the accidents of colonial isolation. England was at war with France or France's allies for much of the first half of the eighteenth century. These conflicts inevitably spilled over into colonial warfare as well, but vast distances and natural obstacles ensured that at least until the late 1750s imperial warfare in North America did not radically disrupt colonial life.[4] Once he was settled in Philadelphia, Franklin was able to witness the chaos of human affairs without suffering significantly from it, at least until his career as an amateur scientist was foreshortened by the pressing political needs of Pennsylvania.

But the protective insulation of provincial existence does not completely account for the successive stages of Franklin's development. He was raised in a household in Boston that recognized and instilled the priorities of Puritan culture: the chief end of man is to glorify God; the proper origin of all public effort is private piety. Religion is not the business of the end of life but of life's beginning, the only foundation upon which adult existence can be safely built. Franklin organized his secular career in a way that Cotton Mather would have found familiar, establishing his "Articles of Belief" and his modes of worship as the basis for a life of works. In the ordering of his existence, he fell as a matter of course into a traditional pattern.

At the same time, the orderly implications of a pattern fit Franklin's historical and literary experience only if the pattern moves, circulates, and recirculates through its phases and stages. Indeed, this veteran compiler of almanacs would probably have acknowledged, in the vicissitudes of his career, elements of the traditional analogy to the seasons of human life. James Thomson's poem—like Antonio Vivaldi's *Il Quatro Siento*—reflects an eighteenth-century passion for seasonal change as a metaphor and framework for understanding virtually all natural and cultural processes. Passages from *The Seasons* appear frequently in *Poor Richard's Almanac,* and Franklin explained to William Strahan in 1745 that Thomson's work had restored his lost "Relish" for poetry: "That charming Poet has brought more Tears of Pleasure into my Eyes than all I ever read before. I wish it were in my Power to return him any Part of the Joy he has given me" (*Papers,* 3:14). This enthusiasm for Thomson—Franklin placed a standing order with Strahan, his London book supplier, for a dozen copies of "Whatever Thomson writes"—stemmed not from a streak of seasonal fatalism but from a love of movement and change, the essential ingredients of Thomson's poetic meditations. Franklin was hungry for "whatever" Thomson produced, not for formulas of cyclic reassurance or the balanced architecture of stability that Anne Bradstreet celebrates in her *Quaternions* of late renaissance culture: the four humors, the four elements, the four seasons, the four "empires" of recorded history. That kind of symmetrical fixity was not the bill of fare to excite Franklin's relish.

In the same letter in which he praises Thomson, Franklin also urges Strahan not to be "too nice," too particular or too discriminating, in the selection of political and philosophical pamphlets he forwards from London: "Let me have everything, good or bad, that makes a Noise and has a Run: for I have friends here of Different Tastes to oblige with the Sight of them." A printer, newspaper publisher, writer, and scientist, Franklin had a practical and liberating grasp of the extent to which interlocking systems of movement shaped the behavior of earthly bodies, just as dramatically as Newton's laws of motion described the behavior of celestial ones. The noise and run of the London press would bring energy and movement to Philadelphia. They were the vehicles of provincial friendship that addressed a spectrum of opinion, food for different tastes, expressions of life.

The goodness or badness of Strahan's pamphlet selections—on political, literary, or moral grounds—mattered little to Franklin simply because their motion secured their nature: whatever had energy would "oblige" the sight of Franklin's circle as part of a universal system of movement, just as the sight, sound, and smell of an electrical discharge from a glass tube or a Leyden jar would soon oblige the same circle of curious acquaintances in Franklin's home with vivid evidence of the noise and run of the invisible electrical "fluid."

William Blake's intuitive exploitation of the image of Franklin in his prophetic apocalypse of empire seems improbable if we think exclusively of the late, avuncular sage of the Duplessis portrait or the iconic visage appropriated by a modern mutual fund. The aged diplomat might convincingly play the role of Enlightenment sage that inspired Turgot's famous epigram on Franklin's extraordinary career: "He takes lightning from the gods and the sceptre from tyrants." But what could such a sober old burgher have in common with the intense, naked, human fire of Orc? The connection seems less unlikely, however—and increasingly essential to the understanding of Franklin's example and impact—the more we reflect upon the young man, glorying in his naked strength, who stripped and swam three and a half miles in the Thames near London, performing aquatic feats to the astonishment and applause of his boat-bound companions, or upon the mature journalist who savored the noise and run of social controversy, whether for "good" or "bad." "Energy is Eternal Delight," proclaims Blake's iconoclastic Devil in *The Marriage of Heaven and Hell*.[5] Franklin's life, in all of its distinct phases or stages, is the fullest expression the eighteenth century provides of the meanings collected and compressed in Blake's aphorism.

Moreover, Franklin's 1745 letter to William Strahan calls attention to the role played in Franklin's development by a very particular phase in his career. Twenty years earlier he found himself in the very midst of the noise and run of the London press, able to savor its activity directly without relying on a well-placed intermediary like Strahan to keep his tastes supplied. Franklin sailed for London in the fall of 1724 with the encouragement and (as he thought) the financial support of William Keith, Pennsylvania's provincial governor, in order to buy the equipment and supplies necessary to establish himself as a printer in Philadelphia. Keith in fact had little to offer Franklin except empty "Expectations." The letters of credit that Franklin planned to use in making his purchases did not exist. Instead, stranded in London, he followed the advice of a fellow passenger, Thomas Denham, found work as a printer, and in the company of James Ralph began to acquaint himself with the resources of the city on the strength of the fifteen pistoles he had brought from America.[6]

In all likelihood, the relish that Franklin professed to have for James Thomson's work derived from this personal immersion in the literary life of the British capital. The first portion of *The Seasons* to appear in print, the 1726 version of "Winter," was published in London a few months before Franklin's return voyage to Philadelphia.[7] In the midst of his duties as a compositor in two prominent London print shops, Franklin paid enough attention to contemporary verse to permit him to quote some instructive lines from Edward Young's newly published satires on fame in an admonitory letter to his ambitious friend James Ralph. Thomson's new poem, like Young's, was also having its run, and almost certainly would have attracted the attention of such an energetic intellectual tourist. For Franklin was not scrupulously saving his wages to return home, confront William Keith, and console Deborah Read, the young woman whom he had expected to marry upon his return to Philadelphia. He was, in effect, on his grand tour, an interval of independent study and travel that had begun in Boston with the third volume of the *Spectator,* Lord Shaftesbury's *Characteristics,* Defoe's *Essay on Projects,* and Cotton Mather's *Bonifacius,* among other key books, and would continue in the bookstalls of London during an especially significant period in English letters.

Franklin dutifully records among the great errata of his life his neglect of Deborah Read during this period of exuberant tourism, but if London indeed seduced him for a time, it did so by appealing less to his carnal appetites than to his intellectual ones. He remembers in his memoirs "one Wilcox a bookseller" with "an immense Collection of second-hand Books" near his lodgings in Little Britain.[8] Just as he had with fellow apprentices and patrons years earlier in Boston, Franklin worked out arrangements with Wilcox that allowed him to borrow from this tempting inventory. He apparently bought books as well as borrowed them, attended plays, visited coffeehouses where he "pick'd up some very ingenious Acquaintance," and "read considerably" (*Writings,* 1353).

Looking back forty-seven years later, in part 1 of the *Autobiography,* he vindicates his father's refusal to help establish him in a printing business that he was clearly not prepared to manage. He takes note of his ignorance and comments on William Keith's well-intentioned duplicity, but Thomas Denham's advice to what must have been a very anxious eighteen-year-old suddenly at loose ends three thousand miles from home proved both sound and prophetic: Go to work for a London printer, Denham urged, "you will improve yourself; and when you return to America, you will set up to greater Advantage" (*Writings,* 1344). London, for the next nineteen months, would present opportunities for self-education that Franklin could not have encountered in such concentrated form in Philadelphia—nor, perhaps, over a similar interval in London itself during some other year in the opening decades of the eighteenth century. The personal improvements that Thomas Denham foresaw may well have been practical or technical, but Franklin's testimony and experience suggest that much richer influences found in him a receptive and resourceful pupil.

In the *Autobiography,* Franklin singles out William Wollaston's *The Religion of Nature Delineated* as the stimulus that launched him on his career as a moralist. He helped set type for a reprinting of Wollaston's book during his first months at Samuel Palmer's London print shop. But while Wollaston's deficiencies may have enticed Franklin to try his hand at metaphysical subjects, the most prominent voices then engaged in the contemporary debate over the ethical nature of human experience were Bernard Mandeville and Francis Hutcheson. Mandeville's *The Fable of the Bees* had appeared in its earliest form in 1705, as a verse narrative called "The Grumbling Hive." But Mandeville in 1723 reissued the 1714 edition of the poem with an expanded set of prose appendixes, including essays on the origins of society and virtue as well as an extensive critique of charity schools. This volume was reprinted in 1724 and 1725, when it received its most influential reply in Francis Hutcheson's first major work, *An Inquiry into the Original of our Ideas of Beauty and Virtue,* itself reprinted almost immediately in 1726. Hutcheson was not the only writer to take issue with Mandeville's formula of private vice and public virtue, but he was the most conspicuous and eloquent successor to Shaftesbury, Mandeville's initial antagonist, whose work Franklin already knew from his apprentice days in Boston.[9]

For the months that Franklin lived in London, Hutcheson's account of the disinterested moral sense in man directly engaged Mandeville's ingenious but reductive psychology of prideful self-interest. Jonathan Swift's imaginatively vivid and complex portrait of human nature in *Gulliver's Travels*—at once grimmer and more hopeful than Mandeville's—did not appear until October 1726, the same month in which Franklin celebrated his return to Philadelphia, and Pope's *Essay on Man* would not begin appearing until 1733, the year of Mandeville's death and also of the first publication of *Poor Richard's Almanac.* If Franklin's most significant personal acquaintance with poetry led him to prize Young's satires and Thomson's seasonal meditations, an equally personal experience with the dialogue between Mandeville and Hutcheson gave him memorable exposure to the contemporary exchange between moral philosophy and practical psychology.

Franklin had in fact prepared for this direct exposure to the intellectual exchange of London by schooling himself in the collected volumes of the *Spectator,* a complete set of which was available in his brother's print shop in Boston. In the first part of his memoir, written in 1771, Franklin specifically mentions the third volume of the *Spectator* papers when he is describing his methods of self-instruction in writing. The particular contents of that volume would prove influential in the formation of his private "Articles of Belief" once he was established in Philadelphia. But in the memoir, Franklin emphasizes the delight he took in repeatedly reading Addison's volume and almost inevitably acquiring a detailed acquaintance with the social and intellectual preoccupations of its audience.

Indeed, it is easier to get a sense of the succession and range of interests in eighteenth-century London—of the shifting climate of discussion in the city's streets and clubs—from a volume of the *Spectator* papers than it is to understand the acquisition of literary method. Franklin would have done better to practice the arts of sentence arrangement and argumentative order by abstracting, reassembling, or versifying the sections of Lord Shaftesbury's essays. Any volume of the *Spectator* will, to some extent, reflect life's disordered variety in much the way that a true correspondence does. Of course, Addison and his colleagues were more deliberate in their approach to moral instruction than a random collection of letters or a daily gazette would suggest, but the papers as a sequence aspire to randomness as often as to order. Individual numbers usually have the methodical ornament of an epigraph from classical literature and come packed with illustrative aphorisms from the same source, but Addison presents his learning as the casual results of his meditative excursions, not as their focal or starting points. The subject of the papers is, finally, the play of the mind in London and not an ethical or intellectual formalism in disguise.[10]

Franklin's account of the use he made of the *Spectator* papers adroitly emphasizes these elements of compositional accident and variety. What seems at first to be a sign of Franklin's youthful love of method is, on closer inspection, a careful incorporation of chance and improvisation within a private system of self-schooling. In the *Autobiography,* Franklin is very particular about noting the casual way in which he "met" with the *Spectator* papers, not through a deliberate inspection of a numbered sequence of books in James Franklin's shop but by happenstance, encountering an "odd volume" in the course of his miscellaneous reading. His delight in the prose style leads to a series of games in which he disassembles "hints" of the papers and tries to reassemble the sentences in his own words and reorder them into complete numbers. This playful self-tuition, however, only involves "some" of the papers, with Franklin uncovering in the process only some of his "Faults" as he works from prose to verse and verse to prose, jumbling "into Confusion" his summary hints of the contents of the "Tales" and reassembling them again.

Out of all of this mixing and matching, Franklin occasionally "had the

Pleasure of Fancying that in certain Particulars of small Import, I had been lucky enough to improve the Method or the Language" (*Writings*, 1320). This disclosure is carefully worded to emphasize how luck, fancy, and vanity formed the unstable foundation upon which Franklin constructed his youthful ambition to be "a tolerable English Writer." Even this final phrase in the *Autobiography*'s account is skillfully weighted to suggest the emptiness of imitative form. Franklin, as he wrote in 1771, was already among the most intolerable of American writers to the English ministry. He portrays his youthful Anglophilia with nostalgic affection but subjects it at the same time to the contingent forces of accident and history.

A distrust of "formalism" is among the chief traits that Addison and his colleagues shared with Shaftesbury's *Characteristics*. In his *Spectator* papers #185 and #201 (both from Franklin's cherished volume 3), Addison associates the spirit of formalism with fanatical enthusiasm, particularly in religion.[11] Working toward a similar end, the first essay in Shaftesbury's collected works is not in fact his earliest piece—the *Inquiry on Virtue or Merit* (1699)—but his *Letter concerning Enthusiasm* (1708), in which he recommends "raillery," ridicule, and good humor as antidotes to the morose single-mindedness of the spiritual zealot. This letter was among the key ingredients in the dramatic constitution of Silence Dogood, but perhaps more important still to the growth of Franklin's mind and style was Shaftesbury's broader identification of temperament with truth.

Not a method of inquiry but a manner of intellectual conduct is the model that Shaftesbury offers his contemporaries: "characteristics," as his title suggests, rather than fixed principles or propositions. A love of doctrines inevitably produces doctrinaire thinking. This would be one primary lesson that any alert reader of Addison, Shaftesbury, or even the highly doctrinaire Mandeville would draw from a consideration of their books in the contentious cities of Boston and London in the first decades of the eighteenth century. Though human disputes might resolve themselves into clearly opposed schools of thought, human disputants tend to reflect incompatible mixtures of ideas and traits of character that are far more confusing and far less consistent than the terms of the disputes might suggest.

Mandeville and Shaftesbury, for example, oppose one another in their assessments of human psychology, with Mandeville taking the extreme position of tracing all human action ultimately to self-love and pride. Yet Mandeville follows Shaftesbury's recommended strategies of raillery and ridicule far more consistently and delightfully than many of Shaftesbury's most ardent defenders. Mandeville's slander of human nature was sufficiently notorious in the eighteenth century to lead Pope to include his name in the 1743 *Dunciad* under the mischievous spelling of "Mandevil."[12] But Mandeville, like Pope, was a religious conservative who, in a pamphlet on public executions printed when Franklin was in London, advocates turning hangings into the kind of instructive religious theater presided over by the prominent ministers of Boston in Franklin's youth.[13]

In sharp contrast to *The Fable of the Bees,* Shaftesbury repeatedly celebrates what he calls the "moral architecture" of man, but like Mandeville he also recognizes that the passions and thoughts of human beings are compound forms, incorporating significant elements of vanity or self-love even in the most apparently disinterested actions. Modern scholars often willfully misread Shaftesbury's successor, Francis Hutcheson, when Hutcheson tries to illustrate human motives by drafting moral "equations" to represent the degrees of self-interest and disinterested goodwill that combine to shape any human action. Hutcheson confesses that his moral algebra seems "extravagant and wild," but even as he makes this concession in his *Inquiry into ... Beauty and Virtue,* he does not completely repudiate the attempt to form a calculus of benevolence. Some day, he thinks, such measurements may be possible. But in proposing an ethical algebra, Hutcheson insists that moral heroism is independent of social station, public prominence, and individual talents. These factors he arranges in such a way that they neutralize one another; his only "algebraic" certainty declares that moral heroism, wherever it occurs, is always a compound of benevolence and self-interest.[14]

When Mandeville, in "Remark N" of his prose commentary on *The Fable of the Bees,* traces "love" to its source in what he calls "our darling Passion, Lust," he is indulging a flair for the outrageously reductive comment that earned him his reputation for being what Franklin terms "a most facetious entertaining Companion" in the London coffeehouses where Franklin met him. But Mandeville goes on in his prose remark to establish more clearly what he means: Love is "an adulterated Appetite, or rather a Compound, a heap of several contradictory Passions blended in one," all of which tend to make the effects of love "so different, whimsical, surprising and unaccountable" (*Fable,* 1:146). If there was wide agreement throughout the seventeenth and eighteenth centuries on the pervasive influence of what A. O. Lovejoy terms "approbativeness," or the love of praise, in human character, an equally broad consensus existed on the image of human character as an adulterated compound, a heap of contradictions.[15]

Franklin's experience and his reading in Boston, Philadelphia, and London prepared him to make the most of this vision of a compound and contradictory humanity, to imitate and then to extend the elements of dramatic agreement that he found among writers who customarily defined themselves, or were perceived by others, simply as opponents. His first exposure to these paradoxes of controversy, during the inoculation debates in Boston in 1721 and 1722, would have instructed a youthful reader of Shaftesbury, for example, in the extraordinary pertinence of the analogy that Shaftesbury draws in the *Letter concerning Enthusiasm* between physical and mental epidemics:

> The Human Mind and Body are both of 'em naturally subject to Commotions: and as there are strange Ferments in the Blood, which in many Bodys occasion an extraordinary Discharge; so in Reason too, there are heterogeneous Particles which must be thrown off by Fermentation. Shou'd Physicians endeavour absolutely to allay those Ferments of the Body, and strike in the Humours which discover themselves in such Eruptions, they might, instead of making a Cure, bid fair perhaps to raise a Plague, and turn a Spring-Ague or an Autumn-Surfeit into an epidemical malignant Fever. They are certainly as ill Physicians in the *Body-Politick,* who wou'd needs be tampering with these mental Eruptions; and under the specious pretence of healing this Itch of Superstition, and saving Souls from the Contagion of Enthusiasm, shou'd set all Nature in an uproar, and turn a few innocent Carbuncles into an Inflammation and mortal Gangrene. (*CMM,* 1:14)

The commotions in the body politic of Boston during its smallpox outbreak were sufficiently intense to turn apparent revolutionaries like James Franklin and his upstart newspaper into the champions of an alliance between conservative science and blind superstition. At the same time, an apparently conservative figure of authority—Cotton Mather—emerged as a bold defender of a revolutionary medical technique that he had confidence in partly because of the testimony about folk remedies that he had gathered from his black servant.[16]

These are the whimsical, surprising, unaccountable results of a heap of contradictory passions, in the midst of which Benjamin Franklin emerges into the print record for the first time with many of the marks of comic tolerance that are evident in Shaftesbury's advice against society's ill physicians—those who are little better than enthusiasts inflaming the contagion of enthusiasm.

From an intellectual standpoint, then, Franklin had begun to live in London long before he had left Boston. He had done much of the reading and thinking necessary for the controversy between Mandeville and Hutcheson to be meaningful. He had begun his lifelong experiment in the projection of a journalistic voice, with a full awareness of the stakes involved among a community of readers who viewed "character" not as a mere rhetorical device or convention of print but as the most urgent of literary, philosophical, and religious subjects. Steven Shapin makes clear in his study of the example of Robert Boyle that seventeenth-century thinkers, and their eighteenth-century heirs, understood character as both an individual construction and a communal resource. It formed the basis for what Daniel Defoe repeatedly celebrates as the complete tradesman's "credit," and it was an indispensable element of social and intellectual cohesion in the expansive commercial and political worlds of the early modern era.[17]

The letters of Silence Dogood reflect Franklin's emerging grasp of the potential of character—understood as a dramatic compound rather than a normative statement—to accommodate the range of human display, to seize the imagination of a reading public, to make a noise and have a run in the service of the widest understanding of charity. To exercise an influence for good involved much more than simply chastising vice or applauding virtue. Those functions had their importance for Franklin's ethical and spiritual imagination but never at the expense of a generous conviction, gleaned from his eclectic reading, that the human individual was a multiple, and not a monolithic, entity.

The *New England Courant* and the Dogood letters both begin with Addisonian self-introductions out of a desire to emulate the practice of the *Spectator* series, but more than a mannerism is involved in this gesture of provincial mimicry. As Shaftesbury's medical analogy suggests, these were times of literal and figurative infection, spread by mysterious means with results that were often catastrophic. Both London and Boston suffered severe smallpox epidemics in 1721 and 1722. Reports of plague spreading from Turkey to southern France agitated the contemporary English press and were reprinted in some of the same numbers of the *Courant* that carried Silence Dogood's letters.[18] Daniel Defoe—already one of young Benjamin Franklin's favorite writers—published *A Journal of the Plague Year* in the same year as Silence Dogood's debut, partly out of a desire to prepare his readers for a possible outbreak of plague in England by reexamining the public and private responses to the great London plague of 1665.[19] Diseases of the spirit became painfully conspicuous when the social fabric confronted the challenges of a great physical epidemic.

These deeper, spiritual contagions of his day came to engage the energies of Benjamin Franklin long before his transformation from private citizen to public servant. Indeed, even before he went into business for himself—while he was still Samuel Keimer's assistant in Philadelphia—Franklin had formed his Junto of young idealists around a core of affirmations originally suggested by John Locke. In a brief sketch of rules for an ethical and intellectual self-improvement society, Locke proposes three key questions as tests for any prospective member:

1. Whether he loves all men, of what profession or religion soever?

2. Whether he thinks no person ought to be harmed in his body, name, or goods, for mere speculative opinions, or his external way of worship?

3. Whether he loves and seeks truth for truth's sake; and will endeavour impartially to find and receive it himself, and to communicate it to others?[20]

In the earliest records that Franklin kept of the proceedings of the Philadelphia Junto, these three inquiries from Locke are copied directly into the club's secular liturgy as its ritual of confirmation (*Papers*, 1:259).

By the spring of 1731, less than three years after opening his own print shop, Franklin began to elaborate upon the example of the Junto in a broad historical and political context. His brief account of these early ambitions introduces the third part of the *Autobiography*, in which Franklin looks back fifty-seven years to a few notes describing a *"great & extensive Project"* recorded on a "little Paper, accidently preserv'd":

OBSERVATIONS on my Reading History in Library, May 9, 1731.

"That the great Affairs of the World, the Wars, Revolutions, &c. are carried on and effected by Parties.—

"That the View of these Parties is their present general Interest, or what they take to be such.—

"That the different Views of these different Parties, occasion all Confusion.

"That while a Party is carrying on a general Design, each Man has his particular private Interest in View.

"That as soon as a Party has gain'd its general Point, each Member becomes intent upon his particular Interest, which thwarting others, breaks that Party into Divisions, and occasions more Confusion.

"That few in Public Affairs act from a meer View of the Good of their Country, whatever they may pretend; and tho' their Actings bring real Good to their Country, yet Men primarily consider'd that their own and their Country's Interest was united, and did not act from a Principle of Benevolence.

"That fewer still in public Affairs act with a View to the Good of Mankind.

"There seems to me at present to be great Occasion for raising an united Party for Virtue, by forming the Virtuous and good Men of all Nations into a regular Body, to be govern'd by suitable good and wise Rules, which good and wise Men may probably be more unanimous in their Obedience to, than common People are to common Laws.

"I at present think, that whoever attempts this aright, and is well qualified, cannot fail of pleasing God, & of meeting with Success.—

B.F."—(*Writings,* 1395)

In many respects, this brief memorandum is just the sort of little paper that accident routinely consumes, but the casual title and date are misleading. Franklin ceremonially encloses his clauses in quotation marks— as if they were to be recited rather than simply filed away—and signed the page, just as Locke had provided for the signatures of his fellow lovers of truth and mankind in the rules upon which Franklin had modeled the Junto.

Like a careful physician schooled in the commotions of the body politic, Franklin surveyed history for its strange ferments and contagions, derived largely from the failure of "Parties" to build upon foundations that were durable enough to withstand the assaults of "particular private Interest." But to oppose the enthusiasm of partisanship would simply be to enflame the passions that drive it. Design, division, confusion, and renewed design constitute the expression of human energy in "the great Affairs of the World"—the scene where Franklin too proposed to exert his influence, uniting across national frontiers a body of uncommon people linked by obedience to uncommon laws.

In his commonplace book for the following year, Franklin envisions life as a traveling agent for his society of "Virtuous Men," promoting private libraries and a "universal Correspondence" among them in the service of "Virtue and Liberty and Knowledge" (*Papers,* 1:193). This is the model of religious itinerancy that evolved into the Great Awakening a few years later, but Franklin conceived of it in his mid-twenties as a collective response to the partisan confusion of history. If coalitions of private and general interest were unstable, if partisan instincts inevitably thwarted their designs, perhaps the solution lay in the very multiplicity and durability of those instincts, just as the energy of human character derived from the unpredictable mixture of its compound elements. Parties were the inescapable means of achieving the great ends of history. The human tendency to form them, coupled with the universal correspondence of readers in a global "Republic of Letters," was the "great Occasion" to which Franklin was already turning his attention at the beginning of his professional life.

"Observations on My Reading History in Library" reflects its young author's understanding that he lived in a Mandevillean world, governed (if it could be said to be governed at all) by the chaotic operations of competitive self-interest. But the lesson that Franklin drew from his reading took a characteristic form: this violently divisive world was ripe for the practice of Shaftesburean brotherhood. The Society of the Free and Easy that Franklin first proposed to himself in these "Observations" would be a secret fraternity of "Moralists" pledged to one another's material and ethical advancement in life, with the aim of redeeming the contest of appetites by which they were surrounded.[21]

This governing dramatic construction of his career was, in large measure, the product of Franklin's earliest years and was shaped by a program of reading and writing that was brought into focus by the influences surrounding his first period of residence in London. The chapters that follow describe how the intellectual apprenticeship of these years revealed its outlines and its implications in the formative decades of Franklin's life. In the *Autobiography,* he purports to have postponed the execution of his great, redemptive design until he had ceased to have the strength to undertake it. In fact, it was precisely the execution of this design, expressed through the products of an unusually diverse and accomplished career, to which Franklin devoted his abundant vitality in the first half of the eighteenth century. Boston in 1722 offered him an opportunity to experiment with the efficacy of "letters" in a climate of passionate division. Franklin's complex vocation gradually emerged over the course of the decade that spans the appearance of Silence Dogood and the 1731 library memorandum that marks the first "Rise" in Franklin's mind of his "Design."

Chapter One

ARTICLES OF BELIEF

Silence Dogood was born at sea, buoyed up by the same "merciless" waves that swept her father overboard as he stood on deck "rejoycing at my Birth." Later she remained equally buoyant in the face of the economic hardships that forced her widowed mother to bind her out as an "apprentice" in the household of a young bachelor minister. This curious apprenticeship to a country cleric must have struck James Franklin and his friends in the office of the *New England Courant,* reading Silence Dogood's initial letter, as a strangely promising misapplication of terms. Cutlers, masons, tallow chandlers, printers, and other skilled tradesmen might take and train apprentices, articled like James' younger brother to long periods of service before advancing to the status of journeymen and perhaps, eventually, to ownership of their own businesses.

But as the Widow Dogood herself observes in the fourth of her letters to James Franklin's newspaper, ministers are not products of the apprentice system. They take degrees in divinity at Harvard College, a course of education that she contemplates for her son William until she is dissuaded by a Bunyanesque dream exposing the worldly corruption of theological education in New England: "I reflected in my Mind on the extream Folly of those Parents, who, blind to their Children's Dulness, and insensible of the Solidity of their Skulls, because they think their Purses can afford it, will needs send them to the Temple of Learning . . . from whence they return, after Abundance of Trouble and Charge, as great Blockheads as ever, only more proud and self-conceited" (*Papers*, 1:17). This sharp criticism of parental vanity underscores the anomalous nature of Silence Dogood's own apprenticeship. She gratefully recalls in her first letter the attentions of her clerical "Master," a "good-natur'd young Man" who "labour'd with all his Might to instil vertuous and godly Principles into my tender Soul, well-knowing that it was the most suitable Time to make deep and lasting Impressions on the Mind, while it was yet untainted with Vice, free and unbiass'd" (*Papers*, 1:10).

New England churches were familiar with the figure of the licentious minister who abuses the intimate privileges of his office. An uncle of Cotton Mather, a son of the revered John Cotton, had lost his pulpit over a sex scandal.[1] It is unlikely that the suggestive nature of Widow Dogood's language, describing her "knowing" master's laborious solicitude for her tender soul, would have escaped the notice of the wits at the office of the *New England Courant.* Could she be hinting at a sexual "apprenticeship" infinitely more damaging to clerical prestige than any number of allegorical satires of life at Harvard? A thought such as this one would account for the unusual urgency and caution with which the publisher of the *Courant* sought more letters from his mysterious correspondent, to be "deliver'd at his Printing-House, or at the Blue Ball in Union Street, and no Questions shall be ask'd of the Bearer" (*Papers*, 1:11n).

Other elements of Silence Dogood's first letter, however, suggest a different sort of apprenticeship altogether, one far less congenial to ribald assaults on clerical authority. The only agents of seduction that she directly acknowledges are those to which her inventor, much later in life, confesses himself to be vulnerable: books. A book, according to Widow Dogood, is "the best of company," a sentiment that her master apparently shares and encourages in his young "apprentice" by giving her the "free Use of his Library." The second of Mrs. Dogood's letters describes how she greeted the initial, clumsy romantic overtures of her master with "unmannerly Laughter," followed by apologies, consent, and seven years of happy marriage—an interval of time that is, indeed, consistent with eighteenth-century terms of apprenticeship.

To the astonishment and scandal of the countryside, an anonymous, orphan servant girl is transformed not into the dutiful helpmate of a country minister—a journeyman's middle condition at best—but into the formidable independence of "a State of Widowhood," the heir of one clergyman and the landlady of another, a master of her own leisure and architect of her own character, a pun which must have provoked some amusement in Benjamin Franklin as he disguised his handwriting, or "character," to announce the full emergence of Silence Dogood as a public figure of very complex origins and intentions:

> "*Know then,* That I am an Enemy to Vice, and a Friend to Vertue. I am one of an extensive Charity, and a great Forgiver of *private* Injuries: A hearty Lover of the Clergy and all good Men, and a mortal Enemy to arbitrary Government and unlimited Power. I am naturally very jealous for the Rights and Liberties of my Country; and the least appearance of an Incroachment on those invaluable Priviledges, is apt to make my Blood boil exceedingly. I have likewise a natural Inclination to observe and reprove the Faults of others, at which I have an excellent Faculty. I speak this by Way of Warning to all such whose Offenses shall come under my Cognizance, for I never intend to wrap my Talent in a Napkin. To be brief; I am courteous and affable, good humor'd (unless I am first provok'd,) and handsome, and sometimes witty, but always, Sir, Your Friend and Humble Servant, SILENCE DOGOOD. (*Papers,* 1:13)

Franklin was barely sixteen when he wrote this extraordinary self-advertisement, so it is not particularly surprising that the rest of the Dogood letters fulfill only in part the promise of this passage. For much of the remaining twelve letters, Franklin is forced to eke out what he recognizes as his slender supply of subjects and knowledge with generous quotation from his reading in Defoe's *Essay on Projects,* the *Spectator,* and the pages of the *London Journal.*

What is remarkable, however, is the instinct that Franklin displays for positioning himself, even at this early age, in complex rhetorical territory. The voice he adopts is neither completely secular nor completely religious. Scarcely the simple entertainer she promises to be in her first letter, Silence Dogood shows by the end of this second "Epistle" (as she calls them) a mastery of prophetic cadences that unite judgment with forgiveness, chastisement with charity, spiritual with political fervor, generosity with jealous passion.[2] The emphatic *"Know then"* with which Franklin announces his escalating ambitions has a biblical finality that prepares for the warning he issues to all whose "Offenses" he detects and whose fate he darkly (if only half seriously) identifies with that of the worthless servant cast into outer darkness at the end of the Parable of the Talents. Unlike such worthless ones, Silence Dogood asserts her determination to put her "talents" to work.[3]

Good-humored and humble, but subject to outbursts of righteous indignation, Franklin's Dogood combines the traditional attributes of an unpredictable Deity with a reassuringly human measure of affability, wit, and personal vanity. The mixture of sublime and commonplace traits, of public and private identities, playfulness and earnestness, secular and religious purposes, is sufficiently heady to prompt the young author of this study in Chaucerian self-characterization to rein himself in at the end of the letter, but not before he gives an indication of the subtle relationship he would later develop with the explosive religious and political forces of his lifetime.

Franklin carefully weaves those forces into the presentation of Silence Dogood's character. She introduces herself by announcing the intention of supplying readers of the *Courant* with an entertaining miscellany of biweekly letters, but this comparatively innocent purpose does not disguise Franklin's keen awareness of the social turmoil within which he writes. James Franklin's paper was embroiled in quarrels with the religious and political establishments in Boston, quarrels that began with the *Courant's* fierce opposition to smallpox inoculation during the epidemic of 1721. This opposition expanded into a general satiric assault on colonial authority, which eventually led to James Franklin's brief imprisonment, midway through the Dogood series, and official efforts in the following year to stop the publication of his paper. In the *Autobiography*, Franklin describes the strategy that James and his friends employed to save the *Courant* by publishing it under Benjamin's name, but he does not give the reasons that a sixteen-year-old apprentice was selected for the task of carrying on the "Management" of a paper that had the energetic support of several "ingenious Men" in the community, all older, more securely established, and more experienced than he.[4]

One reason for this curious decision was almost certainly the skill with which the Dogood letters addressed a climate of partisan division without inflaming passions or compromising principles. These fourteen letters amount to the first diplomatic success in the career of America's most distinguished revolutionary diplomat, a success in some respects as artful as Franklin's more celebrated performance at the French court near the end of his life. Such a precocious accomplishment required him to draw on his reading in ways that are far more subtle than his dependence upon quotation suggests. But even Franklin's use of quotation seems dictated to a significant extent by political sensitivity rather than by journalistic desperation.

The most stringent attack upon political authority that Franklin makes in the Dogood papers, for example, comes not from Silence Dogood but from Thomas Gordon in the *London Journal* of February 1720. An extract from *Cato's Letters,* letter fifteen, comprises virtually the complete text of Silence Dogood's letter of July 9, 1722—the eighth in her series—castigating any public official who seeks to constrain the people's scrutiny of their government. Only traitors and tyrants, the *Journal* extract asserts, have cause to fear freedom of speech. Such ringing sentiments, however, find no immediate echo in Mrs. Dogood's words. Her volatile temper, hatred of arbitrary government, and "jealous" love for rights and liberties express themselves only in the comparatively mild assertion that, for this week at least, she "prefers" Gordon's sentiments to "any Thing of my own" (*Papers,* 1:27).

Franklin quietly permits the English press to defend proverbial English liberties in this first, pointed commentary on Boston politics. Later, he allows Silence Dogood to expand her critique of religious hypocrisy and intemperate zeal, but even in these later instances, Franklin still conducts his sharpest criticism of the Boston establishment through quotation, carefully providing alternative targets for public passion—like the apostate ministers of Connecticut, who abandoned New England's congregational tradition to seek reordination in the Anglican Church. Silence Dogood's excellent faculties of censure and reproof apparently involve a considerable appreciation for the value of tact.

Franklin's formal sophistication is evident, too, in his decision to postpone these direct reflections upon local politics until the first seven Dogood letters establish the character of his speaker as passionate and principled, without being consumed with zeal or self-importance. Once he introduces political subjects directly, he continues to mix the tone and weight of the correspondence with apparently less controversial matter: the usefulness of "friendly" insurance societies for destitute widows, the ridiculous proliferation of euphemisms for drunkenness, the behavior of nighttime "ramblers" on a September evening in Boston. An astute social physician, Mrs. Dogood is not about to risk aggravating what Shaftesbury views as the natural "commotions" of the public mind by an unnecessarily forthright opposition. Let the "strange Ferments" boil away on their own; directly tampering with these "mental Eruptions" could only produce a dangerous social inflammation.

At the same time, even these apparently casual letters have a tendency to turn, surprisingly, into more ambitious comments on the acerbic civic temper. At the end of a long quotation from Defoe's *Essay on Projects* concerning the plight of widows, for example, Mrs. Dogood observes "that the Country is ripe for many such *Friendly Societies,* whereby every Man might help another, without any Disservice to himself." By italicizing Defoe's technical term, Franklin emphasizes its general social connotation of neighborly feeling, for which this contentious city in particular was indeed ripe. A few lines later, Mrs. Dogood closes the tenth letter by observing that her entire estate consists of little more than "Contentment and a few Cows," comically simple circumstances that also suggest the pastoral calm she maintains amid the feverish atmosphere of town.

A source of parodic "friendship" at best, drunkenness is a reprehensible vice in Silence Dogood's eyes not because strong drink is intrinsically evil but because its abuse perverts and exaggerates passions. She observes in her twelfth letter:

'Tis strange to see Men of a regular Conversation become rakish and profane when intoxicated with Drink, and yet more surprizing to observe, that some who appear to be the most profligate Wretches when sober, become mighty religious in their Cups, and will then, and at no other Time address their Maker, but when they are destitute of Reason, and actually affronting him. Some shrink in the Wetting, and others swell to such an unusual Bulk in their Imaginations, that they can in an Instant understand all Arts and Sciences, by the liberal Education of a little vivifying *Punch,* or a sufficient Quantity of other exhilerating Liquor. (*Papers,* 1:40)

The delightful analogy to laundry preserves a sense of domestic comedy, as Franklin exposes the grotesque metamorphoses of tavern culture. Mrs. Dogood is puzzled and troubled more by the complex intellectual distortions of intoxication than by the descent into licentiousness that Hogarth will vividly depict some years later. A drunken egotism of scientific understanding, in particular, marks the *New England Courant* from its first issue during the inoculation controversy. These comments of Silence Dogood are skillfully measured acts of Franklin's self-censure as well as community instruction aimed at more pervasive and, perhaps, more dangerous vices than drinking.[5]

Franklin turns from his examination of the vocabulary of drink to record, in the next to last of the Dogood letters, the experiences of an evening walk that, he hopes, will provide some "Relief to the Labour of the Mind . . . as well as to that of the Body" (*Papers,* 1:41). The more substantial subjects of previous letters, however, remain very much in evidence. Franklin recalls in this evening walk at least one celebrated *Spectator* paper that records the random sights of a twenty-four-hour stroll through London. (Franklin, of course, read his *Spectator* with unusual care.) The larger subject of that London ramble—*Spectator* #454— is a celebration of human love both for the varied life of the city, in which the *Spectator* incessantly delights, and for the beauty and diversity of the women whom the strolling speaker sees. Richard Steele confesses in the third volume of the *Spectator* (#204)—Franklin's composition textbook—that the periodical has increasingly become a "Courier of Love," transmitting the complaints of distressed lovers to one another like a pioneer advice column. In an analogous fashion, this closing series of Dogood letters is concerned not with the distresses of private affection but with the disorders of civic love, to which "Friendly Societies," drunk with self, were vulnerable.

The *Spectator* was in fact a courier and a critic of love in more respects than the role of advice columnist suggests; it exposed the exploitation of prostitutes in London and the cold indifference with which so-called gentlemen abandoned their illegitimate children along with the children's destitute and desperate mothers. It studied the psychology of jealousy and praised the hen-pecked husband who valued domestic tenderness over personal ambition, avarice, or power.[6] In the course of the Dogood series, Franklin twice quotes directly from the third volume of the *Spectator*, and in her own city ramble Mrs. Dogood, like Richard Steele, encounters several instances of what she terms "the Spirit of Love," peculiarly misdirected and misapplied in the streets of Boston.

In the first of these encounters, she overhears a discussion of herself by a company "of both Sexes," in which a female speaker accuses her of "criminal Correspondence with a Gentleman." In reply, a "Gallant" defends her against accusations of sexual irregularity, argues further that "she" is a man, but goes on to accuse the Dogood author of too great an indulgence in satire. Leaving the gallant and his female opponent to work out their differences, Mrs. Dogood next observes a group of drunken sailors and their "Doxies" stumbling through the streets, followed by a party of flirtatious women who seem to be abroad "with no other Design than to revive the Spirit of Love in Disappointed Batchelors, and expose themselves to Sale to the first Bidder" (*Papers,* 1:42). Mrs. Dogood closes the letter by recalling the bawdy reply of a shoemaker to the suggestive inquiry of "a noted Rambler, *Whether he could tell how long her Shoes would last.*" The shoemaker replied that he could indeed make an estimate about their daytime wear "in the common Affairs of the House," but he didn't know how to account for "violent and irregular" nighttime service.[7]

Love seems at best disordered in this portrait of Boston by night, where the excesses of sailors are only a comparatively innocent version of the general excesses of the community. The final Dogood letter explicitly extends this general disorder of the heart to the manipulation of "the Loves and Hatreds of Mankind" by zealous, unscrupulous politicians who embrace piety as a disguise for personal ambition. The formal skill with which Franklin arranges this succession of incidents and quotations over the final three letters of the series effectively turns the local partisan divisions of Boston into broad moral and religious questions that center on the pivotal commandment of the New Testament: the imperative to love God and one's neighbor.

He achieves his ends almost invisibly, as if by an effortless process of association. The distortions of individual character brought on by drink, which Mrs. Dogood examines in the twelfth letter, evolve into the diseased spirit of civic love, reflected in the drunken sailors of the thirteenth and the spiritual extremes of religious zeal with which the Dogood series closes. This ability to move fluidly from an atmosphere of occasional journalism into the rhetoric of the spiritual sublime is another marked attribute of Franklin's first writing master, the third volume of the *Spectator*. Addison, writing on September 22, 1711—nearly eleven years to the day before Silence Dogood's diagnosis of diseased love in Boston—celebrates the value of charity by alluding to a passage in the Bible that would eventually serve as one of Franklin's moral touchstones, Matthew 25, and by quoting extensively from Job:

> What then shall I do when God riseth up? and when he visiteth what shall I answer him? . . . If I have with-held the poor from their desire, or have caused the eyes of the widow to fail; or have eaten my morsel my self alone, and the fatherless hath not eaten thereof: If I have seen any perish for want of cloathing, or any poor without covering: If his loyns have not blessed me, and if he were not warmed with the fleece of my sheep: If I have lift up my hand against the fatherless when I saw my help in the gate: Then let mine arm fall from my shoulder-blade, and mine arm be broken from the bone. (*Spectator*, 3:36)

Franklin never makes so direct and dramatic a biblical appeal in the Dogood letters—his own fictive widow and her fatherless children being singularly self-sufficient—but his exploitation of the rhetorical range of eighteenth-century journalism is every bit as extensive and perhaps more sophisticated than that of Addison and his colleagues. The sophistication is implicit in the complexities of Mrs. Dogood's "silence," which is both a diplomatic strategy of understatement or indirection and a moral posture that draws upon several rich veins in Franklin's reading.[8]

The first of those veins is clearly Cotton Mather's *Bonifacius: An Essay upon the Good* (1710), a book to which Franklin attributes an early and influential "turn" in his thinking. In his chapter "Home and Neighborhood," Mather emphasizes that "a world of *self-denial* is to be exercised" in the practice of neighborly benevolence. He exhorts his readers not to think "of making the good you do, a pouring of water into a pump, to draw out something for yourselves" but, rather, to model themselves on Christ's disinterested example: *"Do good* unto those neighbors who have *done hurt* unto you . . . *do good to them that hate you, and pray for them which despitefully use you and persecute you."* This, says Mather, is the way to *"do good* on a *divine principle; good,* merely for the sake of *good!"*[9] The repeatedly italicized word *good* in Mather's text suggests a source for the surname under which Franklin elected to write, and the context in which Mather presents his advice confirms the importance of Silence Dogood's self-effacing given name.

Silence Dogood, as her creator imagines her, is an avid reader, given the free use of a ministerial library in which the volumes are "well chose" to foster even in the provincial student "great and noble Ideas" (*Papers,* 1:10). It is not, in other words, a library of dry, polemical divinity such as Franklin complained of in his father's house. The idea of a silent, even secretive, benevolence was well established among the great and noble concepts to which Franklin turned for intellectual and spiritual nourishment in his process of self-education. Mather voices, in *Bonifacius,* a standard for disinterested goodness that Franklin found confirmed in the third volume of the *Spectator,* when Steele argues for the importance of applying one's "good Talents among Men" regardless of the glory one might or might not receive from an inattentive or malevolent world (*Spectator,* 3:13). Such "exalted Spirits" of benevolence, he affirms, "would rather be secretly the Authors of Events which are serviceable to Mankind, than without being such, to have the publick Fame of it."[10] In his first extended exercise in secret authorship, Franklin has Silence Dogood declare her determination to exercise her "Talents" openly while she keeps her identity hidden. What is not so well hidden is the fusion of *Bonifacius* and the *Spectator* in the origins of her name and character.

Shaftesbury's *Letter concerning Enthusiasm,* too, endorses disinterested benevolence in language that is eminently enthusiastic: "To love the Publick, to study universal Good, and to promote the Interest of the Whole World, as far as lies within our Power, is surely the Height of Goodness, and makes that Temper which we call *Divine*" (*CMM*, 1:37). Like Mather and Steele a few years later, Shaftesbury emphasizes that this divine temper is far removed from the desire for renown or glory and untroubled that the recipients of its benevolence are ungrateful or even "insensible of the Good they receive." Franklin would prove especially mindful of Shaftesbury's words in the expansive intentions and secretive practices of the Philadelphia Junto—which can strike a modern reader of the *Autobiography* who is unaware of these moral imperatives to silent benevolence as a kind of small tradesmen's conspiracy. For the purposes of understanding the Dogood letters, however, it is important to emphasize the full relationship between the widow's name and the extent of Franklin's personal literary exposure to the great and noble ideas that formed a common heritage uniting Mather, Steele, and Shaftesbury.

A clear index of the importance of the philosophical and ethical issues that Silence Dogood's name evoked for contemporary readers is Bernard Mandeville's critique of the idea of secretive benevolence in his "Enquiry into the Origin of Moral Virtue." Mandeville added this essay to the 1714 edition of *The Fable of the Bees,* which Franklin might indeed have read prior to writing the Dogood letters and which he almost certainly read after meeting Mandeville in London in 1725. Mandeville is pointedly replying to Shaftesbury and Steele when he applies his skepticism to the idea that "there are noble and generous Actions that are perform'd in Silence . . . that among the Heathens there have been Men, who, when they did good to others, were so far from coveting Thanks and Applause, that they took all imaginable Care to be for ever conceal'd from Those on whom they bestow'd their Benefits, and consequently that Pride has no Hand in spurring Man on to the highest Pitch of Self-denial" (*Fable,* 1:55–56).

Such an idea strikes at the heart of Mandeville's psychology of self-interest and private vice. He deals with it at the very end of his "Enquiry" as a kind of climactic blow at Shaftesbury's vision of moral heroism, casting doubt on the purity of motive behind the legendary self-effacement of virtuous heathens:

> But such Men, as without complying with any Weakness of their own, can part from what they value themselves, and, from no other Motive but their Love to Goodness, perform a worthy Action in Silence: Such Men, I confess, have acquir'd more refin'd Notions of Virtue than those I have hi-

therto spoke of; yet even in these (with which the World has yet never swarm'd) we may discover no small Symptoms of Pride, and the humblest Man alive must confess, that the Reward of a Virtuous Action, which is the Satisfaction that ensues upon it, consists in a certain Pleasure he procures to himself by Contemplating on his own Worth: Which Pleasure, together with the Occasion of it, are as certain Signs of Pride, as looking Pale and Trembling at any imminent Danger, are the Symptoms of Fear. (*Fable*, 1:57)

Mandeville's view of the incompatibility of goodness and silence—of the bond between virtue and pride—is so vividly expressed in this passage as to suggest that Franklin may have had some contact with Mandeville's work as he was creating the peculiarly loquacious "silence" of his first narrative persona, perhaps through the agency of James Franklin's witty associates on the *New England Courant.* One of those associates, William Douglass, a European-educated physician who played a conspicuous role in the attacks on Cotton Mather during the smallpox hysteria, shared a profession and a Leyden medical degree with Mandeville, along with their common propensity for controversial writing.[11] Certainly by the time Franklin comments in the *Autobiography* on the stubborn nature of his vanity and pride, he will have had Mandeville's example in mind: "In reality there is perhaps no one of our natural Passions so hard to subdue as *Pride.*" Franklin acknowledges: "Disguise it, struggle with it, beat it down, stifle it, mortify it as much as one pleases, it is still alive, and will every now and then peep out and show itself. You will see it perhaps often in this History. For even if I could conceive that I had compleatly overcome it, I should probably be proud of my Humility" (*Writings*, 1394).

Mandeville drew on an extensive body of writing that linked pride with humility in seventeenth- and early eighteenth-century moral philosophy, from any portion of which Franklin, too, might have drawn to suggest the psychological and moral issues evoked by Silence Dogood's name.[12] Shaftesbury and Steele are the most immediate English sources, but Jacques La Placette's influential *Treatise on Pride* (1674) was translated into English almost as soon as it appeared, and Blaise Pascal commented repeatedly in the *Pensées* on the elusive nature of true humility: "those who write against the desire of glory, glory in having written well." Among New England clergy throughout the seventeenth and eighteenth centuries, this analysis of man's susceptibility to pride was commonplace. Thomas Shepard's confession in the *Parable of the Ten Virgins* is representative: "I pray, but self-love sets me a work; I profess, but praise of men acts me."[13] The words could easily have been spoken by Nathaniel Hawthorne's devout hypocrite, Arthur Dimmesdale, or discovered by Benjamin Franklin in his father's library of divinity.

The best evidence of Franklin's youthful acquaintance with this realistic moral psychology is his portrait of Silence Dogood, which makes up what he calls the "Foundation" of his journalistic edifice in the first three letters of the series. The library of her clerical "Master" was where she developed her taste for great and noble ideas, where she learned to suspect her own motives and to anticipate the suspicions of others. Love, gratitude, pride, "or all three," she confesses, combined to influence her consent to her master's unexpected marriage proposal. The response of her neighbors to the unusual match was equally mixed, "some approving it, others disliking it, as they were led by their various Fancies and Inclinations" (*Papers,* 1:12). The first sign, in effect, of Franklin's awareness of the multiple social and ethical controversies within which he writes is this decision to make Silence Dogood a figure of controversy in her own fictive neighborhood and, through her, to acknowledge the mixture of interested and disinterested motives behind all human passions and judgments.

Mandeville's strategy in "Enquiry into the Origin of Moral Virtue" is to attribute to his idealistic opponents a far purer vision of human character than they in fact possess. None of Franklin's most influential instructors in moral philosophy would have denied that pride plays a significant role in motivating people to virtuous and benevolent acts. Ambition "runs through the whole Species . . . every Man in Proportion to the Vigour of his Complection is more or less actuated by it" (*Spectator,* 3:205). But the human appetite for glory may express itself either in destructive or constructive ways, as a fondness for "nocturnal Exploits, breaking of Windows, singing of Catches, beating the Watch," or as a devotion to the public good (*Spectator,* 3:207).

Education and religion are the proper agents to channel this passionate human force, but the energy of pride and self-love is essential to any social movement. The analogy that the *Spectator* provides is the traditional figure of a sailing vessel harnessing passion's wind, an image that Franklin might have had in mind as he describes the "wild steerage" of his drunken sailors and their Boston doxies in the Dogood letters:

> The Man who is fitted out by Nature, and sent into the World with great Abilities, is capable of doing great Good or Mischief in it. It ought there-

fore to be the Care of Education to infuse into the untainted Youth early Notices of Justice and Honour, that so the possible Advantages of good Parts may not take an evil Turn, nor be perverted to base and unworthy Purposes. It is the Business of Religion and Philosophy not so much to extinguish our Passions, as to regulate and direct them to valuable well-chosen Objects: When these have pointed out to us which Course we may lawfully steer, 'tis no Harm to set out all our Sail; if the Storms and Tempests of Adversity should rise upon us, and not suffer us to make the Haven where we would be, it will however prove no small Consolation to us in these Circumstances, that we have neither mistaken our Course, nor fallen into Calamities of our own procuring. (*Spectator*, 3:209)

Thirty years later, in the second epistle of the *Essay on Man,* Pope gives this analogy its most sublime form, turning the tempests of adversity from the *Spectator* passage into the driving passions themselves:

In lazy Apathy let Stoics boast
Their Virtue fixed; 'tis fixed as in a frost,
Contracted all, retiring to the breast;
But strength of mind is Exercise, not Rest:
The rising tempest puts in act the soul,
Parts it may ravage, but preserves the whole.
On life's vast ocean diversely we sail,
Reason the card, but Passion is the gale;
Nor God alone in the still calm we find,
He mounts the storm, and walks upon the wind.[14]

Language such as this looks forward to the exultation of a romantic sensibility, but it also looks backward to the moral philosophy of the early eighteenth century and still further to John Locke's concern for nurturing the natural, human energies of children in *Some Thoughts concerning Education* (1693). One of the infrequent temperamental disorders in children that most concerns Locke is a mysterious apathy, "a listless carelessness," which Locke terms the "sauntering humor."[15] A naturally rebellious idleness in children does not trouble Locke, for such behavior has its roots in energetic inclinations that might be gently redirected by an observant parent. But a systematic listlessness so contrary to the naturally busy nature of children is cause for worry, because without vigor there can be no virtue.

Out of this inherently complicated kinetic system, Mandeville distills an artificially simplified one in which pride has the only formative influence upon human action. The oceanic passions of man are in a perpetual ferment, but there is very little room in Mandeville's account for the well-rigged, well-governed vessel of reason and culture in the individual will. The writers to whom Franklin turned for instruction tend to invoke much more mixed conceptual models, most notably perhaps Shaftesbury, who in *Sensus Communis* describes human character with a metaphor that employs the idea of mechanism not as a reductive but as an organic image of personality and motive:

> You have heard it (my Friend!) as a common Saying, that *Interest governs the World*. But, I believe, whoever looks narrowly into the Affairs of it, will find, that *Passion, Humour, Caprice, Zeal, Faction,* and a thousand other Springs, which are counter to *Self-Interest,* have as considerable a part in the Movements of this Machine. There are more Wheels and *Counter-Poises* in this Engine than are easily imagin'd. 'Tis of too complex a kind, to fall under one simple View, or be explain'd thus briefly in a word or two. The Studiers of this *Mechanism* must have a very partial Eye, to overlook all other Motions besides those of the lowest and narrowest compass. 'Tis hard, that in the Plan or Description of this Clock-work, no Wheel or Ballance shou'd be allow'd on the side of the better and more enlarg'd Affections; that nothing shou'd be understood to be done in *Kindness* or *Generosity;* nothing in *pure Good-Nature* or *Friendship,* or thro any *social* or *natural Affection* of any kind: when, perhaps, the main Springs of this Machine will be found to be either these very *natural Affections* themselves, or a compound kind deriv'd from them, and retaining more than one half of their Nature. (*CMM,* 1:115)

The system of balanced counterpoise with which A. O. Lovejoy persuasively associates so much eighteenth-century imaginative writing, including the Constitution of the United States, is clearly in evidence in this passage, but Shaftesbury is equally explicit about the limitations of the strict analogy to mechanism. The "Machine" he is discussing is unlike any conceivable man-made engine in its order of complexity. Its "Springs" and "Wheels" effectively represent metaphors within a metaphor, depicting the "enlarg'd Affections" of the heart and becoming a circulatory spring, or fountain, of a far more elaborate organic nature than simple clockwork would suggest.

Frank Manuel notes that during the early eighteenth century the abstract concept of "springs of action" within individuals and societies gradually began to lose its purely mechanistic associations and to incorporate vitalistic ones. He traces the changes to the complex meaning of the term *ressort* in Montesquieu and in Gibbon's youthful *Essai sur l'etude de la litterature* (1761).[16] This passage from *Sensus Communis* is part of the process of change that Manuel detects. In the seventeenth century, Nicholas Malebranche explicitly compares human vanity to the role of the heart in circulation; like the heart, vanity is an endlessly energetic and steady source of the indispensable movement of life as well as an inescapable ingredient of the affections.[17] Shaftesbury's figure of speech, drawing on this complex metaphorical history, evokes a picture of our "compound kind" that is far more generous in its concessions to Mandeville's (or to Hobbes') psychological position than Mandeville finds himself able to be to the moral idealism of Shaftesbury.

This generous, inclusive capacity is responsible for Silence Dogood's attempts to reawaken the spirit of love in the contentious community of Boston and for Franklin's superb depiction of her compound affections at the end of the second letter. She is a great forgiver and a great enemy, a hearty and a jealous lover, a case study in the complex human "Motions." Addison opens the third volume of the *Spectator* with two long letters on the operations of, and the cure for, jealousy—the only two sequential letters on the same subject in that volume. Franklin's presentation of Silence Dogood as "naturally very jealous" in defense of her country's rights reflects Addison's example. Addison, too, ties jealousy closely to love. If Silence Dogood is, in many respects, a political enthusiast for her cause, then she is only expressing the passionate vigor that is virtue's prerequisite. "*Men of Moderation,*" Shaftesbury scornfully notes, are suspiciously self-composed and, finally, untrustworthy: "They are secure of their Temper; and possess themselves too well, to be in danger of ent'ring warmly into any Cause, or engaging deeply with any Side or Faction" (*CMM*, 1:115). It was one of Shaftesbury's delightful paradoxes—considerably more subtle, as a rule, than the formulaic paradoxes of Mandeville—that moderation could as readily be a sign of selfishness as a sign of self-effacement. Franklin seeks to establish, first of all, Silence Dogood's passionate partisanship as a way of affirming what his teacher Shaftesbury would call, with approval, her "associating Genius" (*CMM*, 1:114).

It is that genius, finally, that keeps her blood from coming to a boil, as she confesses it is sometimes all too likely to do. Her inclination "to observe and reprove" is "natural" and, as she later expresses it, gentle. She gives warning not of her powers of judgment but of her "cognizance," her knowingness. And the closing elements of her self-portrait are inviting, if not a little flirtatious, as she inserts into the list of her cordial attributes of character the oddly inconsequent glance into the mirror that tells her that she is still a "handsome" woman. It seems likely that the portrait of Silence Dogood is indebted, as well, to Franklin's affectionate observation of his mother, who was nearly forty when he was born and approaching sixty as he composed his journalistic celebration of the intellectual, moral, and physical vigor of a mother of grown children.[18] Whatever her personal origins might be, Silence Dogood draws together most of the elements of Franklin's emerging public voice as well as the products of his intense, private education. The Dogood letters are genuinely apprentice work only in the sense that it was an apprentice who wrote them.

"Old Master Janus," the composite identity that Franklin contrived early in 1723 as the presiding genius of the *New England Courant* while the paper was being published under his name, is in many respects an extension of Silence Dogood. "A mortal Hater of Nonsense, Foppery, Formality, and endless Ceremony," Janus is, likewise, good tempered, courteous, "chearly" Christian, and uniquely qualified to observe life in an increasingly pluralistic community both because of his capacity to see "two ways at once" and because he is himself a federation of temperaments, having no less than nineteen features to his face (*Papers,* 1:49–50). The comic convention of Janus is both a familiar means of protecting the identities of the *Courant*'s various contributors and a way of emphasizing the same principled posture of mutual accommodation that Franklin expresses through the vigorously mixed nature of Silence Dogood.[19] Mortal hatred goes hand in hand with extensive charity in each of these fictive entities; spiritual and political fervor coexist with a generous appreciation for social complexity and a predisposition to get along—though not to get along at any price.

Franklin's first-hand experience with the spiritualized politics of Boston taught him both the exhilaration and the costs of the close identification of religious with political argument. In "Rules for the *New England Courant,*" printed three months after the last of the Dogood letters had appeared, he confesses that "Religion is our safety and security . . . no small part of our Strength and Glory," particularly as it is expressed through the unusual energy and ability of the ministers who represent it. But Franklin recognizes, too, that though New England's ministers "are the *Best of Men,* yet they are but Men at the Best," a compound of religious sympathies and political passions who are themselves quite capable of exercising much earthly influence to suppress their earthly critics. Silence

Dogood, Doctor Janus, and Timothy Wagstaff—another of Franklin's fictive *Couranteers*—are his earliest experiments at creating a similarly compound character, uniting the moral vigor associated with religious faith to the social energies represented by the intellectually curious, politically passionate Widow Dogood.

All three of these identities express Franklin's precocious pleasure in the diversity of human life and opinion, his opposition to what Wagstaff calls "Precisians," people who are in favor of "cutting or stretching all Men to their own Standard of Thinking." Religious orthodoxy is Wagstaff's particular concern, and he quotes with approval a lengthy passage from the essays of the celebrated English Deist, Thomas Pope Blount, affirming that "Religion is of an Active Principle . . . it admits of Mirth, and pleasantness of Conversation, and indulges us in our Christian Liberties" rather than terrorize "like one of the Furies, with nothing but Whips and Snakes." It is Shaftesbury's conviction, as well, that mirth or raillery is perfectly consistent with religious debate as "a kind of Specific against Superstition and melancholy Delusion": "There is a great difference between seeking how to raise a Laugh from every thing; and seeking, in every thing, what justly may be laugh'd at. For nothing is ridiculous except what is deform'd: Nor is any thing Proof against *Raillery*, except what is handsome and just" (*CMM*, 1:128).

Franklin thought so highly of Blount's sentiment, in particular, that he returns to it five years later in the third of the "Busy-Body" papers, where he admonishes the vindictive philosophy of "Cretico" in favor of the "seriously chearful" humility and charity of "Cato," an obscure Pennsylvania countryman whom Franklin creates as a Christian paragon. Throughout this early journalism, Franklin is in the first stages of formulating an ideal of religious heroism so ingratiatingly social as to be readily confused with religious indifference. The Dogood letters exemplify an emerging mastery of these apparently antithetical postures: to speak with the spiritual and intellectual authority of "the Best of Men" but on behalf of the limitations inherent to existence lived among those who remain "but Men at the Best." As Franklin's understanding of his religious and literary life matures, it takes philosophical, liturgical, and artistic forms that underscore the extent to which his dramatic departures from the tradition of New England piety—represented by Silence Dogood's liberating widowhood or by Franklin's actual and symbolic flight from Boston—are equally dramatic instances of the extent to which he remained drawn to many of those same traditions from his background and his reading, reconfigured to meet new personal and social needs.

Within three years of writing the Dogood letters, Franklin undertook the most ambitious metaphysical inquiry he would ever attempt, *A Dissertation on Liberty and Necessity, Pleasure and Pain,* printed in London in 1725 when Franklin worked for Samuel Palmer's press. The *Dissertation,* along with the surviving fragment of Franklin's "Plan of Conduct" of 1726, captures in both characteristic and uncharacteristic ways his steady advance toward the "Articles of Belief and Acts of Religion" of 1728, the definitive expression of Franklin's commitment to religion as an active principle. The most uncharacteristic feature of the *Dissertation* is its deductive method, the construction of what Franklin grandly pronounces to be a "Chain of Consequences" emerging from two straightforward propositions about the nature of God. In all the other intellectual enterprises of his long life, Franklin invariably expressed a preference for inductive methods, reasoning upward and outward from directly observed experience, accumulating facts or recording experiments without displaying what one of his early papers for the *Courant* whimsically refers to as *"Hypothesimania."* His letters on electrical phenomena are models of this commitment to empirical methods.

In this respect, *A Dissertation on Liberty and Necessity* would seem to be a youthful aberration. Franklin encourages readers of the *Autobiography* to think so and includes the pamphlet among his errata—not, curiously enough, because it was full of error (though Franklin suspects it might be) but because its conclusions were not very useful in the conduct of social life. In fact, the *Dissertation* is much more social in its origin and effects than Franklin appears to recall as he writes his memoirs, without a copy of the text at hand and at a distance of almost fifty years. As early as 1746 he repudiated "the horrible Errors I led my self into when a young Man, by drawing a Chain of plain Consequences as I thought them, from true Principles" (*Papers,* 3:88–89). But what the *Dissertation* leads to in reality, within what must have been only a few months of its composition, is a plan of conduct that derives directly from the critique of human pride that the *Dissertation* presents.

Taking its rise from what Franklin believed to be the two elements of a religious consensus uniting "people of almost every Sect and Opinion," the *Dissertation* presents a radical understanding of eighteenth-century moral and spiritual existence. Out of this understanding, Franklin derived the curiously appealing mixture of political expediency and unconditional faith represented by the constitutional "articles" and legislative "acts" of his private system of belief. His original intent, however, was that the *Dissertation* be public, extending the scope of human agreement, at first to its own admittedly limited audience but, eventually, to readers of "every Sect and Opinion" to whom its inclusive doctrines might appeal.[20]

The earliest sign of the *Dissertation's* rhetorical and social complexity is Franklin's rather adroit use of key psychological and theological terms from the body of his text in the brief dedication to James Ralph. Pleasure and pain are not, initially, objects of dispassionate study in Franklin's essay. They are important social ingredients in its composition. In assembling and organizing his thoughts, Franklin explains, he has taken some "Trouble," some pains, to respond to a friend's request purely in order that his friend might derive some "Pleasure or Satisfaction" from the reading. Nor is the author's pain entirely at an end when the writing is over, for Franklin is clearly self-conscious about the extent to which he may have overreached his youthful powers by offering to expose his "*present* Thoughts of the *general State of Things* in the Universe." One works hard to write in the first place, only to run the risk of ridicule by one's readers—or so Franklin understands the untoward consequences of authorship to work, especially when the author is unprotected by a pen name as well as seduced by his own grandiloquence. Despite the danger and the labor, he goes ahead: "The whole I leave entirely to you," he writes faithfully to Ralph, "and shall value my self more or less on this account, in proportion to your Esteem and Approbation" (*Writings,* 57).

Humanity's psychological appetite for "Approbation" is the definitive insight of eighteenth-century moral science. Franklin is signaling, at the close of the dedication to the *Dissertation,* that, while his literary pretensions may indeed be modest, he is well aware that he is addressing a central ethical preoccupation of the time, in his person as well as in his text. "Esteem," like pleasure and pain, will also prove to be a critical term in Franklin's description of the human predicament. The creator views all of his creatures with equal and unvarying "Esteem." That is the substance of Franklin's ninth proposition in the first part of the *Dissertation.* James Ralph has an opportunity, as reader, to emulate the "Great Parent of Nature" and teach Franklin to value himself by accepting and praising a handful of pages that the author readily confesses are at least as hypothetical as they are conclusive. If the *Dissertation* does finally present a "chain" of consequences, it is a very loose chain indeed, binding only in the sense that this dedication suggests the depth and durability of the bond that Franklin had established with James Ralph.

Youthful ambition and youthful friendship are responsible for the existence of this document. It was not prompted into life and form simply by some antecedent pain to which it was a response and which it sought to alleviate. In the baldest sense, that is the argument that Franklin's text makes concerning human motivation, drawing upon the relationship between appetite and will that Locke describes in the *Essay Concerning Human Understanding* as well as upon Addison's description of Socrates' relief when his fetters were removed prior to his suicide. In the *Spectator* account of that scene, Addison describes Socrates' speculations "on the Nature of Pleasure and Pain in general and how constantly they succeed one another," concluding the paper with an allegorical fable describing the descent of Pleasure and Pain to Earth and their difficulties in dividing mankind between them. The two states "are such constant Yoke-fellows ... that they either make their visits together, or are never far asunder" (*Spectator*, 3:57–59). Determining the proportion of each that is present in a given individual provokes "endless Disputes" between the two deities, despite their apparently supernatural powers of judgment.

William Wollaston agrees about this inextricable mixture of pleasure and pain in human experience. In *The Religion of Nature Delineated*—the book that Franklin was helping to reprint as he was writing his own thoughts for James Ralph—Wollaston expresses the inevitable uncertainty that we must always acknowledge concerning one another's happiness or misery, virtue or wickedness: "the true characters of men must chiefly depend upon the unseen part of their lives," Wollaston notes, and even the part that one can see is a confusing mixture of degrees of pleasure and pain perpetually slipping out of balance. "It rarely happens," Wollaston concludes, "that we are competent judges of the good or bad fortune of other people."[21] Franklin had the work of Wollaston, Addison, and Locke among others as models to draw upon and to diverge from in his brief account of pleasure and pain, just as he had a rich tradition of Calvinist, necessitarian thinking to influence his views of human liberty.

What the dedication to James Ralph establishes, even before Franklin begins sorting through this complex of ideas, is that no pure doctrine of necessity (like "the Fall of a heavy Body to the Ground") or narrow psychology of reactive sensation can account for the full social gesture that the *Dissertation* represents. Though the pain of unsatisfied ambition certainly played a part in its writing, so did the youthful generosity that Franklin expresses by answering a request from a friend that inevitably exposes painful insecurities as well as grand aspirations. The young man who writes the dedication, then, is significantly richer in what Shaftesbury would call the generous affections than many of the *Dissertation*'s doctrines and propositions would seem to allow for in human character.

To write is to be generous—such, at least in part, is Steele's understanding of the *Spectator*'s role when he notes the paper's function as a courier of love. In some measure, Franklin's metaphysical *Dissertation* is just such a courier of the heart. This implicit generosity at the basis of the transaction between writer and reader is put to memorable use by Shaftesbury when he mockingly replies to Thomas Hobbes on the contradiction inherent not in Hobbes' philosophy of naked self-interest but in his posture as a philosopher:

> Sir! The Philosophy you have condescended to reveal to us, is most extraordinary. We are beholden to you for your Instruction. But, pray, whence is this Zeal in our behalf? What are *We* to *You*? Are You our *Father*? Or if You were, why this Concern for Us? Is there then such a thing as *natural Affection*? If not; why all this Pains, why all this Danger on our account? Why not keep this Secret to Your-self? Of what advantage is it to You, to deliver us from the Cheat? The more are taken in it, the better. 'Tis directly against Your Interest to undeceive Us, and let us know that only private Interest governs You; and that nothing nobler, or of a larger kind, shou'd govern us, whom you converse with. Leave us to our-selves, and to that notable *Art* by which we are happily tam'd, and render'd thus mild and *sheepish*. 'Tis not fit we shou'd know that *by Nature* we are all *Wolves*. Is it possible that one who has really discover'd himself such, shou'd take pains to communicate such a Discovery? (*CMM*, 1:92–93)

Shaftesbury's exposure of contradiction here differs considerably in its formal argumentative polish from the personal dedication of Franklin's literary pains to James Ralph, but the principle involved is in many respects identical: the social conditions of writing are inevitably an ingredient in meaning. In particular, the writer is always asserting, in some degree, the same associating genius that Franklin exploits with such deliberation in the figure of Silence Dogood.

Shaftesbury emphasizes these social assumptions by framing his argument as a dialogue—a form that he prizes for a number of complicated reasons—with a writer who has been dead for thirty years. The strategy was sufficiently appealing to prompt Francis Hutcheson to adopt it, somewhat less effectively, in his indignant response to the relentlessly manipulative materialism of Bernard Mandeville, a "late witty Author" (as Hutcheson calls him) who denied the existence of disinterested social action, attributing all apparent acts of public virtue to a successful program of indoctrination through statues and panegyrics: "So easy a matter it seems to him," Hutcheson scoffs, "to quit judging of others by what we feel ourselves!—for a person who is wholly *selfish,* to imagine others to be *publick-spirited!* . . . Yet this it seems *Statues* and *Panegyricks* can accomplish!"[22]

Hutcheson and Shaftesbury agree that something deeper must be at work in the transaction between speaker and audience, author and reader, than the stark doctrines of appetite and self- interest alone suggest. Something deeper is evident as well in Benjamin Franklin's decision to reply to James Ralph's request for his present thoughts not in a personal letter but in a philosophical tract, set in type, of which Franklin printed one hundred copies, unprotected by one of his witty Boston pen names. *A Dissertation on Liberty and Necessity* is not a response to his Boston experience, of course, but it is in some sense a fulfillment of the reading that Franklin began there.

In 1725 he found himself in the midst of a literary and political culture that, before, he had only been able to observe from afar. In contemporary London, Shaftesbury's legacy was a matter of open debate between Mandeville and Hutcheson, who recast in some degree the antagonistic roles filled by Shaftesbury and Hobbes two decades earlier.[23] The corruption of public and private life by a thirst for fame was the subject of Edward Young's recent verse satires on what he called "the universal passion." The arrest and execution of the notorious Jonathan Wild during Franklin's first year in London suggested to observers like Young and others that the human need for praise had begun to neutralize the difference between virtue and vice:

> What is not proud? The pimp is proud to see
> So many like himself in high degree:
> The whore is proud her beauties are the dread
> Of peevish virtue, and the marriage-bed;
> And the brib'd cuckold, like crown'd victims born
> To slaughter, glories in his gilded horn.

> Of folly, vice, disease, men proud we see;
> And (stranger still!) of blockheads' flattery;
> Whose praise defames; as if a fool should mean,
> By spitting on your face, to make it clean.[24]

Young may have been thinking of Jonathan Wild in particular, but certainly of the spectacle of public executions in general, in his image of crowned victims borne to slaughter in a sea of folly, vice, and disease.

Even Mandeville, insulated as he was by his cynical assessment of human motives, was shocked by the grotesque fair of the passions and appetites that accompanied execution days. In a pamphlet he published in 1725 on the causes of the frequency of public executions, Mandeville describes the terrible chaos of Newgate Prison and the procession to Tyburn through drunken mobs, who seized these occasions as "Jubilees" of petty theft, sex, and gin in the city's filthy streets. "Young villains" pressed forward to take leave of the condemned and to secure their own rising reputations for crime or hurled the carcasses of dead animals overhead in order to enjoy the "Mischief promis'd by the Fall" when their "meteors" landed in the crowd:

> It is incredible what a Scene of Confusion all this often makes, which yet grows worse near the Gallows; and the violent Efforts of the most sturdy and resolute of the Mob on one Side, and the potent Endeavours of rugged Goalers, and others, to beat them off, on the other; the terrible Blows that are struck, the Heads that are broke, the Pieces of swingeing Sticks, and Blood, that fly about, the Men that are knock'd down and trampled upon, are beyond Imagination, whilst the Dissonance of Voices, and Variety of Outcries, for different Reasons, that are heard there, together with the Sound of more distant Noises, make it a Discord not to be parallel'd.[25]

The ingenious causal relationship between private vice and public virtue that Mandeville celebrates in *The Fable of the Bees* does not reassure him before the hellish spectacle of Tyburn.

Execution day called forth one extreme of human character, as Shaftesbury's celebration of the generous affections called forth another. When Franklin suggests to James Ralph his interest in "the *general State of Things*" as a preface to the *Dissertation*, it is these painful and pleasurable extremes that his literary predisposition and background would cause him to have in mind—particularly as they were encapsulated in the contrast between Hobbes' wolves and Shaftesbury's natural affections, or between Mandeville's pride and Hutcheson's love. The complexities of the dedication to Ralph already indicate the extent to which Franklin was prepared to weave together vanity and humility, pride and affection, in his own portrait of the springs of human action. He tries out another compressed account of his purposes, again addressed directly to Ralph, about halfway through the *Dissertation*:

> You have a View of the whole Argument in a few familiar Examples: The *Pain* of Abstinence from Food, as it is greater or less, produces a greater or less *Desire* of Eating, the Accomplishment of this *Desire* produces a greater or less *Pleasure* proportionate to it. The *Pain* of Confinement causes the *Desire* of Liberty, which accomplish'd yields a *Pleasure* equal to that *Pain* of Confinement. The *Pain* of Labour and Fatigue causes the *Pleasure* of Rest, equal to that *Pain*. The *Pain* of Absence from Friends, produces the *Pleasure* of Meeting in exact proportion. &c.
>
> This is the *fixt Nature* of Pleasure and Pain, and will always be found to be so by those who examine it. (*Writings*, 65)

At first, this summary view of the texture of human feeling seems to reduce life to a mechanics of stimulus and response modeled upon hunger, but the surprising introduction of more complex affections in Franklin's last example makes the "fixed" nature of pleasure and pain seem far less reductive and fatal than the first example implies.

The pain of absence from friends establishes a "hunger" for social and emotional intimacy as fundamental as the need for food. Franklin's text confirms the antecedent pleasures of companionship just as his dedication to James Ralph does before Franklin undertakes the considerable pains of writing. Other complex antecedent pleasures play roles in the first three illustrations as well. The antagonists in the first, for example, seem to be hunger and repletion, but Franklin also employs the words "Abstinence" and "Desire" as if a deliberate determination to court bodily hunger for some larger spiritual purpose were involved. The discipline, as well as the creation, of desire is part of the background of human experience from which Franklin draws his cases.

Confinement is posed against "Liberty," a much more complex term than the simple idea of release would suggest, and Franklin's phrasing in "the *Pain* of Confinement" inevitably evokes a pun on childbirth that the more prosaic pains of imprisonment would not contain. To such a pun "the *Pain* of Labour" is a logical successor, further enriching the suggestions of the affectional world that Franklin will introduce directly in the pleasures of human meeting as he closes his list of "familiar" examples. They are indeed familiar in many senses—household "familiars" in the experience of most readers, who would recognize in them the ingredients not of a reductive materialism but of an expansive humanity. The *Dissertation* as a whole tries to accommodate the extraordinary range of human need and expression upon which this brief passage touches.

Of the nine propositions in the first section of Franklin's pamphlet, the last two are the most interesting and, from Franklin's point of view, the most fruitful. The first section, "Of Liberty and Necessity," draws a number of traditional conclusions from a standard description of the key attributes of the first mover: that he is all wise, all good, and all powerful. On these grounds, Franklin quickly proceeds to dismiss evil as nonexistent and to characterize all human action both as governed by necessity and as necessarily good. These are conventional elements of the "Argument from Design," which Shaftesbury, Hutcheson, and Wollaston invoke with varying degrees of eloquence. "The Order and Course of Things will not be affected by Reasoning of this kind," Franklin concedes, partly out of the recognition that his discussion has many philosophical predecessors. Crime and punishment will continue to take place; virtue and vice will continue to play their roles in the makeup of human character, but with the important change that the "distinction" between them is "excluded," as Franklin puts it at the end of the *Dissertation*.

Just what he means by this exclusion is made clearer by the first section's eighth proposition: "If there is no such Thing as Free-Will in Creatures, there can be neither Merit nor Demerit in Creatures." The consequence Franklin immediately draws, to conclude this portion of his pamphlet, is that the Creator must esteem and use all creatures equally. Unlike the seven propositions that precede them, these last two do indeed begin to affect the order and course of things. Franklin prefaces his pamphlet with an epigraph from Dryden, including the line that Alexander Pope would later reformulate in the famous conclusion to the first epistle of the *Essay on Man*:

> Whatever is, is in its Causes just
> Since all Things are by Fate; but purblind Man
> Sees but a part o' th' Chain, the nearest Link,
> His Eyes not carrying to the equal Beam
> That poises all above.[26]

Dryden's ontological and epistemological "Chain" is a direct ancestor both of the "dread *Order*" that Pope celebrates in the *Essay on Man* and of the imperial iron chain that William Blake scorns a century later in "America: A Prophecy." But though Franklin clearly identifies much of his thinking with Dryden's stoic resignation in the epigraph, the emphasis of the first section of his youthful *Dissertation* falls on those closing propositions, where he affirms not human blindness and divine justice but human equality and divine esteem.

Merit and demerit are as empty of meaning in Franklin's metaphysics as evil is. In this first respect, his eighth proposition is as much a product of his upbringing in Puritan Boston as it is a reflection of the logic that he professes to be following or the reading that he has been doing in various natural philosophers and moralists. Cotton Mather is as scornful of "merit-mongers" in his *Bonifacius* as he is horrified by those wicked persons to whom the Devil's service is as congenial as the worship of God through good works.[27] Franklin arrives by "pure reason" at a conclusion about the inefficacy of mere works that is reassuringly traditional in form but from which he draws the pleasingly untraditional doctrine of the equal distribution of divine esteem.

Pure reason, however, cannot account for Franklin's delightful leap from what seems to be a description of divine indifference to an assertion of divine esteem. Creatures who possess neither merit nor demerit would seem to have little basis for soliciting the Deity's regard. Franklin arrives at his remarkable ninth proposition on the Creator's equal esteem for every creature by dramatically condensing a number of elements in the "Argument from Design," beginning with Shaftesbury's celebration of the complex counterpoises of the world's "clockwork." Indeed, in the following passage from the *Dissertation* Franklin virtually paraphrases Shaftesbury's *Sensus Communis,* or common sense, the term with which the *Dissertation* ultimately closes its case:

> How exact and regular is every Thing in the *natural* World! How wisely in every Part contriv'd! We cannot here find the least Defect! Those who have study'd the mere animal and vegetable Creation, demonstrate that nothing can be more harmonious and beautiful! All the heavenly Bodies, the Stars and Planets, are regulated with the utmost Wisdom! And can we suppose less Care to be taken in the Order of the *moral* than in the *natural* System? It is as if an ingenious Artificer, having fram'd a curious Machine or Clock, and put its many intricate Wheels and Powers in such a Dependance on

one another, that the whole might move in the most exact Order and Regularity, had nevertheless plac'd in it several other Wheels endu'd with an independent *Self-Motion,* but ignorant of the general Interest of the Clock; and these would every now and then be moving wrong, disordering the true Movement, and making continual Work for the Mender; which might better be prevented, by depriving them of that Power of Self-Motion, and placing them in a Dependance on the regular Part of the Clock. (*Writings,* 61)

This passage immediately precedes the eighth and ninth propositions of Franklin's first section and prepares for them by suggesting the ludicrous incompatibility between the ideas of free will and natural design. Human reason and will, left to their own devices, would "be perpetually blundering about in the Dark," Franklin argues, if their motions were not prescribed.

It seems curious that in the proverbial Age of Reason Franklin would find cause to impugn reason, but that is one consequence of his century's developing appreciation for the elaborate complexity of natural mechanisms. One explanation for Francis Hutcheson developing the concept of the "moral sense" in man—in addition to his interest in refuting Mandeville without falling afoul of Locke—is his appreciation for the cumbersome nature of thought, in particular its inability to account for the sudden operation of "those delightful Sensations" of approval and "esteem" that occur both in the witnesses and in the agents of moral action:

Notwithstanding the mighty *Reason* we boast of above other Animals, its Processes are too slow, too full of doubt and hesitation, to serve us in every Exigency, either for our own Preservation, without the *external Senses,* or to direct our Actions for the *Good* of the *Whole,* without this *moral Sense.* Nor could we be so strongly determin'd at all times to what were most conducive to either of these Ends, without these *expeditious Monitors,* and *importunate Sollicitors;* nor so nobly rewarded when we act vigorously in pursuit of these Ends, by the calm dull Reflections of *Self-Interest,* as by those delightful Sensations.[28]

Delightful moral sensations, especially the sensation of love, form the starting point for the earliest stages in Hutcheson's study of virtue. We love those who are possessed of "moral" goods, Hutcheson observes, and we do not love those who are possessed merely of natural ones, such as property. What is the basis of this experiential difference? The skillful rhetoric of governors, the canny deductions of reason or self-interest do not provide Hutcheson with satisfactory answers to the developing inquiry. Esteem and contempt, he concludes, are "occult" qualities, as mysterious as any of the fundamental operations of life. They are parts of the natural mechanism of the universe, not expressions of uncontingent human will, and as such they are elements in a vast system the purpose of which is not to degrade human liberty by subjecting it to blind necessity but to generalize the concept of the miraculous.

Hutcheson introduces his 1725 inquiry on virtue with a separate essay on beauty in the same volume precisely so he can directly challenge the hierarchal "chains" of ontological status with an emphasis on systematic law that derives its justification from beauty rather than from power. The passage from Hutcheson's first treatise that is most critical to an understanding of Franklin's thought sums up the "Argument from Design" by explicitly subordinating human needs not only to the Deity's purposes but partially also to the operations of order in inanimate nature:

> The wonderfully simple *Mechanism* which performs all Animal Motions, was mentioned already; nor is *that* of the inanimate Parts of *Nature* less admirable. How innumerable are the Effects of that one Principle of *Heat*, deriv'd to us from the *Sun*, which is not only delightful to our Sight and Feeling, and the Means of discerning Objects, but is the Cause of *Rains, Springs, Rivers, Winds,* and the universal Cause of *Vegetation!* The *uniform Principle of Gravity* preserves at once the *Planets* in their *Orbits,* gives *Cohesion* to the Parts of each *Globe,* and *Stability* to *Mountains, Hills,* and *artificial Structures* . . . it gives an *uniform Pressure* to our *Atmosphere,* necessary to our Bodys in general, and more especially to *Inspiration* in Breathing; and furnishes us with an *universal Movement,* capable of being apply'd in innumerable Engines. How incomparably more *beautiful* is this Structure than if we suppos'd so many *distinct Volitions* in the DEITY, producing every particular Effect, and preventing some of the accidental Evils which casually flow from the *general Law!* And yet this latter manner of Operation might have been more useful to us, and would have been no distraction to *Omnipotence:* But then the great *Beauty* had been lost, and there had been no more Pleasure in the Contemplation of this Scene which is now so delightful. One would rather chuse to run the hazard of its *casual Evils,* than part with that *harmonious Form* which has been the unexhausted Source of Delight to the successive *Spectator*s in all Ages.[29]

The idea of a universal extension of divine esteem is rooted, then, in what Hutcheson identifies as the increasingly sophisticated, scientific empiricism of his day. It is not through distinct volitions that God chooses to work, any more than it is through independent volition that men live. Evil is merely a casual hazard rather than a demonic or providential intervention in history. The elegance of "harmonious Form," infinitely varied but uniform in its laws, is the aesthetic and spiritual end to which creation tends and in which individual human character inevitably participates.

Upon this passage in Hutcheson, as well as upon its forerunners in Shaftesbury, Franklin bases both his assertion of the Creator's equal esteem for all creation and his challenging claim, early in the second section of his treatise, that "no Condition of Life or Being is in itself better or preferable to another" (*Writings,* 66). Not only are all men created equal; all being is created equal. Neither Shaftesbury nor Hutcheson before him, nor Jefferson afterward, draws the egalitarian conclusion from this line of thinking with Franklin's blunt determination.

What the first section of his *Dissertation* in fact excludes, then, is not the difference between virtue and vice so much as the invidious distinctions among people that human beings have been prone to derive from those terms. A source of sectarian rhetoric simply melts away in the face of a celestial regard in which, Franklin asserts, all creatures have a common share. This dramatic leveling of the conservative, vertical universe of Dryden and Pope becomes still more pronounced in the second section of Franklin's text, "Of Pleasure and Pain," where he concludes (among other things) that no experiential or ethical basis exists for distinguishing between conscious life and insensible matter.

Whereas the first section of the *Dissertation* works downward from the divine attributes toward human equality, the second section works upward from infancy through a gestational psychology in which Franklin (following Locke) traces all human effort to the ubiquitous sensation of uneasiness or pain. Uneasiness is "the first Spring and Cause of all Action," a kind of first mover of the human soul without which life would be inconceivable: "We are first mov'd by *Pain,* and the whole succeeding Course of our Lives is but one continu'd Series of Action with a View to be freed from it. As fast as we have excluded one Uneasiness another appears, otherwise the Motion would cease. If a continual Weight is not apply'd, the Clock will stop. And as soon as the Avenues of Uneasiness to the Soul are choak'd up or cut off, we are dead, we think and act no more" (*Writings,* 63).

Though Franklin adopts the favorite mechanical metaphor of Enlightenment thought in this passage, his last sentence (like Shaftesbury's application of the metaphor in *Sensus Communis*) suggests that the multiple springs of all action, the soul's avenues of uneasiness, form a circulatory system of motivation and response that more closely resembles a human body than a clock. The fluid exchange between states of uneasiness and relief, pain and pleasure, constitutes the critical business of life, without which "we should all be reduc'd to the Condition of Statues, dull and unactive." Moreover, Franklin concludes through a series of five propositions that human desire ensures a degree of exact proportion between the sensations of pleasure and pain: they always attain a perfect equilibrium in every lifetime, though the absolute amounts of pain or pleasure occurring in any individual existence may vary. This last conviction—which Franklin confesses runs contrary to much "common Experience"—establishes the psychological groundwork for his earlier assertion that God uses or esteems all creatures equally.

None of Franklin's major sources of influence suggest such a radical equilibrium in human experience. Addison's mythic fable concludes with Pleasure and Pain in perpetual imbalance in the lives of individuals. William Wollaston goes to great lengths to illustrate how degrees of pleasure and pain might on occasion cancel one another, but in the end the spectacle of history leads him to insist on the necessity for an afterlife where earthly injustices will be redressed: "Can anyone then with Reason imagine, that *reason* should be given, tho' it were but to a few, only to be run down and trampled upon, and then extinguish'd? May we not rather conclude that there must be *some world*, where *reason* will have its turn, and prevail and triumph? Some Kingdom of *Reason* to come?"[30]

Wollaston's uncharacteristic burst of eloquence in this passage suggests his sensitivity to the close relationship between philosophy and drama in the early decades of the eighteenth century. Shaftesbury praises and employs dramatic monologue and dialogue in the *Characteristics* both in homage to the example of Socrates and out of his conviction that dramatic dialogue is the form best suited to the psychological multiplicity of man. In *Soliloquy; or, Advice to an Author* (1710), his title alone almost inevitably leads Shaftesbury to single out *Hamlet* for its moral and spiritual power, and *Hamlet* seems as well to have been Wollaston's inspiration in his plea for the compensatory afterlife of Reason:

> What is a man,
> If his chief good and market of his time
> Be but to sleep and feed? A beast, no more.

Sure, He that made us with such large discourse,
Looking before and after, gave us not
That capability and godlike reason
To fust in us unused.
(5.4.33)

The direct pertinence of *Hamlet* to Franklin's *Dissertation on Liberty and Necessity* involves more complex issues than William Wollaston's tentative experiments with the moral sublime. But for the moment, it is important to emphasize that Franklin differs from Wollaston and Addison on the issue of a compensatory afterlife primarily out of his desire to make the discussion of providential rewards and punishments seem beside the point. The perfect equilibrium of earthly pleasure and pain confirms and extends Franklin's view of the Creator's equal esteem for all creatures at the same time that it elegantly dispenses with the drama of reward and punishment.

Franklin acquired his suspicions of reward and punishment from Locke and Shaftesbury, though in each case Franklin draws more radical conclusions than his immediate predecessors. In *Some Thoughts concerning Education*, Locke emphasizes repeatedly that children are to be guided in the path of virtue but not by a barrage of rules accompanied by parental threats and enticement; such a system might produce a cunning adult but never a virtuous or a happy one. Instead, Locke recommends an educational strategy skillfully adapted to a child's love of activity and variety, gently shaping habits in such a way that play and study come to have an equal "relish" in the child's mind. Locke structures his book to repeat this central message on as many occasions as possible. The following passage is representative:

> The natural temper of children disposes their minds to wander. Novelty alone takes them; whatever that presents, they are presently eager to have a taste of, and are as soon satiated with it. . . . A lasting continued attention is one of the hardest tasks can be imposed on them: and therefore, he that requires their application, should endeavour to make what he proposes as grateful and agreeable as possible; at least, he ought to take care not to join any displeasing or frightful idea with it. If they come not to their books with some kind of liking and relish, it is no wonder their thoughts should be perpetually shifting from what disgusts them, and seek better entertainment in more pleasing objects, after which they will unavoidably be gadding. . . . It is true, parents and governors ought to settle and establish

their authority, by an awe over the minds of those under their tuition; and to rule them by that: but when they have got an ascendant over them, they should use it with great moderation, and not make themselves such scarecrows, that their scholars should always tremble in their sight. Such an austerity may make their government easy to themselves, but of very little use to their pupils. . . . It is as impossible to draw fair and regular characters on a trembling mind, as on a shaking paper.[31]

It is the "great skill" of a teacher or a parent, Locke concludes, to get and keep his student's attention: "To this he should add sweetness in all his instructions; and by a certain tenderness in his whole carriage, make the child sensible that he loves him and designs nothing but his good."

The parent in such an ideal household remains a subtle and affectionate providential force, even without the employment of the more overt instruments of power—reward and punishment. Locke's educational system, in effect, applies the benevolent conclusions of the "Argument from Design" on a domestic scale. In similar fashion, Franklin diminishes the elements of awe and fear in his parental "Design," fixing pleasure and pain in an absolute proportion and then assigning an "equal Quantity of each" to every creature, "so that there is not, on that Account, any Occasion for a future Adjustment" (*Writings,* 66). The need for William Wollaston's restorative "Kingdom of Reason" does not exist. The books, in short, are balanced.

Franklin invites the bookkeeper's analogy with a certain, flippant gusto in the *Dissertation* not because he lacks a metaphysical imagination but because he is taking into account Shaftesbury's description of the challenges posed by a skeptical audience. It is not "devout Mysticks" predisposed to belief who solicit one's persuasive powers in a metaphysical dialogue but "these cooler Men," as Shaftesbury calls them in *The Moralists* (1709), doubters inclined to label religion mercenary and slavish: "For how shall one deny, that to serve God by Compulsion, or for Interest merely, is *Servile* and *Mercenary?*" (*CMM,* 2:272). It is tactically and intellectually naive to offer such questioning spirits the bait of an afterlife as a reward for earthly virtue, Shaftesbury argues. They must be made to see order and providence in history before being able "to conceive a further Building": "A Providence must be proved from what we see of Order in things present. We must contend for Order; and in this part chiefly, where Virtue is concerned. All must not be refer'd to *a Hereafter.* For a disorder'd State, in which all present Care of Things is given up, Vice uncontroul'd, and Virtue neglected, represents a very *Chaos,* and reduces us to the be-lov'd Atoms, Chance and Confusion of the Atheists" (*CMM,* 2:277). Shaftesbury is not willing that all should be referred to a Hereafter, but he is content that eventually some should be, once the skeptic has been lured back to faith. Franklin's contention for order is more extreme. Future adjustments to the account of virtue are unnecessary.

One discordantly conservative result of this description of human equilibrium is that life is stripped of all of its possible grievances: as Franklin puts it, the monarch and the slave, the beggar and Croesus, are equally happy and equally miserable. But at the same time, Croesus and the monarch have lost any fixed position they might have held in a stable hierarchy of disinterested order. They are not distinguished, in the Creator's esteem, from their meanest subjects or servants and serve no particular role in the distribution of divine favor to human communities. Individual consciousness, enmeshed as it is in the cycles of pleasure and pain, is the only metaphysically significant agent in Franklin's radically democratic scheme.

In his general discussion of pleasure and pain, Franklin urges that no reason exists to prefer one state or condition of life over another, a claim clearly influenced by the reductive psychology of Mandeville's *Fable:* "How can any Action be meritorious of Praise or Dispraise, Reward or Punishment," Franklin writes, "when the natural Principle of *Self-Love* is the only and irresistible Motive to it?" Pope expresses much the same commonplace of eighteenth-century thought in the second epistle of the *Essay on Man,* when he proclaims that "Self-love, the spring of motion, acts the soul." But Pope goes on (by a poetic counterpoise) to complete the couplet: "Reason's comparing balance rules the whole." Despite the suggestive equilibrium of pleasure and pain that Franklin proposes, a system of stable, mechanistic counterpoise is exactly what his *Dissertation* does not supply. In figurative terms, there is all the difference in the world between the rule of comparative balance suggested by Dryden's "equal Beam" and the ongoing conditions of exchange in Franklin's physical and metaphysical equilibrium. "Order is Heaven's first law," in Pope's universe, but in Franklin's (as in Isaac Newton's) motion is—motion not channeled by human merit or the princely prerogatives of reward and punishment but simply directed by the inescapable experience of pain.

In some respects, the picture Franklin paints of the human predicament is a puritanically grim one. It is marked by elements of tragic resignation, which he partly acknowledges in the last of the *Dissertation's* sum-

mary conclusions: "No state of life can be happier than the present, because Pleasure and Pain are inseparable." But the deeper implications of
Franklin's 1725 pamphlet are anything but static and resigned. Indeed, in
his own terms, his is a classically "interested" appeal, perfectly suited to
the circumstances of an obscure, unpropertied, nineteen-year-old printer
looking to rise in the world. The *Dissertation* places few restraints upon
that desire to rise; it is in fact an intensely activist document, a feature that
Franklin will recognize when he comes to revise it as a Junto paper five
years later.

Once reward and punishment become subservient to a democratic on-
tology—as, for all intents and purposes, they do in Franklin's pages—then
the necessary metaphysical conditions exist for a reconsideration of social
arrangements to reflect the inclusive extension of divine esteem. Gerald
Stourzh notes the apparent inconsistency in Franklin's mature political
thinking between his willingness to accept, even to praise, the institution
of monarchy and his lifelong contempt for aristocracy.[32] But the inconsistency conforms perfectly to Franklin's youthful metaphysics. A king who
strives to emulate the Deity's egalitarian sympathies metaphorically enacts
the order of things; a legislature or a parliament seeking to impose a network of privileges and exclusions upon mankind illegitimately falsifies
that order. At least implicitly in the *Dissertation*, a "great Occasion"
emerges for founding a broad distribution of political liberty upon a sense
of the relentless necessities of the universe. When Franklin sits down to
draft his library memorandum in Philadelphia six years later, his vision of
human history draws its scope and sense of possibility from these reflections.

The immediate actions to which the *Dissertation* appears to invite us,
however, are merely licensed rather than encouraged. We are free to satisfy
the desires bred in us by life's multiple sources of uneasiness, but there are
few incentives to the exercise of that freedom beyond simply local and
temporary relief. New uneasiness will always follow, no praise or merit
will ever be due to any of our unusual or singular achievements, God's
esteem will never flow more generously to us than to any other entity in
creation. Franklin's *Dissertation* finally argues that human life is not a radically individualized pursuit of gratification but a fundamentally communal plight, endlessly in motion and, paradoxically, unchanging in its
earthly circumstances and metaphysical status. A key outcome of the
pamphlet, then, is the recognition of the human community of interest,

not a competition among the selfishly interested. A Creator who delights in action, in motion, and who uniformly esteems all creation is precisely the sort of deity to preside over what is shortly to become Franklin's personal cult of virtue.

The dedication to James Ralph opens the *Dissertation* precisely on this note of community. Ralph had, for all his faults, been Franklin's emotional link to Philadelphia during the early months in London. He helped Franklin spend his money, he used Franklin's name, he resented Franklin's "familiarities" with his mistress. But through all of these complications, they remained warm "familiars" and would remain so for the rest of Ralph's life. In Ralph's company, Franklin took in the plays at London's theaters, where together they might have seen, in 1725, a production of *Hamlet* staged at the Royal Theater in Drury Lane, along with *Macbeth, The Tempest,* and Addison's *Cato.*[33] Indeed, the dedication to Ralph echoes some of the spirit with which Hamlet affectionately dismisses Horatio's profession of unworthiness:

> Nay, do not think I flatter.
> For what advancement may I hope from thee,
> That no revenue hast but thy good spirits
> To feed and clothe thee? Why should the poor be
>   flattered?
> (3.2.62)

James Ralph was entirely too much passion's slave for the rest of Hamlet's encomium to apply, but the joint lack of revenue cheerfully endured by two spirited young "philosophers" fits the case of Franklin and Ralph quite well. Shaftesbury had already prepared Franklin to view *Hamlet* as a philosophical form, and Francis Hutcheson drew from Hamlet's famous soliloquy on the player's tears to reinforce his own argument for the existence of sudden, disinterested moral passions in man: "What's Hecuba to him, or he to Hecuba, / That he should weep for her?"

For many reasons, then, it is natural for Franklin to turn to Shakespeare's most reflective play as he addresses an imaginary reader's ultimate objection to his assertion that pleasure and pain are always equal in human life. Surely "common Experience" refutes this claim! But Franklin replies to this objection first by paraphrasing William Wollaston on the unknowable nature of another's private experience and then by echoing the relationships between inner guilt and outer performance that occupy

Shakespeare in the cases of Claudius and Hamlet. "When we see Riches, Grandeur, and a chearful Countenance," Franklin writes,

> we easily imagine Happiness accompanies them, when oftentimes 'tis quite otherwise: Nor is a constantly sorrowful Look, attended with continual Complaints, an infallible Indication of Unhappiness. In short, we can judge by nothing but Appearances, and they are very apt to deceive us. Some put on a gay chearful Outside, and appear to the World perfectly at Ease, tho' even then, some inward Sting, some secret Pain imbitters all their Joys, and makes the Ballance even; Others appear continually dejected and full of Sorrow; but even Grief itself is sometimes *pleasant,* and Tears are not always without their Sweetness. . . . Others retain the Form and outside Shew of Sorrow, long after the Thing itself, with its Cause, is remov'd from the Mind; it is a Habit they have acquir'd and cannot leave. (*Writings,* 67)

Among Franklin's literary preceptors, it is not Wollaston but Hamlet who displays such a vivid appreciation for the "forms, moods, shapes of grief," the outward show of sorrow. Franklin's interest in the theater of the passions, in this passage, draws directly on the opening exchanges in the play between Hamlet and his mother, even to Franklin's careful echo of Gertrude's reassuring modifier in his imaginary antagonist's appeal to the authority of "common" experience: "Thou know'st 'tis common," Gertrude observes to her son, "All that lives must die." Hamlet's grim reply, of course, underscores the complex reverberations of "common."

In the final passages of the *Dissertation,* Franklin presents his sense of an afterlife and of the immortality of the soul by comparing death to a sleep in which all cessation of thought amounts to cessation of being, regardless of the fate of that "Faculty" of contemplation one calls the soul. His analysis seems curiously cold, until we recall Franklin's disclaimers of certainty at the beginning of the *Dissertation.* But perhaps as important as his philosophical modesty is the linguistic and dramatic ambition that prompts Franklin to identify his own thoughts on immortality with the meditations that lead Hamlet to pause on the brink of nothingness. "But suppose," Franklin writes, "we pass the greatest part of Life in Pain and Sorrow, suppose we die by Torments and *think no more.*" It may still be the case (he concludes) that pleasure will compensate even for "an Age of Pain," not through the comforts of an afterlife but through infinite compression, "as one cubic Inch may be made to contain . . . as much Matter as would fill ten thousand cubic Feet." One thinks of Hamlet's admiration for the ability of Fortinbras and his army to compress all the passion of their lives into a contest for "a plot / Whereon the numbers cannot try the cause."

The fate of the soul, in Franklin's account, is nearly a transliteration of Hamlet's celebrated fears: "tho' incapable of Destruction itself," Franklin acknowledges, "to cease to *think* is but little different from *ceasing to be*" (*Writings,* 69). The soul survives the body's dissolution but not the self. These closing passages of the *Dissertation* require a reader to be attentive to the echoes of dramatic poetry that Franklin's exuberance and youth, as well as the friendly eye of James Ralph, encourage him to attempt in his account of human suffering and human joy.

The four surviving resolutions from the "Plan of Conduct" that Franklin drew up as he sailed home to Philadelphia in 1726 reflect quite closely this interplay between the reductive and the expansive aspects of the *Dissertation.* Franklin introduces these resolutions with a comparison between "the art of poetry" and the art of life. Just as a plan is indispensable to the writing of "what may be worth the reading," so those who aspire to some greater coherence in life must also observe a "regular design" (*Papers,* 1:99). It is both an illuminating and a confusing comparison, for two of the surviving four resolutions—the first and the third—seem to be drawn from a purely material economy of pain and pleasure that has nothing in common with the poetic heights of human experience. "It is necessary for me to be extremely frugal for some time, till I have paid what I owe," Franklin dutifully notes in the first of the four resolves; accordingly, in the third he undertakes "to apply myself industriously to whatever business I take in hand, and not divert my mind from my business by any foolish project of growing suddenly rich; for industry and patience are the surest means of plenty." Practical, economic necessity alone—or what the *Dissertation* will recognize as an austere form of self-love—appears to dictate such narrow goals.

The second and fourth resolutions, however, though not without their tinctures of self-interest, spring from the *Dissertation*'s emphasis on the neutrality of human merit and the community of human need. Franklin exhorts himself in these grander resolves always "to endeavor to speak truth . . . [to] aim at sincerity in every word and action—the most amiable excellence in a rational being," but at the same time to emphasize charity over truth. The last of the four resolutions, in particular, compromises its absolute ethical demands in the interest of communion: "I resolve to speak ill of no man whatever, not even in a matter of truth; but rather by some means excuse the faults I have charged upon others, and upon proper occasions speak all the good I know of everybody" (*Papers*, 1:100).

John Locke's three tests for membership in his society for the promotion of truth and Christian charity jointly emphasize the love of man and the love of truth as necessary conditions for participation in free inquiry. But Locke's tests did not envision the possible collision of his loves, the breakdown of his society along lines of stress created by deep and competing loyalties.[34] Even this early in his life, Franklin recognizes the latent energies of division in the "matter of truth." His own four resolves invoke amiable excellence as a restraint upon the exercise of absolute rectitude. Excellence that is not amiable may finally fail of achieving its ends and serving the cause of reason. An emerging tradesman's tact is certainly part of the basis of this last commitment. But just as evident in these words is Franklin's recognition of an obligation to imitate, as well as he can, the divine pattern of uniformly distributed esteem. Good and ill, human fault and its extenuation or excuse, form an ethical equilibrium in life, corresponding to the circulation of pleasure and pain and prohibiting the exercise of dogmatic judgment. Fragmentary though it is, Franklin's "Plan of Conduct" forms a recognizable stage in the transformation of pure belief into active principle—a transformation that he systematically extends through his commercial and public life in Philadelphia over the next thirty years.

Chapter Two

ACTS OF RELIGION

The language of Franklin's precocious *Dissertation on Liberty and Necessity* suggests the extent of his youthful susceptibility to moments like the one in Francis Hutcheson's *Inquiry*, where faith in a sublime moral harmony sustains human consciousness against the "casual Evils" of earthly existence. Hutcheson's language represents the theoretical core of the Augustan idea of order, an idea to which Franklin responds with the zeal of an enthusiast.[1] His own experiments with the moral sublime, however, are more restrained than those of Hutcheson or Shaftesbury, at least partly as a result of Franklin's keen awareness that he must live in a tradesman's world as well as in that of a philosophical poet and rhapsodist. His representative audience is James Ralph rather than the elite circle of scholarly noblemen and clerics for whom Samuel Palmer was reprinting William Wollaston's book on the religion of nature. But just as Silence Dogood moves comfortably among sublime and humble subjects, Franklin proves adept at negotiating between the rarefied climate of the *Dissertation* and the practical "Plan of Conduct" that he drafted to shape his future.

As Franklin coped with the unexpected challenges of readjusting to colonial life in 1726, he continued to build into his daily habits and into his writing this blend of common and uncommon elements, elite intellectual appetites side by side with quite ordinary preoccupations. What emerged as the distinctive property of Franklin's greatest prose—his capacity to embody the most sophisticated ideas in the simplest language—began as a distinctive property of his daily life in Philadelphia. This complex enactment of style has its roots in Franklin's wide reading, but it becomes most visible in his portrayal of his "speech" in the *Autobiography* as well as in his carefully scripted and religiously performed the "Articles of Belief and Acts of Religion."[2]

Speech—as Franklin acknowledges in his 1726 "Plan of Conduct"—is the essential medium of amiable excellence, the means by which character discloses itself and cements the bonds of rational community. Though he purported to treat it merely as a tactical convenience throughout much of his public life, Franklin recognized speech as the primary social evidence of self-government through which individuals could dramatize the loyalties of their moral nature. Codes of civil conversation were among the apparatus of gentility that political clubs or scientific societies in the seventeenth century adapted to the needs of intellectual life in England and Europe.[3] John Ray, one of Franklin's favorite physicotheological authorities, suggests that the tongue is one of only two anatomical members for which nature provides a natural "bridle" as an indication of its rebellious tendencies.[4] The successful management of speech, then, began to serve as a sign of the subjection of all of the body's passions to a higher conception of human purpose. This subjection, in turn, closely resembled the kind of uncommon ethical discipline that Franklin foresaw as the basis for breaking the destructive patterns of partisanship in human history. Out of the simple elements of his "Plan of Conduct," Franklin crafted a detailed ethical and religious discipline, which reflected this rapidly expanding sense of personal vocation and moral purpose.

When Franklin returned to Philadelphia in October 1726, his patron and surrogate father, Thomas Denham, took a store in Water Street and promptly drowned—not literally, of course, but figuratively. Denham was seized by a sudden "Distemper" and "carried off," as Franklin succinctly puts it in the *Autobiography*. But the abruptness of Denham's illness and the impact of his death, as well as Franklin's own near-fatal pleurisy, suggest the cataclysmic deluge that marks winter's onslaught in James Thomson's vivid poem:

> Prone, on th' uncertain Main,
> Descends th' Etherial Force, and plows its Waves,
> With dreadful Rift: from the mid-Deep, appears,

Surge after surge, the rising, wat'ry, War.
Whitening, the angry Billows rowl immense,
And roar their Terrors, thro' the shuddering Soul
Of feeble Man, amidst their Fury caught,
And dash'd upon his Fate.
(ll. 163–70)[5]

The stormy destiny that Thomson describes is more suited in its ocean setting to the fictive death of Silence Dogood's father, but in some respects Thomas Denham's fatal illness after barely four months of near-familial intimacy with his young clerk reenacts the imagined state of orphanhood with which Franklin began his literary career. "He left me once more to the wide World," Franklin soberly recalls of Denham's death. The account of these events in the *Autobiography* even includes a suggestion of heartless "executors" who took Denham's store into their "Care" while abandoning the young man for whom Denham had felt such a "sincere Regard" (*Writings,* 1354).

The theatrical note that Franklin strikes in these recollections underscores his own rebirth from serious illness to find himself once again without work or prospects, thrown back upon Samuel Keimer and the business of printing. A similar revolution in circumstances had overtaken Deborah Read in Franklin's absence. On the advice of her parents, she had married a potter named Rogers, who deserted her shortly after Franklin's return to America and fled to the West Indies, where he, too, soon died. The *Autobiography* presents these transformative events—death, desertion, critical illness, abandonment—in the space of little more than a paragraph. The several crises seem, in a small way, to take up this handful of obscure human beings and dash them upon their varied fates in a manner that makes Franklin's touch of melodramatic language in his memoir seem perfectly appropriate.

Indeed, Thomson's sublime storms are curiously well suited to the mortal and emotional upheaval that Franklin describes with such marked restraint nearly fifty years after the fact. The reflective autobiographer of 1771 would find in Thomson's lines a consistent subordination of the foolish dreams of men to the vast, recurrent "biography" of the natural universe:

Now, fond *Man!*
Behold thy pictur'd Life: pass some few Years,
Thy flow'ring SPRING, thy short-lived SUMMER's Strength,

Thy sober AUTUMN, fading into Age,
And pale, concluding, WINTER shuts thy Scene,
And shrouds *Thee* in the Grave—where now, are fled
Those Dreams of Greatness? those unsolid Hopes
Of Happiness? those Longings after Fame?
(ll. 364–70)

These lines are pertinent to Franklin's mature political and diplomatic experience in ways that they understandably could not be, to quite the same
extent, for the young printer of 1726 and 1727. But Franklin was attracted
to Thomson's stern account of human hope as early as 1749, when he
quotes these lines in *Poor Richard's Almanac*. Even a gifted young merchant's clerk or printer's assistant might deeply feel the vulnerability of a
"pictured" future to the forces of fate. In the *Dissertation on Liberty and
Necessity*, Franklin offers his own dramatic account of the diminutive state
of men, esteemed by their Creator but not providentially favored over any
other feature of the universal design.

The rhapsodic lines of "Winter" treat many of the same themes that
engaged Franklin's mind during his London residence in a seasonal context that is, in some respects, suggestively linked to the seasonal events
that shaped his existence at these critical junctures. Thomas Denham died
in midwinter, just as it had been early winter—Christmas Eve, in fact—
when Franklin discovered that William Keith had effectively left him to
live by his wits in London. Thomson's poetic speaker, like Franklin,
weathers the worst psychic storms by reading in Plutarch, Plato, and
Homer, musing on Socrates, Solon, Aristides, and Cato in the company
of a special friend of "exalted Faith, / Unstudy'd wit, and Humour ever
gay." With a little prudent qualification (particularly with respect to the
state of his good "faith"), these terms might be said to characterize James
Ralph. One reason that Thomson's poetry was able to move Franklin as
deeply as he confessed to William Strahan that it did was because Thomson's first version of his most celebrated work both coincided with and
corresponded to Franklin's London predicament.

Thomson was much more traditional than Franklin in his assertion
that providence's "ever-waking Eye" pities "Mortals, lost to Hope, and
lights them safe, / Thro' all this dreary Labyrinth of Fate." The close of the
April 1726 version of "Winter" looks forward to a "wish'd *Eternity*," in
which the "licens'd *Pain*" of this world would be compensated with "Life
undecaying, Love without Allay, / Pure flowing Joy, and Happiness sin-

cere." In the *Dissertation on Liberty and Necessity,* Franklin's view of human fate is metaphysically much more rigorous and tragically austere, but he shares with Thomson more than just an aptitude for addressing, in their literary work, the general state of things in the universe. The indications of Franklin's ear for dramatic verse that mark the close of the *Dissertation* suggest another important basis for his response to Thomson's extravagantly dramatic monologue: not a poet himself, Franklin was nevertheless alert to the appeal and usefulness of poetry, particularly when it undertakes to express the great, passional "enthusiasms" of eighteenth-century life.

Thomson's "Winter" is enthusiastic verse in this eighteenth-century sense, rhapsodic utterance of the sort that Shaftesbury explores in his longest discrete work, *The Moralists, a Philosophical Rhapsody* (1709).[6] This is the dialogue "on Natural and Moral Subjects" with which Shaftesbury ends the second volume of the *Characteristics.* The third volume, consisting of "miscellaneous reflections," identifies the first two volumes as the central literary enterprise of Shaftesbury's life, which *The Moralists* brings to a conclusion by incorporating the concerns of the preceding four treatises, beginning with the *Letter concerning Enthusiasm.* Shaftesbury's primary speakers in *The Moralists,* Philocles and Theocles, engage in a dispassionate metaphysical dialogue during a dinner party at Theocles' rural estate, which continues the following morning as Theocles recites a "celestial Hymn" to the "*Sovereign* MIND" whose grandeur is expressed in nature. The hymn is a deliberate performance rather than a spontaneous prayer. Theocles periodically interrupts himself to inquire about the dramatic effect he is producing or to carry on a more temperate intellectual dialogue: "Now, Philocles, said he, inform me, How have I appear'd to you in my Fit? Seem'd it a sensible kind of Madness, like those Transports which are permitted to our Poets? or was it downright Raving?" (*CMM,* 2:347).

Of course, the question is disingenuous. What Shaftesbury strives to exemplify through Theocles' extensive rhapsody is sensible "enthusiasm," a mixture of near-liturgical self-discipline with spontaneous poetic effusion and religious ecstasy, which Philocles will later strive to label when he expresses concern over how a quiescent public might perceive "those who are deep in this *Romantick* way" (*CMM,* 2:394). Shaftesbury is using the term *romantic* here in a context that distinguishes it from late seventeenth-century usage. Even Samuel Johnson, four decades later, continues to derive the word's meaning almost exclusively from the idea of extravagant fictions represented by medieval and Renaissance romance forms. But Shaftesbury identifies romantic utterance with the celebration of an experience of religious sublimity that fuses science, faith, and artistic control into the beginnings of a new kind of speech. Theocles establishes these ingredients early in the third part of the dialogue, as he and Philocles are taking their morning walk:

> O GLORIOUS *Nature!* supremely Fair, and sovereignly Good! All-loving and All-lovely, All-divine! Whose Looks are so becoming, and of such infinite Grace; whose Study brings such Wisdom, and whose Contemplation such Delight; whose every single Work affords an ampler Scene, and is a nobler Spectacle than all which ever Art presented!—O mighty *Nature!* Wise Substitute of *Providence!* impower'd *Creatress!* Or Thou impowering DEITY, Supreme Creator! Thee I invoke, and Thee alone adore. To thee this Solitude, this Place, these Rural Meditations are sacred; whilst thus inspir'd with Harmony of Thought, tho unconfin'd by Words, and in loose Numbers, I sing of Nature's Order in created Beings, and celebrate the Beautys which resolve in Thee, the Source and Principle of all Beauty and Perfection. (*CMM*, 2:345)

The "Nature" that Theocles addresses is a complicated entity: scientific "Spectacle," loving "Creatress," and "Wise Substitute" of the "Supreme Creator." In certain respects, Shaftesbury appears to be proposing a new trinity, blending genders and disciplines with an unprecedented freedom that calls for a corresponding latitude in expression. Theocles is understandably self-conscious about the formal qualities of this passage; "unconfin'd by Words, and in loose Numbers" though it may be, it is still a poetic performance—a singing in celebration of created beauty and perfection.

Milton is Shaftesbury's immediate model in these rhapsodic passages, as Franklin's selections of verse for his own morning rites of celebration will soon make evident. But it is Shaftesbury, in turn, who directly stimulates James Thomson in his later hymn to the splendor of natural design.[7] The engendering, divine presence of Thomson's "Winter" is, like Shaftesbury's mighty Nature, a fluid blend of male and female powers. Winter, "Sullen, and sad; with all his rising Train," is a distinctly masculine entity of formidable, but limited, authority. The "opening Chambers of the South" that birth the new spring, the "lone Quiet" whom the poet woos "in her silent Walks," the "fair Moon" who kisses passing clouds, the clouds themselves "in whose capacious Womb" the storms of winter and the rejuvenating waters of spring reside are all definitive female elements and much more critical to the "physiology" of seasonal change than is winter's feudal pomp.

The images of female potency that Thomson employs are scientifically modern; the images of masculine authority are intellectually and historically regressive. The trinitarian pattern that marks Theocles' invocation of the great "Creatress" in *The Moralists* is directly responsible for Thomson's own poetic apostrophe:

> NATURE! great Parent! whose directing Hand
> Rolls round the Seasons of the changeful Year,
> How mighty! how majestick are thy Works!
> With what a pleasing Dread they swell the Soul,
> That sees, astonish'd! and, astonish'd sings!
> (143–46)

Thomson's numbers are, perhaps, less loose than Shaftesbury's, but both passages express the exhilarating response to a new integration of empirical with metaphysical experience. And both identify this perceived relationship with a necessity for new, worshipful speech. To this necessity, Franklin likewise responds, when, in 1728, he drafts the "Articles of Belief and Acts of Religion" in ways much more consistent with the heightened utterance of Shaftesbury and Thomson than his account of his linguistic powers in the *Autobiography* would lead one to expect.

Speech, in Franklin's memoir, often seems to be exclusively a convenience for conducting rational arguments or conveying information. This is the light in which he casts it when he discusses his adoption and, finally, his rejection of Socratic modes of discussion. "While I was intent on improving my language," Franklin recalls, he met first with an English grammar that led him to Xenophon's *Memorable Things of Socrates.* Xenophon in turn taught him to drop "Contradiction" as an argumentative style and to "put on the humble Enquirer and Doubter" (*Writings,* 1321). This strategy, too, Franklin dropped once he discovered that it often brought him unmerited victories. He retained only those habits "of expressing Myself in Terms of modest Diffidence" that were, tactically, most useful. The whole discussion, in fact, seems purely utilitarian: here is how to improve your powers of persuasion by adopting these useful forms. Indeed, Xenophon is probably not the important influence that Franklin claims he is, simply because Xenophon's Socrates is much more given to contradiction, and much less to humble doubt, than Plato's Socrates usually proves to be.[8]

The *Spectator* (#197) provides a much more revealing discussion of how to manage disputes "handsomly," from which Franklin undoubtedly drew when he devised his own public manner:

> Avoid Disputes as much as possible. In order to appear easie and well-bred in Conversation, you may assure your self that it requires more Wit, as well as more good Humour, to improve than to contradict the Notions of another: But if you are at any time obliged to enter on an Argument, give your Reasons with the utmost Coolness and Modesty, two things which scarce ever fail of making an Impression on the Hearers. Besides, if you are neither Dogmatical, nor shew either by your Actions or Words, that you are full of your self, all will the more heartily rejoice at your Victory. Nay, should you be pinched in your Argument, you may make your Retreat with a very good Grace: You were never positive, and are now glad to be better informed. This has made some approve the Socratical way of Reasoning, where while you scarce affirm any thing, you can hardly be caught in an Absurdity, and though possibly you are endeavouring to bring over another to your Opinion, which is firmly fix'd, you seem only to desire Information from him. (*Spectator*, 3:108)

Eustace Budgell, the author of this number, concludes his observations by emphasizing that the "true End of Argument" is information.

Franklin's account of his social tactics clearly draws on the *Spectator*, once more from the well-thumbed third volume, but at the same time Franklin broadens the narrowly utilitarian spirit of Budgell's advice. *Argument* is the term that both Franklin and the *Spectator* initially consider. In the *Autobiography*, however, Franklin expands his reflections to cover what he calls "Conversation," a more general application of the powers of speech that includes (Franklin notes) the giving and receiving of "Pleasure" as well as knowledge. As if to underscore this expansion of verbal possibilities, Franklin follows his endorsement of the pleasures of conversation with a playful exercise in the emendation of two lines from Pope. The process of emendation is delightfully instructive, for it allows Franklin to dramatize his nondogmatic principles by surrendering to "better Judgments" the very critical points that he so deftly makes (*Writings*, 1323).

Simple conversational pleasure is still significantly different from the rhapsodic ecstasies of Thomson's verse or Shaftesbury's moralists. Indeed, one anecdote from the first part of the *Autobiography* seems explicitly intended to fix in the reader's mind a picture of Franklin, even in his less temperate youth, as stolidly unpoetic. As with much of Franklin's memoir, however, the anecdote requires a careful reading. Franklin's first circle of acquaintances in Philadelphia—Charles Osborne, Joseph Watson, and James Ralph—were in some respects similar to Theocles and Philocles: a Shaftesburean brotherhood of young clerks and tradesmen given to reflective rambles "on Sundays into the Woods near Skuykill," where they would practice on one another their skills in eloquence or poetry.

On one such occasion they agree to a contest in creating versions of the Eighteenth Psalm as a test of their comparative powers in "Language and Expression." Franklin, "having little Inclination" for such exercises, agrees to present Ralph's psalm as his own in order to trick the envious Osborne into revealing an honest reaction to Ralph's gifts. The joke is a complete success, partly because of Franklin's embellishments: "I was backward, seem'd desirous of being excus'd, had not had sufficient Time to correct; &c. but no Excuse could be admitted, produce I must" (*Writings*, 1341).

The reaction both to Franklin's presentation and to Ralph's lines is gratifying. Osborne's praise is fulsome, and Franklin slips into dramatic voice to render his friend's response a half-century after the events he is recalling, when all of the participants except Franklin are dead: "But who would have imagin'd, says he, that Franklin had been capable of such a Performance; such Painting, such Force! such Fire! he has even improv'd the Original! In his common Conversation, he seems to have no Choice of Words; he hesitates and blunders; and yet, good God, how he writes!" (*Writings*, 1342). Some of the complexity of Franklin's account is already evident in the distinctions he is drawing, through Osborne, among three modes of "speech": common conversation (in which Franklin's Socratic humility comes off poorly), a polished text, and live performance. There is, Franklin subtly asserts, no hesitation or blundering in either the false modesty of his preamble or the force and fire of his reading. One may speak one's lines, as Hamlet reminds us, either in fits of clumsy bombast or with genuinely measured passion. Osborne's words, as Franklin presents them, are intended to celebrate the actor as well as the speech. Franklin performs a brief part, and in the memoir he writes a brief "play" to suggest that his inclination for the dramatic sublime is much more highly developed than he wishes to assert openly.

The description of this poetic contest ends with Franklin's apparently casual account of how fate dealt with two of his friends, Osborne and Watson, both of whom died young. With Osborne, Franklin establishes his comic pact for a postmortem visit to settle once and for all the nature of the afterlife. Though Osborne becomes an eminent lawyer in the West

Indies before his untimely death—and so, presumably, is sensitive to contractual obligations—Franklin complains that he never does fulfill the
terms of their "serious Agreement." Watson, on the other hand, the most
reticent participant in the psalm contest, abruptly and poignantly resur-
faces in Franklin's memory as "the best of our Set," who "died in my Arms
a few years after." The mixture of tenderness, elegiac regret, and comic
recollection in this closing passage would challenge any performer's dramatic powers.

Franklin's awareness of the pertinence of these memories as examples of
his artistic accomplishments and inclinations may be reflected, as well, in
the choice of the Eighteenth Psalm as a poetic challenge. In the *Autobiography*, he observes with considerable understatement that this psalm describes the descent of a deity. And so it does, an apocalyptic descent in answer to the psalmist's cry of distress as his enemies assail him, the "cords of
death" and "torrents of perdition" surround him. The Earth reels and the
mountains tremble as the Lord descends, with "thick darkness" under his
feet, wielding thunder, hailstones, coals of fire, and lightning to rout the
psalmist's enemies: "Then the channels of the sea were seen, and foundations of the world were laid bare, at thy rebuke, O LORD, at the blast of
the breath of thy nostrils."

These lines have an unmistakable application to the turbulent political
circumstances of 1771, in the midst of which the autobiographer is writing, and an equally marked connection both to Thomson's poetic apocalypse of the seasons and to Franklin's close association in the contemporary mind with lightning. The conspicuous understatement in his
allusion to the psalm's contents seems an invitation to fit those contents
into the complex dramatic and rhetorical texture of the *Autobiography*,
particularly since Franklin so clearly establishes, in his recollections of Osborne, Watson, and Ralph, a mastery of the multiple levels of performance available to him in language. At the close of the "Articles of Belief
and Acts of Religion," Franklin ranks among the "innumerable Benefits"
for which he thanks his "good God" three of the chief blessings of his existence: "Life and Reason, and the Use of Speech" (*Writings*, 90). The first
two blessings seem self-evident in their importance, but it is the third that
marks Franklin's close adherence to the tradition of moral and spiritual
rhapsody that Thomson exemplifies and that Shaftesbury consciously
evokes and deploys in the private exercises of faith.

Articles of belief, then, pass into acts of religion through the medium
of enthusiastic speech, which is both a means of expression and a means

of incitement, both spontaneous and prescribed, spoken as well as written. Indeed, actor and author need not be the same person for the spiritual and social ends of religious speech to be met, for the "performance" of faith to be sincere and efficacious, as Franklin's rendering of Ralph's psalm apparently was for Charles Osborne. Franklin would not require the young Irish minister, Samuel Hemphill, to be the author of his own sermons, provided the sermons were beautifully written and powerfully uttered. When in 1728 he assembled his own "little Liturgy" for private worship, Franklin freely mingled the words of others with his own formulations of prayer and petition. A candid acceptance of the close relationship between worship and theater marks the private religious exercises with which Franklin undertook to replace the vacuous ceremonies of Jedidiah Andrews's Presbyterian congregation.

The "Articles of Belief and Acts of Religion" begins by establishing, in the broadest sense, the "stage" on which individual human beings enact their piety: a spectacular, polytheistic cosmology. "The Infinite has created many Beings or Gods, vastly superior to Man," Franklin supposes, "who can better conceive his perfections than we, and return him a more rational and glorious praise." Alfred Owen Aldridge points out that Franklin undoubtedly borrows this supposition, and with it the idea of a plurality (or, as Franklin puts it, a "Chorus") of celestial worlds, from a number of contemporaries and predecessors, including Isaac Newton.[9] William Wollaston, too, in *The Religion of Nature Delineated,* celebrates what he likewise terms the "chorus" of the planets, as Shaftesbury does in his rhapsodies on celestial order.[10]

Part of the customary rhetoric in presenting the "Argument from Design" invariably entails interplanetary excursions of the imagination. Cotton Mather's popularization of the discoveries of contemporary science, *The Christian Philosopher,* voices the same wonder that Franklin expresses at the infinitude of space. Mather calculates, in a whimsically vivid analogy, that it would take a cannonball moving at maximum velocity 700,000 years to reach the nearest fixed star, a considerable underestimate, which, even so, provokes Mather's impassioned exclamation: "*Great God,* what is thy Immensity!"[11] The inconceivable sublimity of space leads Franklin also to conclude the Earth "to be almost Nothing, and my self less than nothing, and of no sort of Consequence," sentiments with which several generations of Puritan ministers, as well as Franklin's catechistically inclined Uncle Benjamin, would have heartily and soberly agreed. "A *Resignation* is requir'd," Shaftesbury's dialoguist Philocles observes, subordinating the human ego to the grandeur of universal order: "Man . . . resigns his Form a Sacrifice in common to the Rest of Things" (*CMM,* 2:214).

But Franklin's allusion to a "Chorus of Worlds," superior in some respects to human culture, confirms that one direct source of his cosmology is Milton. Midway through the "Articles of Belief and Acts of Religion," Franklin quotes Milton's choral hymn to the Creator from book 5 of *Paradise Lost,* which Franklin undertakes to sing as part of his own daily ritual. Milton's lines, in fact, conclude the first section of the "Articles of Belief," which Franklin labels "Adoration." The sections of "Petition" and "Thanks" follow, but the "Choral Symphonies" that Milton invokes were sufficiently influential with Franklin not only to suggest the outlines of the preamble to the "Articles of Belief" but also to compose the largest single section of the text. Franklin selects nearly fifty lines of blank verse, an unusually bulky quotation for a writer so closely associated with the aphorism, but perhaps not so daunting a performance for this experienced singer of the much longer Eighteenth Psalm:

Thou Sun, of this great World both Eye and Soul,
Acknowledge him thy Greater, sound his praise
In thy eternal course, both when thou climb'st,
And when high Noon hast gain'd, and when thou fall'st.
Moon, that now meet'st the orient Sun, now fli'st
With the fixt Stars, fixt in thir Orb that flies,
And yee five other wand'ring Fires that move
In mystic Dance not without Song, resound
His praise, who out of Darkness call'd up Light.
Air, and ye Elements the eldest birth
Of Nature's Womb, that in quaternion run
Perpetual Circle, multiform, and mix
And nourish all things, let your ceaseless change
Vary to our great Maker still new praise.
(5:171–84)

The full passage comprises most of the joint prayer made by Adam and Eve as they awake on the morning of their last day of unfallen life. Franklin cut a total of eight lines near the beginning and end of the hymn in order to exclude from his private celebration allusions that Milton makes to the invisible remoteness of God and to the possibility of some lurking evil in Paradise, suggested by Eve's troubling and prophetic dream. Evil, as *A Dissertation on Liberty and Necessity* makes clear, plays no role in Franklin's

universe, nor do hymns to natural design, such as Franklin is constructing, place much emphasis on divine remoteness. The universe may be
vast, but the celebrant, in a kind of paradoxical inversion, feels the vastness intimately as both an exterior and an interior spectacle.

Shaftesbury's rhapsody on the sun from *The Moralists* is a direct homage to Milton but emphasizes more than Milton's lines do the relationship between celestial "bodies" and earthly ones. The sun's expense of
energy in this passage is both miraculously vast and erotically human in
its scale:

> PRODIGIOUS ORB! Bright Source of vital Heat, and Spring of
> Day!—Soft Flame, yet how intense, how active! How diffusive, and how
> vast a Substance; yet how collected thus within it-self, and in a glowing
> Mass confin'd to the Center of this *Planetary* World!—*Mighty* Being!
> Brightest Image, and Representative of *the Almighty!* Supreme of the Cor-
> poreal World! Unperishing in Grace, and of undecaying Youth! Fair, Beau-
> tiful, and hardly Mortal Creature! By what secret ways dost Thou receive
> the Supplys which maintain Thee still in such unweary'd Vigour, and un-
> exhausted Glory; notwithstanding those eternally emitted Streams, and
> that continual Expence of vital Treasures which inlighten and invigorate
> the surrounding Worlds? (*CMM*, 2:371–72)

Nature's "womb," in Milton's text, is certainly the figurative destination of
Shaftesbury's solar ejaculations, but Franklin's liturgical interest in Milton's lines does not seem to reside primarily in their sexual imagery, except
perhaps as such imagery might be an admonitory (and motivational)
preamble to the portion of Franklin's ritual that follows: "the Reading of
some Book or part of a Book Discoursing on and exciting to MORAL
VIRTUE."

The lines from *Paradise Lost* that Franklin selects are conspicuous
chiefly for their exuberant pleasure in movement and in the participatory
equality of all created matter in the song of praise. From the four elements
on up the scale of being to the "Sons of Light" circling God's throne, the
entire universe is circulating and recirculating in a "mystic Dance" that
vividly illustrates what Franklin describes in the second of his articles of
adoration (just prior to the Miltonic song) as the "prodigious Motion"
through which the "Energy" of the divine will expresses its laws. The old
idea of a hierarchy of being influences Milton's language to a significant
degree, but the hierarchical terms are moving with dizzying speed in a
multiplicity of forms and directions. Subordination is not Milton's subject

in this hymn, a fact he may intend to suggest by refusing to distinguish between Adam and Eve in its singing.

Instead, the scientific models of circulatory interdependence and complexity govern this cosmology. Franklin, in fact, introduces the singing of Milton's lines in his private liturgy by suggesting the reading of passages from selected texts arguing the attributes and existence of God through appeals to natural history. Milton was writing *Paradise Lost* as Isaac Newton was completing his appropriately meteoric rise from a charity subsizar at Trinity College, Cambridge, to the Lucasian Chair of Mathematics. It is not surprising, then, that Milton's images might look forward to the scientific piety of the eighteenth century as well as backward to the theologically contested ground of the seventeenth.

For Franklin's purposes, these lines are as much a hymn to prodigious motion as to God, though not in the sense that Henry Adams would grimly forecast as he contemplated a twentieth-century iconography of the impersonal, spinning dynamo. The deity whom Franklin presents at the center of the Miltonic dance is, like the human agents of *A Dissertation on Liberty and Necessity*, exquisitely responsive to the dual psychological impetus of pleasure and pain: "O Creator, O Father," Franklin prays at the beginning of the "Articles of Belief," "I believe that thou art Good, and that thou art *pleas'd with the Pleasure of thy Children*." It was to generate this reciprocal pleasure that life was created in the first place, Franklin suggests, and since experience teaches that human happiness is impossible without virtue, Franklin concludes virtue to be at once a pragmatic necessity and a mode of praise, the joint source of divine and human delight. This mutuality of delight is, in effect, the "bright circlet" of praise that Milton elaborates upon in his hymn and that Franklin sketches out in the circulation of "delights" with which he closes the opening prayer to the "Articles of Belief":

> And since he has created many Things which seem purely design'd for the Delight of Man, I believe he is not offended when he sees his Children solace themselves in any manner of pleasant Exercises and innocent Delights, and I think no pleasure innocent that is to Man hurtful.
>
> I love him therefore for his Goodness and I *adore* him for his Wisdom.
>
> Let me then not fail to praise my God continually, for it is his Due, and it is all I can return for his many favors and great Goodness to me; and let me resolve to be virtuous, that I may be happy, that I may please Him, who is delighted to see me happy. Amen. (*Writings*, 84–85)

In some respects, Franklin appears to be striking a further note of resignation in these resolves. Since human beings are "of no sort of Consequence" to the great design, their powers of service and return are limited. But the limitation swiftly gives way to the extraordinary assertion of
the human capacity to give God "delight," a confirmation of the shared
moral nature of Creator and created being that Francis Hutcheson emphasizes in his construction of the moral sense as the common basis of
natural design and of the unexhausted "Delight" experienced by its human witnesses. In his *Inquiry into...Beauty and Virtue,* Hutcheson establishes pleasure and delight at the basis of the natural system, and he extends that notion, as Franklin will, to a concept of interplanetary
benevolence that will spontaneously prompt the inhabitants of the Earth
to delight in the happiness of rational agents even on "the most distant
Planets."[12] From Hutcheson's hint, Franklin constructs his elaborate spectacle of a universe of "Beings or Gods" praising the inaccessible "INFI-
NITE" but "not above caring for us."

When Franklin describes the project for achieving moral perfection in
his *Autobiography,* all discussion of this system of mutual delights disappears, and that fact may be part of the reason that many readers of the
Autobiography find those pages to be mechanistically cold.[13] But there is
nothing at all cold about the "Articles of Belief." Franklin is confessedly
looking for ritualistic and rhetorical means of "exciting" himself to the
practice of "Moral Virtue." Outward behavior needs to be subject to the
government of duty, but Franklin is also very much interested in his inward state, in the calmness, serenity, and joy of his soul, the humility and
sincerity of his heart. Formality and hypocrisy, he proclaims in the first of
his petitions, are as "odious" to him as they were to a long tradition of
American Protestants who despised ceremonies that stood in place of a
living experience of grace.

There is very little anxiety about the conversion experience in the "Articles of Belief," but Franklin's devotional text is nevertheless shaped both
by the strong desire to prepare oneself for each individual day and by an
equally strong desire for the ultimate attainment of "perfect Innocence"
and "good Conscience," true virtue and magnanimity. It makes sense,
then, to view the "Articles of Belief" in the context of the broad awakening of piety that marks the middle decades of the eighteenth century in
America. Gilbert Tennent was beginning his career as a revivalist at about
the same time Franklin composed his personal liturgy, and just as a revivalist's sermon is avowedly preparational in nature—a rhetorical incite-

ment to religious enthusiasm—so too are Franklin's prayers, hymns, and petitions.

The goal of Franklin's fourteen requests, or "Petitions," in the middle portion of the "Articles of Belief" is to prompt himself to become a social agent for extending to others the extraordinary charity that reason convinces him has been extended to all created being. Keenly aware that he is but man at the best, he offers an elaborate portrait of what it might involve to be the best of men in a world in which disinterested virtue is an impossibility and from which human culpability as well as human liberty have been banished.

The prelude to the "Petitions" is carefully worded as a reminder that the appeals that follow make no claim to identifying "Real Goods" or genuine blessings. They plead not for Grace but for assistance in the exercise of moral graces, in the creation of a "character" far more extensively presented than the self-portrait of Silence Dogood six years earlier but equally rich in dramatic suggestion. Franklin is thinking ahead to the contingent and complex nature of the actual petitions that follow this prelude, but he is also glancing back at his reading in the third volume of the *Spectator*, where Addison discusses the proper spirit of devotion by describing the prayer that Socrates teaches to Alcibiades: "Give us those things which are good for us, whether they are such things as we pray for, or such things as we do not pray for; and remove from us those things which are hurtful, though they are such things as we pray for" (#207). The analogy that Addison notes between Socrates' instructions in how to pray and Christ's framing of the Lord's Prayer may have suggested to Franklin the heroic linkage that he later draws between Jesus and Socrates in the motto to "Humility" from his list of thirteen virtues.

But Addison's anecdote preserves as well Socrates' comic recognition that human prayer is all too frequently "human": that is, the devotions of men are shaped by ignorance and self-interest, just as Mandeville insists every feature of life is shaped. Socrates avoids both the cynicism of Mandeville and the sacrilege of self-interested prayer by adopting the childlike form of divine petition that Addison quotes. Franklin's prelude to prayer addresses the same need:

> In as much as by Reason of our Ignorance We cannot be Certain that many Things Which we often hear mentioned in the Petitions of Men to the Deity, would prove REAL GOODS if they were in our Possession, and as I have Reason to hope and believe that the Goodness of my Heavenly

Father will not withold from me a suitable Share of Temporal Blessings, if by a VIRTUOUS and HOLY Life I merit his Favour and Kindness, Therefore I presume not to ask such Things, but rather Humbly, and with a sincere Heart express my earnest Desires that he would graciously assist my Continual Endeavours and Resolutions of eschewing Vice and embracing Virtue; Which kind of Supplications will at least be thus far beneficial, as they remind me in a solemn manner of my Extensive DUTY. (*Writings*, 88)

In one sense, this language seems completely to eliminate the metaphysical dimension of prayer, as if Franklin were intent on conducting a purely social exercise in drafting moral memos to himself. The distinct echo of Socrates' devotions in the *Spectator*, however, establishes Franklin's recognition that all prayer is necessarily a performance in which, to one degree or another, the words fly up and the thoughts remain below. Part of Socrates' moral heroism involves his capacity to recognize this predicament and yet still incorporate it, with gentle humor, into acts of devotion.

The ideal of Socratic piety persists in Franklin's petitions insofar as they reflect the dramatic richness of human life rather than the fixed nature of an ethical formalism. Shaftesbury, too, singles out Socrates as the "divinest Man who had ever appear'd in the Heathen World" precisely because of his ability to mingle sublime metaphysical speculation with comic realism and self-abnegation. When Aristophanes mocked him in the theater, Socrates attended the performance in a singular display of "good-humour," and though he often appeared to invite Aristophanes's "cloudy" mockery, Shaftesbury concedes, he nevertheless unites "*the heroick, and the simple, the tragick* and *the comick Vein*" in human character, forming in the dialogues a "*Pocket-Mirrour*" of humanity: "In this, there were *Two* Faces which wou'd naturally present themselves to our view: *One* of them, like the commanding Genius, the Leader and Chief above-mentioned; the *other* like that rude, undisciplined, and head strong Creature, whom we ourselves in our natural Capacity most exactly resembled" (*CMM*, 1:195). Franklin frames his own series of petitions in the "Articles of Belief" as just such a complex reflection, capturing the generous range of "natural Capacities" in human character.

A conviction of individual sinfulness is completely absent from the moral inventory that Franklin sketches out. Instead, a profile of ethical activism emerges as full of motion as Milton's celestial dance and surprisingly free of the rhetoric of human debasement so critical to the sermons of the Great Awakening. Franklin's requests for divine assistance begin with a recognition of his complex relationship to authority:

That I may be preserved from Atheism and Infidelity, Impiety and Profaneness, and in my Addresses to Thee carefully avoid Irreverence and Ostentation, Formality and odious Hypocrisy, Help me, O Father

That I may be loyal to my Prince, and faithful to my Country, careful for its Good, valiant in its Defence, and obedient to its Laws, abhorring Treason as much as Tyranny, Help me, O Father

That I may to those above me be dutiful, humble, and submissive, avoiding Pride, Disrespect and Contumacy, Help me, O Father

That I may to those below me, be gracious, Condescending and Forgiving, using Clemency, protecting *Innocent Distress,* avoiding Cruelty, Harshness and Oppression, Insolence and unreasonable Severity, Help me, O Father (*Writings,* 88–89)

Franklin's most conspicuous references to humility and submission come into play only when the petitioner departs from heavenly and earthly "courts" to enter his immediate social surroundings. Before God and his "prince," Franklin shows all the dignified confidence one would expect of a creature fully assured of his Creator's esteem and of his essential equality with monarchs. He is, above all, a "careful" subject rather than a deferential and submissive one. Loyalty and obedience are Franklin's professed goals in the first two petitions, but he makes equally clear his commitment to certain human prerogatives that include a propensity to critical independence and resistance as well as a degree of scorn for the hypocritical "forms" of subordination. In this context, the social deference of the third request includes an oblique acknowledgment of human stubbornness, resiliency, and pride. The forgiving spirit of the fourth petition does not preclude some degree of tolerance for reasonable severity and indifference to culpable distress.

Franklin presents virtue in these petitions not as a network of contractual obligations or authoritarian rules but as a dynamic system of energies, self-denying and self-asserting, subject to lapses and contingencies, a matter of moral passions as well as spiritual knowledge and enlightened reason:

That I may refrain from Calumny and Detraction; that I may avoid and abhor Deceit and Envy, Fraud, Flattery and Hatred, Malice, Lying and Ingratitude, Help me, O Father

That I may be sincere in Friendship, faithful in Trust, and impartial in Judgment, watchful against Pride, and against Anger (that momentary Madness), Help me, O Father

That I may be just in all my Dealings and temperate in my Pleasures, full of Candour and Ingenuity, Humanity and Benevolence, Help me, O Father

That I may be grateful to my Benefactors and generous to my Friends, exerting Charity and Liberality to the Poor, and Pity to the Miserable, Help me, O Father

The human agent pictured here recognizes that an aptitude for calumny (as well as a susceptibility to anger) has a certain kinetic resemblance to the extraordinary "exertions" of charity or the vigorous abhorrence of vice. The exercise of justice and temperance may lead directly to an expression of nearly intemperate satisfaction at the sense of one's own virtuous "fullness." The point is not that Franklin's petitions are compromised by marks of self-interest. Human beings, as presented in the pages of *A Dissertation on Liberty and Necessity,* are inevitably compromised. Ethical precisianism—the cutting and stretching of human character to fit the demands of an abstract standard of thought—was never part of Franklin's intention in composing the "Articles of Belief." "I believe thou hast given Life to thy Creatures that they might Live," he writes in the "Adoration" section, "and art not delighted with violent Death and bloody Sacrifices," with dogmatism and a morbid emphasis on ritualistic atonement.

A God who created the human character could presumably tolerate the spectacle of its mixtures and inconsistencies, the struggle to convert weaknesses into strengths. Franklin willingly exhibits that struggle even in the jumbling of sublime with banal traits that comprises the final group of petitions:

That I may possess Integrity and Evenness of Mind, Resolution in Difficulties, and Fortitude under Affliction; that I may be punctual in performing my Promises, peaceable and prudent in my Behaviour, Help me, O Father

That I may have Tenderness for the Weak, and a reverent Respect for the Ancient; That I may be kind to my Neighbours, good-natured to my Companions, and hospitable to Strangers, Help me, O Father

That I may be averse to Craft and Overreaching, abhor Extortion, Perjury, and every kind of Wickedness, Help me, O Father

That I may be honest and Openhearted, gentle, merciful and Good, chearful in Spirit, rejoicing in the Good of Others, Help me, O Father

The author of these fourteen appeals would seem to have some cause to plead for evenness of mind, but Franklin is not striving for the mnemonic convenience of a catechism. The petitions reflect an obvious delight in the humanity of their author as well as in the humane ideals they express; the circle of metaphysical delights with which the "Articles of Belief" opens—man in God and God in man—takes a poetic form in Milton's hymn and a prosaic one in Franklin's fourteen choral petitions.

The insistent uneasiness of human existence so vital to the young author of *A Dissertation on Liberty and Necessity* keeps these ethical aspirations from hardening into a lifeless monument. When Franklin takes up in the *Autobiography* his closely related project for achieving moral perfection, he risks the appearance of lifeless rigidity in order to emphasize the unrealistic idealism of his youthful goal. The thirteen virtues he itemizes there Franklin claims to generate from his reading and to order in such a way as to construct a sequential method or program for the management of behavior. The result has sometimes impressed readers as artificial and inhuman—a classic instance of moral precisianism—despite Franklin's efforts to present the entire project in a comically humane context and to cast the virtues in the more complex psychological atmosphere created by the prose mottoes that he attaches to each. A similar problem of mistaken intention or tone is impossible with the fourteen petitions in the "Articles of Belief," which are tied much more closely to the complex life of the petitioner, to the inescapable mixture of motives in human behavior, and to the disorder of actual existence.[14]

The expressions of gratitude with which Franklin closes the "Articles of Belief" underscore the universal charity that animates them. Taking his cue from Milton's celebration of the nourishing cycles of elemental nature, Franklin thanks his "Good God" for all the benefits of material life, "for useful Fire and delicious Water" as well as for the social consolations of knowledge and literature, reason and speech. Rather than pray for deliverance from evil, he thanks his Creator "for the fewness of my Enemies" and rejoices not in the prospect of eternal life but in the health and joy of "every Pleasant Hour." The brevity and simplicity of Franklin's "Thanks" inevitably suggest some reduction in scope at the conclusion of the "Articles of Belief," a return to the relentlessly necessary conditions of existence. But it is a return liberated by the extraordinary imaginative journey that Franklin has taken from the "first principles" of infinite space at the beginning of his text to the modest, hourly compensations at its end—boldly revising the political metaphors of the Lord's Prayer but in a manner perfectly consistent with Christ's scorn for those who "heap up empty phrases" in prayer, thinking "that they will be heard for their many words" (Matthew 6:7). Sustained rather than diminished by the broad dramatic and conceptual expanse of his articles of spiritual government, Franklin is newly prepared to undertake the conduct of life.

The initial sign of this sense of readiness in Franklin is the directness and sophistication that he brings to his portrait of moral heroism in the Busy-Body papers, the first extensive pieces of writing that he undertook after his return from London to Philadelphia. This series of letters to Andrew Bradford's *American Weekly Mercury* grew to thirty-two numbers, of which Franklin wrote only the first eight, but in many respects this performance is more ambitious and more authoritative than the Dogood letters. The Busy-Body is not so vivid an individual as the Widow Dogood, but he is less dependent than she on direct quotation, and he is consciously preparing himself to undertake a career as a journalist and publisher once the unwelcome competition with Samuel Keimer's presumptuous *Universal Instructor in All Arts and Sciences; and Pennsylvania Gazette* is concluded.

In the last of the Busy-Body papers that he wrote, Franklin prepares as well for his career as an almanac writer and for his role as a political pamphleteer by ridiculing the pseudoscience of astrology in the person of "Titan Pleiades" and by projecting some of his preliminary conclusions about paper currency. Titan Leeds is the actual almanac maker with whom Franklin initially competes and whose untimely death Richard Saunders cheerfully predicts in the first prefaces to *Poor Richard's Almanac* (1733). Franklin's first political pamphlet, *A Modest Inquiry into the Nature and Necessity of a Paper-Currency* (1729), appears less than a week after the last of the Busy-Body numbers to which Franklin contributed.

In the *Autobiography*, Franklin loosely associates these public roles of journalist and almanac maker with his private plan of forming a united party for virtue, but he suggests that his "narrow Circumstances" at the time prevented him from combining his private and public goals. In fact, these disparate activities form a single, complex vocation, emerging as they do in extraordinarily close conjunction with one another very early in Franklin's career. Within a space of three years, he assumes control of the *Pennsylvania Gazette,* issues his first almanac, and distributes his first pamphlet on a matter of public business. Almost precisely in the middle of this three-year period, he composes his 1731 memorandum on the succession of design and confusion in history, in which he proposes the present as a great occasion for change in human affairs. Franklin's early "circumstances" and intentions, it would seem, were anything but narrow. Though his celebrated 1728 epitaph proclaims his identity as a simple "tradesman," Franklin's trade from the beginning was instrumental to larger social and ethical ends.

The Busy-Body, then, is a self-conscious preamble to the career that Franklin intends to make for himself in Philadelphia, as both a printer and a public figure, but it is also an indication of the metaphysical assumptions behind these broad secular ambitions. In the portrait of the virtuous "Cato" that Franklin offers in the third number of the Busy-Body, he emphasizes private piety and character as the necessary foundation for public benefits. Cato, as Franklin presents him, inverts the Mandevillean formula that private vice is public virtue. Indeed, the criticism that the Busy-Body levels at "Cretico"—the "sowre Philosopher" and "cunning Statesman" who is Cato's moral opposite—seems far more suited to a figure of Mandeville's stature than to the inconsiderable Samuel Keimer, whom modern scholars seem generally to accept as the Busy-Body's intended target (*Papers,* 1:121). Franklin directly associates Cato with the Shaftesburean axiom that "Virtue alone is sufficient to make a Man Great, Glorious, and Happy" (*Writings,* 96). And he might have added, as well, his endorsement of Shaftesbury's conviction that virtue is both an ethical and a dramatic achievement.

At first, the Busy-Body presents Cato merely as a deserving countryman, but his abrupt appearance "at a House in Town" among "Men of the most Note in this Place" takes on an increasingly vivid and apocalyptic dimension. His rap at the door has a "peculiar" authority, and though his dress is common it is also suggestive of a saintly Wanderer: "his Beard perhaps of Seven Days Growth, his shoes thick and heavy" (*Writings,* 97). A group of worldly men are struck by the "Air of his Face" with a spontaneous "Veneration" wholly sustained by the rich panoply of Cato's virtues: humanity, benevolence, resolution, "strict Justice and known Impartiality":

He always speaks the Thing he means, which he is never afraid or asham'd to do, because he knows he always means well; and therefore is never oblig'd to blush and feel the Confusion of finding himself detected in the Meanness of a Falshood. He never contrives Ill against his Neighbour, and therefore is never seen with a lowring suspicious Aspect. A mixture of Innocence and Wisdom makes him ever seriously chearful. His generous Hospitality to Strangers according to his Ability, his Goodness, his Charity, his Courage in the Cause of the Oppressed, his Fidelity in Friendship, his Humility, his Honesty and Sincerity, his Moderation and his Loyalty to the Government, his Piety, his Temperance, his Love to Mankind, his Magnanimity, his Publick-spiritedness, and in fine, his *Consummate Virtue,* make him justly deserve to be esteem'd the Glory of his Country. (*Writings,* 97)

The virtues of Franklin's hero are not primarily the classic ones suggested by his name but the religious ones dramatically incarnated in the New Testament. They are likewise singularly appropriate to the role of crusading journalist that Franklin shortly hopes to assume. Yet Cato remains securely rooted in a "Country," a political culture of which he is both citizen and judge, an "Arbitrator and Decider" of worldly differences, Franklin assures us, not of the ultimate disposition of souls.

This complicated identity is subsumed under the virtue of temperance. It is largely as a dramatic temperament that Franklin presents Cato, with qualities of character that literally "temper" one another, as innocence and wisdom do in forming the mixed condition of serious "chear" that distinguishes Cato's demeanor. Temperance was the first of the thirteen virtues that Franklin assembled in his project for achieving moral perfection because, he claimed, a mastery of physical appetites like eating and drinking was a prerequisite to acquiring any other virtuous habit. But temperance has more than a tactical importance in Cato's character. As Shaftesbury presents it in *The Moralists,* temperance is the master virtue, an elder "sister" of political liberty and "nursing Mother of the Virtues; who like the Parent of the Gods . . . wou'd properly appear drawn by rein'd Lions, patient of the Bit, and on her Head a Turret-like Attire: the image of defensive Power, and Strength of Mind":

Is not this the Sum of all? the finishing Stroke and very Accomplishment of *Virtue?* In this Temper of Mind, what is there can hinder us from forming for our-selves as Heroick *a Character* as we please? What is there either *Good, Generous, or Great,* which does not naturally flow from such a modest TEMPERANCE? Let us once gain this simple plain-look'd *Virtue,* and see whether the more shining *Virtues* will not follow. See what that *Country of the Mind* will produce, when by the wholesom Laws of this Legislatress it has obtain'd its *Liberty!* You, PHILOCLES, who are such an Admirer of *Civil Liberty*...can you imagine no Grace or Beauty in that original *Native Liberty,* which sets us free from so many inborn Tyrannys, gives us the Privilege of our-selves, and makes us *our own,* and Independent? A sort of Property, which, methinks, is as material to us to the full, as that which secures us our Lands, or Revenues. (*CMM,* 2:251–52)

In the Busy-Body's portrait of Cato, Franklin follows Shaftesbury quite closely by deriving the shining virtues from the "plain look'd" ones, by fusing politics, property, and faith, in the country of the mind, to form a concept of heroic character far more ambitious in its public scope than the reform of Samuel Keimer's devious personality.

Keimer was an ideal candidate for satire during Philadelphia's early years, but satire was not a form that Franklin's personal education encouraged him to adopt. It was, Shaftesbury observes in his essay of advice to authors, a kind of literary blood-sport: "our *Satirists,*" he writes, are "Slaughtermen" whose instincts derive from ancient *"Amphitheatrical Spectacles"* (*CMM,* 1:270). The more noble goal of authorship and publication is the one that Franklin recommends, and promptly practices, at the end of the eighth Busy-Body paper: the settlement of the public's mind, "the Abatement of their Heats, and the Establishment of Peace, Love, and Unity, and all the Social Virtues" (*Writings,* 118).

These are the same goals—though more directly and cogently expressed—that shaped the Dogood letters as well, and Franklin explicitly unites them to his metaphysics in a brief speech that he makes to his Junto colleagues in 1730 entitled "On the Providence of God in the Government of the World." This speech, too, is part of the transformative discovery of vocation that Franklin was experiencing in the years between 1729 and 1732. Less complex than *A Dissertation on Liberty and Necessity* and less elaborate than the "Articles of Belief," Franklin's discourse on providence is nevertheless a further important sign of his readiness to assume the civic and spiritual authority with which his various comic voices were experimenting.

The "Articles of Belief and Acts of Religion" remains essentially private, a place where Franklin exposes more freely than he might in public the full range of his religious sentiments. In the discourse on providence, before an audience of his "intimate Pot Companions," however, he returns to the metaphysical subjects that engaged his interest during the last few years with a much higher degree of self-consciousness and sense of social context than either the *Dissertation* or the "Articles of Belief" displays. Franklin is addressing the Junto and not a single intimate friend like James Ralph, to whom he dedicated the *Dissertation,* or the parental Creator whose infinite goodness elicits the free disclosure of Franklin's adoration and petitions for aid. He has already become a figure in the Philadelphia community, and this public identity has begun to produce the constraints and compunctions Franklin professed to feel all his life when faced with the prospect of public speaking.

Laboring under the "great Disadvantages and Discouragements" of his speaker's role, Franklin comments for the last time in his life, in a systematic way, on the relationship between the attributes of God and the course of human events. Dispensing with all artifical aids to argument and asserting a dependence on reason alone, he recapitulates the dual basis of the *Dissertation* and the "Articles of Belief," confirming that "whoever considers attentively and thoroughly" the wonders of nature "will be astonish'd and swallow'd up in Admiration" at the infinite wisdom, goodness, and power of God. One does not need to "sing" these conclusions, Franklin observes, in order to convince a thoughtful audience of their truth.

In light of the Deity's certain attributes, Franklin considers three propositions about the nature of God's relationship to human history and concludes that we are "necessarily driven" to accept a fourth: "That the Deity sometimes interferes by his particular Providence and sets aside the Events which would otherwise have been produc'd in the Course of Nature, or by the Free Agency of Men" (*Writings,* 167). It would be absurd to believe, Franklin argues, that a God distinguished by the active energy of his creative power would cease to exercise that love of action and surrender the universe to fate. And it seems equally unlikely to Franklin that a God who exults in his freedom would trouble to produce a creature "in some Degree, Wise, potent, and good" who was not also, in some degree, free.

These are arguments drawn from an experience of human character projected by analogy upon God, just as Isaac Newton portrays the human understanding of divinity at the close of the third edition of the *Principia:* "God is said to see, to speak, to laugh, to love, to hate, to desire, to give, to receive, to rejoice, to be angry, to fight, to frame, to work, to build; for all our notions of God are taken from the ways of mankind by a certain similitude."[15] The statement in Genesis that God made man in his image, "after our likeness," is the basis of Newton's similitudes in the "General Scholium" and of Franklin's adroit defense of the efficacy of human will: "Now if 'tis unreasonable to suppose it out of the Power of the Deity to help and favor us particularly or that we are out of His Hearing or Notice or that Good Actions do not procure more of his Favour than ill Ones. Then I conclude that believing a Providence, we have the Foundation of all true Religion" (*Writings*, 168). The most critical of the consequences that Franklin derives from this understanding of divine character, however, is his respect for the operations of the religious sentiment in human communities, acting as a "Powerful Regulater of our Actions," producing internal peace and external behavior that is "Benevolent, Useful, and Beneficial to others."

The foundation that he actually constructs in his Junto speech is a platform for action rather than for calm adoration. The Deity is prone to interfere, to set aside the "course of Nature" and human agency when it suits his will. By a certain similitude, men too might set aside the course of custom in the service of benevolent ends. When, a few years later, Franklin attacks the Presbyterian Synod of Philadelphia over its treatment of Samuel Hemphill's covenant of works, or when he defends his own devotion to good works in letters to his family and acquaintances, it is this larger occasion for action that he is defending against a resurgent spirit of dogmatic formalism among Philadelphia's prominent clergy.

In 1735 the synod sought to discipline a young emigrant preacher whose doctrines more closely resembled the Parable of the Talents than the Westminster Confession. Franklin opposed the synod both in the interests of the pluralistic community that Philadelphia was in the process of becoming and in the service of his understanding of the charitable providence of God.[16] But his opposition is couched in much more vigorous terms than he employs in the Dogood letters of twelve years earlier. Franklin's defense of Samuel Hemphill takes the form of a sequence of anonymous pamphlets, structured in large measure as point-by-point refutations of the proceedings of the synod and the public vindications of its pamphleteers. He does not subordinate his own voice to that of the *London Journal* or to the dramatic requirements of a fictive persona. And though by convention he does not sign his contributions to the Hemphill debate, they are intensely personal work, acutely aware that the reader's "Opinion of the Veracity and Judgment of the Relater" will determine the effect of Franklin's words.

In these passionate defenses of the efficacy of works, Franklin appeals not to the operations of reason—or to the sublime infinitude of the Creator—but to the fervent example of Christ. In his private cosmology, he requires a mediating divinity between himself and the incomprehensible intelligence that he sees reflected in the vastness of created space. The proprietor of the solar system, the resident spirit of the sun, seems to Franklin a reasonable conception to offer in this mediatorial role: "For I conceive that he has in himself some of those Passions he has planted in us, and that, since he has given us Reason whereby we are capable of observing his Wisdom in the Creation, he is not above caring for us, being pleas'd with our Praise, and offended when we slight Him or neglect his Glory" (*Writings*, 84).

This is the God who participates in the psychology of pleasure and pain—by a "certain similitude," as Newton suggests—and to whom Franklin's fourteen petitions in the "Articles of Belief" are addressed, a partly incarnated Creator who corresponds precisely to no single element of the traditional Trinity but who strongly suggests the susceptibilities of Christ. This, too, is the dramatic model of "Consummate Virtue" that produces the spiritually ideal figure of Cato in the Busy-Body papers. Repeatedly, when he seeks to convince an unsympathetic reader about the priority of works over faith—faith is always associated in Franklin's mind with intense sectarian debate—he recurs to the Sermon on the Mount or to the prophecies and parables of judgment in Matthew 25 as irrefutable examples of the relationship between divine delight and human action.

The extraordinarily dramatic character of Christ appealed directly to this aspect of Franklin's temperament, his suspicion of ethical precepts that had become detached and codified outside the entanglements of personality, his appreciation for the fusion of virtue with human vigor: "Come, O blessed of my Father, inherit the kingdom prepared for you from the foundation of the world; for I was hungry and you gave me food, I was thirsty and you gave me drink, I was a stranger and you welcomed me, I was naked and you clothed me, I was sick and you visited me, I was in prison and you came to me. . . . Truly, I say to you, as you did it to one of the least of these my brethren, you did it to me" (Matthew 25:34–40). This intensely personal assertion of the religious importance of charitable works—coupled with Christ's caution, at the close of the Sermon on the Mount, against those who content themselves with the mere profession of faith—are Franklin's favorite authorities both in defense of Samuel Hemphill's priestly emphasis on morality and in defense of what some members of his family took to be Franklin's personal indifference to spiritual things.

Indeed, the unusual lengths to which Franklin goes to defend Hemphill, over the spring and summer of 1735, suggest the extent to which he recognizes Hemphill's case as a version of his own. The elegant and characteristic "Dialogue Between Two Presbyterians," Franklin's first contribution to the Hemphill controversy, makes all of his essential points on the theological issues involved with great economy and cites the critical biblical texts that sustain Franklin's conviction about the priority of works—about religion as an active principle. "I should as soon expect," Franklin writes, "that my bare Believing Mr. Grew to be an excellent Teacher of the Mathematicks, would make me a Mathematician, as that Believing in Christ would of it self make a Man a Christian" (*Writings*, 257).

If deftness of argument alone had been at stake, this analogy might have closed the discussion. But Franklin's two speakers continue their examination of the cluster of fundamental issues entangled in Hemphill's plight: Is the Reformation a fixed and static accomplishment or an ongoing process of spiritual development? What are a majority's legitimate powers over a minority in matters of belief? How should human fallibility affect the self-preserving instinct of institutions? Important political, as well as religious, questions complicate the issue of Samuel Hemphill's personal fate, questions with a direct bearing upon the degree of success Franklin might reasonably hope to achieve in the vast, redemptive design to which he had tentatively, and only recently, committed himself.

As long as some possibility of accommodation among the opposed parties existed, Franklin hoped that his "Dialogue" would foster it:

> In the present weak State of humane Nature, surrounded as we are on all sides with Ignorance and Error, it little becomes poor fallible Man to be Positive and dogmatical in his Opinions. No Point of Faith is so plain, as that *Morality* is our Duty, for all Sides agree in that. A virtuous Heretick shall be saved before a wicked Christian: for there is no such Thing as voluntary Error. Therefore, since 'tis an Uncertainty till we get to Heaven what true Orthodoxy in all points is, and since our Congregation is rather too small to be divided, I hope this Misunderstanding will soon be got over, and that we shall as heretofore unite again in mutual *Christian Charity*. (*Writings*, 261)

The aspirations for "settlement," for the abatement of public heat and the restoration of all the social virtues, that Franklin identifies with the writer's calling from the beginning of his youthful career still govern his approach to the Hemphill case in the "Dialogue." The form recalls the Shaftesburean commitment to "tempered" passion that the dialogue structure of *The Moralists* hoped to foster.

Once the opportunity for charitable union is gone and the synod has permanently suspended Hemphill, Franklin responds with some of the most impassioned prose he would ever write, a defense of Hemphill and an answer to the investigative commission of the synod, which swells into the longest of his published works. Only the *Autobiography,* among all Franklin's papers, is longer, and even the *Autobiography* obscures the depth of Franklin's passion and his scorn not only for the political presumption of the synod's action but also for their spiritual poverty. The *Defense of the Reverend Mr. Hemphill's Observations* attacks the commission's motives, their selective patterns of admitting evidence, and addresses the six articles of accusation against Hemphill, accusing the commission of erecting the Presbyterian Confession of Faith into an idol.

Franklin categorically dismisses original sin as "a Bugbear set up by Priests" and urges the central importance of good works on aggressively religious grounds. The respectful atmosphere of reasoned exchange from the "Dialogue" is gone but not the determination to argue from reason and the Gospel alone. Franklin is defending what his contemporaries would have considered to be a covenant of works, as opposed to grace, but he is defending it like a Puritan, in language that closely resembles that of the revivalists who were soon to begin their assault on spurious forms of human dependence. Franklin is, in important respects, an Awakener in these sentences, though of a very special sort. Sharply critical of the dubious enthusiasms springing from paroxysms of faith—as Charles Chauncy and others were soon to criticize the enthusiasms of the Awakening—he is nevertheless an enthusiast in his own cause, who suspects the synod of loyalty to dead forms at the expense of what George Whitefield and his colleagues would soon present as a vital, heartfelt piety:

> It is most astonishing to find those who pretend to be christian Ministers finding Fault with Hemphill, p. 40, for teaching, that *to preach Christ is not to encourage undue and presumptuous Reliances on his Merits and Satisfaction, to the Contempt of Virtue and good Works! This,* say they, *is a most dangerous Doctrine.*

And wou'd they really have Hemphill preach the contrary Doctrine? Wou'd they have him encourage impenitent Sinners with the Hopes of Salvation, by teaching them an undue and presumptuous Reliance on Christ's Merits and Satisfaction? And was it for this that God sent his Son into the World? If then Christ has shed his Blood to save such as wilfully continue in their Sins, and obstinately persist in a vicious Course of Action, then in Order to evidence our Trust and Reliance upon the Merits and Satisfaction of our Lord Jesus Christ, we must continue quietly in a State of Impenitence and Wickedness, and promise ourselves Favour and Acceptance with God, notwithstanding all our Sins.

If this be not Antinomianism, if it be not to preach the Doctrine of Devils, instead of the Gospel of Jesus, I know not what is. . . . But when Men continue in a vicious Course of Action, and imagine that God, notwithstanding their Impenitence, will save them at last, and that because of the Merits and Satisfaction of our Lord and Redeemer Jesus Christ, provided they at particular Times, when they happen to fall into a Paroxysm of Devotion, confidently declare their Trust and Dependence thereupon, and apply them to themselves, as our unmeaning Authors sometimes talk; when Sinners, I say, trust and rely upon this; it is a foolish, presumptuous and extravagantly unreasonable Reliance, and it is obvious to the meanest Capacity (our Authors still excepted) that such a Dependance is no way founded upon the Gospel. (*Papers*, 2:117–18)

In the "Dialogue Between Two Presbyterians" of a few months earlier, Franklin is explicit in his conviction that faith is a means only. Good works comprise the end of Christian life, a point of view he supports by appealing to St. James and Christ, whose only comment upon faith when discussing the grounds for admission to Heaven was negative. Not cries of "Lord, Lord" but the duties of morality, Franklin asserts, will fit us to be "the Heirs of Happiness." But in the "Dialogue," Franklin still holds out hope that the synod might display its good sense and piety by refraining from disciplining Hemphill.

A similar restraint marks the early stages of Franklin's presentation of the issues in the pamphlet exchanges of the summer of 1735. The line is drawn, in his own mind, not between civic pragmatism and sectarian zeal—between the reason and the passion of Augustan psychology—but between antithetical "religious" passions, only one of which is genuine. Hemphill's performances are directed toward incitements to virtue, while those of the synod are directed toward the preservation of doctrine. In effect, formalists and enthusiasts are attempting to inhabit the same institutional body. By the end of the controversy, this fundamental antagonism drives Franklin's prose much closer to the bodily invective practiced among his English contemporaries than even the pressure of the Revolution was able to do. "Such Inconsistency!" Franklin explodes at the synod's arguments, "Such Self-contradiction!"

> Surely these Men's Spirits must be strangely muffled up with Phlegm, and their Brains, if they have any, *encompass'd with a Fence of a most impenetrable Thickness....* For if to justify a known Perjury, to lye openly and frequently in the Face of the World; if to condemn Doctrines agreeable to the main End and Design of the Gospel, and calculated for the common Welfare of Men; if to stamp an Appearance of Sanctity upon Animosity, false Zeal, Injustice, Fraud, Oppression, by their own open Example as well as Precept; and to behave as bitter Adversaries instead of impartial Judges; if to do all this be truly *christian Candour, Charity and Truth,* then will I venture to say, these Rev. Gentlemen have given the most lively Instances of theirs. For all these Things have been so strongly charg'd and fairly prov'd upon 'em, that they must of Necessity confess their Guilt in Silence, or by endeavouring a Refutation of the plain Truth, plunge themselves deeper into the Dirt and Filth of Hypocrisy, Falsehood and Impiety, 'till at length they carry their quibbling Absurdities far enough to open the Eyes of the weakest and most unthinking Part of the Laity, from whom alone they can expect Support and Proselytes. (*Papers,* 2:125)

Fifty-three years later, in the third section of the *Autobiography,* Franklin acknowledges that he became Hemphill's "zealous Partisan" in this struggle, but the partisanship is clearly in behalf of Franklin's own religious convictions. He describes the conflict, in his old age, much more exclusively in political terms than in religious ones and gives a comic prominence to Hemphill's plagiarism that the *Defense* of 1735 completely ignores. What the autobiographer chooses to present as a matter of secular tactics, the young pamphleteer addresses with revivalistic urgency. The language that Franklin employs in 1735 demonstrates that it is not his politics that shape his religion but his religious vision—already drawing upon the enlarged scope of his 1731 memorandum on history—that energizes his politics.

Franklin returns to the issues of the Hemphill controversy eighteen years later in a letter to Joseph Huey that recapitulates the essential points of the 1735 *Defense.* Hemphill was even less in the forefront of Franklin's mind in 1753, in the midst of his extraordinary and rapid metamorphosis from amateur electrician to world politician, than he was two decades earlier. But the character of Christ and the implications of the Sermon on the Mount remained just as definitive and powerful for Franklin on the verge of preparing the Albany Plan of Union as they were to the publisher of the *Pennsylvania Gazette.*

In the 1753 letter, the "outward Appearances and Professions" of faith seem more than ever the appurtenances of a corrupt courtliness rather than a genuine devotion. They are, Franklin declares, "Flatteries and Compliments, despis'd even by wise Men, and much less capable of pleasing the Deity" (*Writings,* 476). Charity continues to occupy the center of Franklin's spiritual landscape, "but nowadays we have scarce a little Parson, that does not think it the Duty of every Man within his Reach to sit under his petty Ministrations, and that whoever omits them offends God." The term "Ministrations" here evokes the secular "ministries" of English politics that will occupy Franklin's persuasive and antagonistic energies for much of the rest of his life. But the Huey letter helps establish still more clearly the extent to which Franklin shared in the general movement of eighteenth-century American culture from a passionate, vitalized piety to political revolution.[17]

Within a few years of the Hemphill controversy, Franklin felt called upon to reassure his parents, in a carefully composed letter, that the rumors they had been hearing of their reprobate son in Philadelphia were no cause for anxiety about his soul. Writing sixteen years to the month after his debut as Silence Dogood, Franklin displays a "character" in 1738 that seems alert to continuities between the established printer and publisher and the Boston apprentice. Just as Silence Dogood asserts her basic good nature and courtesy, so Franklin begins his letter to his concerned parents on a courteous note, acknowledging his vulnerability to error and weakness but quickly establishing that he views these propensities as general human failings rather than primarily personal ones. Franklin is now able, in his early thirties, to link his sense of the necessity governing human life to the "extensive Charity" that Silence Dogood proclaims as one of her chief virtues. The letter begins by suggesting—on somewhat deterministic grounds directly borrowed from Locke, Shaftesbury, and the *Spectator*—that our beliefs are matters of fate rather than choice. Error is not voluntary:

I am sorry you should have any Uneasiness on my Account, and if it were a thing possible for one to alter his Opinions in order to please others, I know none whom I ought more willingly to oblige in that respect than your selves: But since it is no more in a Man's Power *to think* than *to look* like another, methinks all that should be expected from me is to keep my Mind open to Conviction, to hear patiently and examine attentively whatever is offered me for that end; and if after all I continue in the same Errors, I believe your usual Charity will induce you rather to pity and excuse than blame me. In the mean time your Care and Concern for me is what I am very thankful for. (*Writings*, 426)

It may have taken Franklin more than the two or three drafts of this letter that have survived to achieve its mixture of dutiful affection with firm self-assertion. Language that attempts only to placate its readers could not achieve such a balance of filial tenderness with the independent reserve to which a grown child is entitled in matters of belief.[18] But the singular power of the individual, whose mind is as unique as his face, is less important to Franklin here than are the allowances (as he calls them in a 1743 letter to his sister) that are necessary to the conduct of affectionate, collective life on the most public as well as the most intimate scale: charity, care, and concern. These three key attributes of the heart generate the syntactical inversion with which Franklin closes the passage above, as he closes the "Articles of Belief," on a gesture of thankfulness, embracing the insistent self in a framework of love and gratitude.

There is no possibility that Benjamin Franklin will consent to conceal his talents under a napkin. It is out of his power to do so, as evil is out of the power of men in *A Dissertation on Liberty and Necessity.* But "vital Religion," as Franklin calls it in a phrase from this same letter (which becomes inseparable from the debates of the Great Awakening), is much more a matter of works than of heresies and orthodoxies in faith. A reference to the Sermon on the Mount brings Franklin's filial defense to a close, touching on the most recent of his religious writings, much as the initial paragraphs in the letter draw upon some of his earliest ones. To an extraordinary degree, he sums up for his parents a course of thought that stretches across the span of years since his departure from Boston and, in the process, suggests the quite specific meaning he had in mind when he drafted the motto for "Humility," the last of the virtues in his project for achieving moral perfection: "Imitate Jesus and Socrates."

It is not precisely clear from the *Autobiography* just when Franklin composed his little book of virtues, but it was "about" the time of the "Articles of Belief." The virtues may well have been the "Acts of Religion," which the surviving manuscript of the "Articles of Belief" omits. In any case, the thirteenth virtue, and its expansive motto, were the last parts of the program to be written, and they reflect Franklin's personal attraction to Christ's advocacy of works in Matthew and his awareness of one of the most influential spiritual guidebooks of the early renaissance, Thomas à Kempis's *Imitation of Christ*. Franklin may well have read the *Imitation* during his months in London in 1725 and 1726. An updated version of the 1530 Whitford translation, prepared by an English Jesuit, Anthony Hoskins, was widely reprinted in the seventeenth century and was readily available in early eighteenth-century London. Hoskins presented his edition of Kempis anonymously, writing as "F.B."[19] The inversion of Franklin's own initials might have caught the eye of a young printer who was already displaying some curiosity about the Roman Catholic discipline of a seventy-year-old devotee of St. Veronica who shared one of his London lodgings.

Editions of the *Imitation of Christ*, translated into German, circulated in the Philadelphia German-speaking community during Franklin's first years in business, when he took some printing jobs in German and may have recognized a familiar text in an unfamiliar language, much as he did *The Pilgrim's Progress*, printed in Dutch, fished out of Long Island Sound with its drunken owner on Franklin's first journey to Philadelphia. However he encountered Kempis's book, Franklin knew it well enough by 1745 to make an irreverent joke out of a corruption of Kempis's Latin text in a letter to his wife's cousin, James Read:

> Your copy of *Kempis,* must be a corrupt one, if it has that passage as you quote it, *in omnibus requiem quaesivi, sed non inveni, nisi in angulo cum libello.* The good father understood pleasure (requiem) better, and wrote, *in angulo cum puella.* Correct it thus, without hesitation. I know there is another reading, *in angulo puellae;* but this reject, tho' more *to the point,* as an expression too indelicate. (*Writings,* 429)

The inclination to bawdy humor here is probably a reflection of the fact that James Read is newly married, living with his bride in his mother's house, next door to Franklin, and has written his older relative for advice in handling a family quarrel. The line from Kempis that James apparently referred to is not, in fact, part of the *Imitation of Christ*. "Pleasure," as Franklin is well aware, is a very strained translation of "requiem" (rest or peace), and *"in angulo puellae"* is at best clumsy anatomy.

But the allusion to Kempis is neither clumsy nor gratuitous. The advice that Franklin finally gives James derives (Franklin claims) from Socrates: "In differences among friends, they that make the first concessions are the wisest." But just as pertinent to James' situation is Kempis's advice in a true matter of "requiem": that "we must sometimes set aside our own will (though it seem good) so that we may have love and peace with others." Franklin could easily have some particular words of Socrates in mind for James' instruction, but the resemblance between the advice in his letter and the text of the *Imitation of Christ* seems too close to be accidental, and Franklin would certainly relish the representative conjunction between his two models of "Humility."

Beyond the suggestion contained in the odd wording of Franklin's motto—to "emulate" Jesus and Socrates would seem a more natural recommendation than to "imitate"—there is little direct evidence beyond the letter to James Read that Franklin was interested in the *Imitation of Christ*. Kempis wrote in a monastical tradition of *contemptus mundi*, which seems at first glance to have little in common with Franklin's involvement in schemes of worldly amelioration. But in the 1738 letter to his parents, Franklin presents his defense of works in language that approximates a famous passage from the *Imitation* that dismisses mere learning in favor of deeds. "The Scripture assures me," Franklin writes, "that at the last Day, we shall not be examin'd what we *thought* but what we *did*; and our Recommendation will not be that we said *Lord, Lord*, but that we did GOOD to our Fellow Creatures" (*Writings*, 426). Kempis writes in the third section of his first book, "On the day of judgment we will not be asked what we have read, but what we have done; not how well we have discoursed, but how religiously we have lived."[20] Both Kempis and Franklin are expanding on the implications of Christ's sermons and parables in Matthew, but their verbal resemblance to one another is not founded in a common biblical source.

Franklin prized this traditional subordination of intellect to action highly enough to expand on it in a prose meditation at the end of *Poor Richard's Almanac* for 1757:

> *Learning* is a valuable Thing in the Affairs of this Life, but of infinitely more Importance is *Godliness,* as it tends not only to make us happy here but hereafter. At the Day of Judgment, we shall not be asked, what Proficiency we have made in Languages or Philosophy; but whether we have liv'd virtuously and piously, as Men endued with Reason, guided by the

Dictates of Religion. In that Hour it will more avail us, that we have thrown a Handful of Flour or Chaff in Charity to a Nest of contemptible Pismires, than that we could muster all the Hosts of Heaven, and call every Star by its proper Name. For then the Constellations themselves shall disappear, the Sun and Moon shall give no more Light, and all the Frame of Nature shall vanish. But our good or bad Works shall remain for ever, recorded in the Archives of Eternity. (*Writings*, 1294)

Piety and godliness play unusually conspicuous roles in this passage, but the great emphasis falls as always for Franklin on charity. "He is truly great who has great charity," Thomas à Kempis also affirms, and he shows an equally vivid conception of the evanescence of earthly knowledge: "Tell me, where now are all the great students and famous scholars whom you have known? . . . Would to God their life had accorded well with their learning, for then would they have studied and read well. How many perish daily in this world by vain learning who care little for a good life and for the service of God. And because they desire to be great in the world rather than to be humble, they vanish away in their learning as smoke in the air."[21]

Like Franklin in his thirteen virtues, the *Imitation of Christ* emphasizes the psychological role of habit, or daily resolutions and accountings, in the prosecution of a virtuous life and dismisses the anguished self-examination for signs of grace that was characteristic of Protestant piety throughout Franklin's lifetime and that formed a chief basis for Franklin's opposition to the Presbyterian Synod and his separation from organized religion. "Trust in God, and do good deeds," is Kempis's simple formulation, an aphorism well suited to appeal to the temperament of Richard Saunders: "A good Example is the best Sermon," Franklin's almanac affirms, "What is serving God? 'Tis doing Good to Man."

After the first section of the *Imitation,* "Admonitions Useful for a Spiritual Life," Kempis turns his attention inward, to imaginary dialogues with Christ and to an exposition of the importance of the sacrament of communion, none of which would have appealed so directly to Franklin as the utilitarian admonitions with which the book begins. But in them, he found a fifteenth-century voice strikingly in harmony with his own eighteenth-century commitment to a life lived by the light of reason and the dictates of religion, complementary elements in Franklin's moral devotions.

Chapter Three

HUMANITY'S POCKET MIRROR

By 1756, when he paraphrased Kempis's book of devotions in *Poor Richard Improved* for the following year, Franklin had been retired from his printing business for nearly a decade. He had become a scientist, a politician, and (briefly) a soldier. He would shortly accept his first diplomatic commission and compile his last almanac as he was sailing to London, much earlier in the crowded year of 1757 than any of the preceding issues of *Poor Richard* had been prepared.

Since the time of Franklin's retirement in 1748, the almanac had taken on a more expansive, miscellaneous format, becoming a kind of substitute for his short-lived *General Magazine* of 1741 and conforming more closely in its subjects and its themes to the growing prestige of Poor Richard's creator. But from its inception, *Poor Richard* had been an ambitious and expansive document. As Bernard Capp amply and entertainingly shows, almanacs had accumulated a complex social history by Franklin's time, which far exceeded their nominal roles as calendars, diaries, weather predictors, and vendors of astrological prophecy.[1] Franklin takes full advantage of the flexibility and popularity of the almanac to give dramatic, public extension to his moral and religious enthusiasms.

In particular, he is quick to exploit the vestigial narrative elements of the almanac, to treat it as a serialized story with a unique capacity to advance a number of plots simultaneously. James Thomson's conventional identification of the "biographical" resonance of the seasons suggests the most obvious way in which an almanac invariably subsumes a general human narrative, but Franklin incorporates personal, historical, and moral narratives into this essential seasonal plot. To some degree, this process of incorporation is typical of Anglo-American almanacs. *Poor Richard* begins its series by imitating a celebrated "story" associated with English almanacs and almanac makers of the early eighteenth century. Franklin's narratives, however, are distinguished by their inclusive nature, by the ambition that quickly leads him to use the pages of *Poor Richard* not strictly as devices for segmenting the year into convenient units of time but as emblems of the complex intersection of interests and experience that the days of the year represent.

The aphorisms, too, play a critical role in this creation of a cumulative, human narrative. Walter Benjamin observes that the storyteller's craft is, in many ways, best exemplified by the proverb, a verbal ruin, as Benjamin puts it, "which stands on the site of an old story and in which a moral twines about a happening like ivy around a wall."[2] The almanac format gives Franklin a means of linking his own proverbs—the aphorisms he culled and polished from a range of sources—with the narrative sites that could best reawaken their full potential for counsel. *Poor Richard* is built upon this sense of coincidental significances, which collectively assert the common, rather than the divided, ground of human experience.

Indeed, the work of compiling the first issue of *Poor Richard* roughly coincides with a momentous private event in Franklin's life: the birth of his son, Francis Folger, on October 20, 1732. Franklin was neither a new nor, at age twenty-six, a particularly young father. His first child, William, had come to live with Franklin and Deborah Read shortly after their common-law marriage in 1730. When William's legitimate half-brother was born two years later, William was a little over three years old. It was an emotionally complicated, as well as a crowded, household, but in late 1732 Franklin must have felt an exhilarating sense of having come through potentially damaging experiences if not unscathed at least intact and in a position to make some moral and emotional restitution for past pain.

Francis Folger's birth was a new beginning, an amendment, the special significance of which would not have been lost on the neighbors and patrons of Franklin's press, who were well aware of William's predicament and of Deborah Read's multiple disappointments. The astrological verses that Franklin prints on the third page of the 1733 almanac seem, in part, a faintly disguised acknowledgment of his family's unusual, erotic biography, as if the dramatis personae of Franklin's personal life had taken on

the costumes of one of John James Heidegger's eighteenth-century masquerades:

> *Saturn* diseas'd with Age, and left for dead;
> Chang'd all his Gold to be involv'd in Lead.
> *Jove,* Juno leaves, and loves to take his Range;
> From whom man learns to love, and loves to change.
> ♂ is disarm'd, and to ♀ gone,
> Where *Vulcan's* Anvil must be struck upon.
> That *Luna's* horn'd, it cannot well be said,
> Since I ne'er heard that she was married.
> (*Papers*, 1:290)

The deities and love triangles evoked in these lines form an account of
the entangled courtship of Benjamin Franklin and Deborah Read that is
neither flippant nor apologetic, addressing the presumed fate of the unfortunate Rogers, Deborah's first husband "left for dead," and the obscured
parentage of William Franklin, as well as the consolatory birth of Francis
Folger, who partly compensates for the stigma—the "horns"—that Deborah may understandably have felt in raising her husband's illegitimate
child. Franklin himself, something of a free-ranging Jove where "low
women" were concerned, is "disarmed" and united to a prolific Luna,
whose marriage is untainted by her husband's changeful ways, habits
which had come to a ceremonial end with William's adoption into the
household.

The deities and love triangles Though the first almanac did not appear until mid-December 1732—
late by almanac standards but a forgivable delay in a house with a new
baby—Poor Richard's dramatic posture in his first preface, his newly acute
monetary necessities, his appeal for the support of his neighbors, all directly reflect Franklin's personal circumstances, charging the preface with a
rich mixture of intimate and generic significance. In a catalogue of the
principal monarchs of Europe with which Franklin closes this first almanac, he announces the nativity of Poor Richard Saunders: "an American
Prince, without Subjects, his Wife being Viceroy over him, 23 October,
1684, [age] 49." The birth date he selects for his fictive almanac maker is
three days after the birthday of Francis Folger Franklin, much as if some of
the private celebration of his expanding family spills over into the energy
and the literary aspirations of his text.[3]

These autobiographical elements are critical to Franklin's emerging
self-portrait as Richard Saunders, but they give a misleading impression of

the singularity of *Poor Richard*. Originality in an almanac is not a virtue. Every essential feature of *Poor Richard*'s appearance in 1733 was prescribed by traditions of almanac making developed in England during the tumultuous decades of the seventeenth century, the golden age of English almanacs. Making predictions is uncertain business under the best of circumstances. In a century of political and religious upheaval, it was particularly hazardous. But the market for certainty is also strongest in uncertain times. Predictability—not predictions—is the basis of the almanac maker's appeal to the common reader. Even Jonathan Swift's celebrated attack on judicial astrology in Isaac Bickerstaff's *Predictions for the Year 1708*, a text that Franklin openly imitates in his first almanac, is inherently conservative in its witty abuse of Bickerstaff's astrological "competitor," the Whig almanac maker, John Partridge. Almanacs commonly abused their competitors' astrological skills, along with their politics, their religion, and their character. Swift and Franklin were fully aware of this tradition of disparagement, though they exploit the tradition in revealingly distinct ways.

The almanac, then, is a generically conservative repository of forecasts—a peculiarly mixed identity with which Franklin's emerging ethical vision was especially sympathetic and which the opening issue of *Poor Richard* clearly proclaims. None of Franklin's major competitors for the Philadelphia almanac market in 1733—Titan Leeds, John Jerman, Thomas Godfrey—chose to publish under an alias. Franklin did so not as a disguise but as an advertisement of the complex network of traditional roles and purposes that he intended his almanac to serve. Among the inclusive voices of his career, Richard Saunders is Franklin's most ambitious dramatic creation, in large part because he is no creation at all. Even his name was borrowed directly from a celebrated, seventeenth-century English astrologer who was closely associated with the innovation of printing public anniversaries in the almanac calendar.[4]

The most conspicuous sign of Franklin's interest in the literary history of almanacs is his adaptation of Swift's hoax of 1708, predicting the death of Titan Leeds as Isaac Bickerstaff predicts the death of John Partridge. Very few members of Franklin's educated audience will have missed his indebtedness. The *Bickerstaff Papers* were reprinted in Swift's *Miscellanies in Prose and Verse* in 1711, 1713, and 1727. A 1736 edition was in the collection of the Library Company, where members of Franklin's immediate circle could easily consult it to compare.[5]

Reproducing that comparison in the widest possible context exposes the range of qualities that quickly secured *Poor Richard's* place in the affections of its readers. In the acerbic atmosphere of public life to which Jonathan Swift's Bickerstaffian pseudonym alludes, "Richard Saunders'" voice is reassuringly fallible and human, that of a generous, nonprescriptive moralist for whom the exercise of wit is a secondary consideration. The temperamental resources that foster unity rather than division are much more conspicuous in Saunders' makeup. Just as the exemplary Cato from the Busy-Body papers represents the intersection of a number of moral attributes, so the almanac in Franklin's hands becomes a means of embodying the compound character of humanity in a document that, by nature, incorporates the wisdom of the serpent and the innocence of the dove in the heterogeneous calendar that forms its outline. Religious holidays and historic anniversaries fuse, in the almanac's pages, with the vestigial narrative of the seasons and the implied stories of Franklin's aphorisms to form a pocket mirror of sublime and common attributes quite similar to the mixture of traits that Shaftesbury associates with Socrates in his *Soliloquy; or, Advice to an Author.* Just as Franklin's first preface dramatizes the complex failures and triumphs of his personal life, *Poor Richard* as a whole dramatizes those of humanity itself, in miniaturized form.

Other predecessors, in addition to Swift, were on Franklin's mind in his choice of the pseudonym, which he almost certainly expected would fool no one. The name "Richard Saunders," and its familiar contraction of "Poor Richard" in the almanac's title, position Franklin in an elaborate lineage of almanac makers, beginning with William Lilly, the most celebrated of seventeenth-century prognosticators, whose almanacs ran without interruption from 1644 to 1682. *Merlinus Anglicus* or *Merlini Anglici Ephemeris,* the title of Lilly's longest almanac series, is the source of John Partridge's two most established almanac titles at the end of the seventeenth century, *Merlinus Redivivus* and *Merlinus Liberatus.*

Richard Saunders of London, a protégé of Lilly, issued his own almanac, *Apollo Anglicanus,* from 1656 to 1675.[6] Lilly and Saunders, like Partridge, were deeply enmeshed in contemporary politics in the middle decades of the seventeenth century. Both were parliamentarians who managed to show sufficient sympathy with the plight of the Stuarts to carry on their almanacs without serious political interference through the Civil War, the Protectorate, and the Restoration. Both were, as well, noted practitioners of astrological medicine and took their astrology seriously, a reverence for the pseudoscience that was not shared by Saunders' successor, and near namesake, Richard Saunder, who continued the *Apollo Anglicanus* of Saunders from 1684 to 1700. This same Richard Saunder also published an almanac under Partridge's title, *Merlinus Redivivus,* for 1687, and in 1712 compliments the fictive Isaac Bickerstaff on his successful jest at Partridge's expense.[7]

Franklin embraces elements of all of these interlinked predecessors in the performance of Richard Saunders of Philadelphia. Like Isaac Bickerstaff and Richard Saunder, Franklin approaches the astrological heritage of almanacs with a bemused skepticism, reflected, in part, in Bridget Saunders' impatience with her husband's profitless stargazing. But Franklin likewise persists in illustrating *Poor Richard* with the human figure of the "Man of Signs," or "Old Anatomy" as he is often called, correlating parts of the body to the twelve constellations and to the motions of the moon and planets in the calendar, just as the astrological physicians Saunders and Lilly, along with most of their contemporaries and predecessors, do. Eminent seventeenth-century scientists like Thomas Browne and William Harvey, in their medical practices, took into account the movements of celestial bodies. Franklin's eighteenth-century readers continued to expect to consult Old Anatomy in their almanacs, regardless of the diminished intellectual stature of astrology, and Franklin cheerfully complied.[8]

Richard Saunders of London was among the first of the English almanac makers to print anniversaries in his calendar—the saints' days of the Church of England, birthdays and accession dates of monarchs, the anniversaries of notable events in history. Franklin continued this traditional and widespread practice of his namesake, but he enriched its range of suggestion by frequently linking anniversaries to aphorisms in ways that underscore the complexity of memory.

In his first almanac, for example, Franklin memorializes the date of the execution of Charles I (January 30) not as the customary red-letter day of martyrdom, which most of his predecessors employed, but in plain black characters, "K. Cha. I. decoll." from the Latin *decollare,* to behead. Beside that date, in the column reserved for his aphorisms, Franklin printed "Kings and Bears often worry their Keepers"—a sentiment seemingly in sympathy with the English regicides but, at the same time, revealing a disquieting acknowledgment of the role of the dutiful citizen as "keeper" of the "king." He liked this saying well enough to repeat it in subsequent almanacs, but its conspicuous presence in the first one is an indication of Franklin's ongoing intention to position many of his aphorisms and his anniversaries in a conversational relationship to one another.

That relationship is almost never simpleminded or superficially conclusive. The effect of this first exchange, for example, is to extend the consideration of Charles' fate beyond the partisan rituals of mourning or celebration, in directions that the aphorism refuses to predict or direct. *Poor Richard's* politics invariably prove to be subtle, but as Franklin duly records in the almanac for 1745, "A soft Tongue may strike hard," provoking thought without alienating its audience with obstinate certainties. The point of the almanac's exchange, as Walter Benjamin might have put it, is to extend the "story" of antagonistic sovereignties that Charles' execution reflects. Though the event was distant, its passions and anxieties remained very much alive among Franklin's colonial readers. It is the ongoing life of this story, rather than its premature resolution, to which the aphorism appeals.

For much of his extensive acquaintance with almanac practice and with its various practitioners, Franklin is undoubtedly indebted to his Boston upbringing. Colonial almanacs originated exclusively in Boston until William Bradford printed his first Philadelphia almanac in 1686. Cotton Mather produced an almanac in 1683 to take advantage of their extraordinary popularity as a vehicle of religious instruction. No apprentice to a Boston printer in the early eighteenth century could have avoided an intimate acquaintance with the contents and the physical appearance of the annual run of "ephemeri," as they were often termed.[9] During his months in London in 1725 and 1726, Franklin had an opportunity to examine closely the English almanacs upon which the colonial compilers freely drew. The names of Richard Saunders and William Lilly continued to be used, long after they were dead, by eighteenth-century English publishers in an effort to capitalize on their popularity.

Lilly's autobiography, first published in 1715 and reprinted in 1721, is just the sort of curiosity likely to have attracted Franklin on the shelves of Wilcox's secondhand bookstore in Little Britain, both because of Franklin's familiarity with colonial almanacs and because of an intriguing similarity in the circumstances of the two young men, introduced to the great metropolis almost precisely a century apart. Indeed, Lilly lived a life that is nearly a burlesque of Franklin's celebrated rise from obscurity to fame. The son of a poor farmer in Leicestershire, Lilly made his way to London in April 1620, arriving in town on Palm Sunday with "seven shillings and sixpence" after paying his coach fare, "one suit of cloaths upon my back, two shirts, three bands, one pair of shoes, and as many stockings." After delivering an introductory letter to his new master in Fleet Street, Lilly recalls, "I saw and eat good white bread, contrary to our diet in Leicestershire," a symbol of the change in his circumstances that eventually leads to a career in astrological medicine, prognostication, and almanac making.[10]

The resemblance between Lilly's Palm Sunday arrival in London and Franklin's famous Sabbath-day stroll in Philadelphia, shabbily attired, reduced to "a Dutch dollar and about a Shilling," eating his great puffy rolls, is striking enough to suggest Franklin's awareness of the parallel when he composes his *Autobiography*. Like Franklin, Lilly was diligent in his calling and stood before kings, though Franklin's scientific credentials far exceed those of the seventeenth-century English Merlin.

Franklin's *Poor Richard* departs from the examples of Partridge, Lilly, Saunders, or Saunder—initially at least—in the simplicity of his title. These four English predecessors relished their grandiose Latin identities—Merlinus and Apollo, Liberatus and Redivivus—perhaps out of a desire to attach an atmosphere of deep learning to their astrological calculations. In contrast, Franklin follows the lead of his brother, James, publisher of at least two almanacs in Newport, Rhode Island, and derives his authorial identity, in part, from the most notorious of the seventeenth-century burlesque almanacs, *Poor Robin*. Begun by William Winstanley in 1662, *Poor Robin* was continued by a succession of English and American compilers throughout the eighteenth century and well into the nineteenth. Winstanley was the originator of the considerably more earnest *Protestant Almanac,* as well, from which Franklin borrowed the idea of the expansive historical chronology that he reproduced on the title page of *Poor Richard*, but *Poor Robin* proved to be Winstanley's more durable enterprise. Burlesque almanacs printed facetious as well as serious chronologies, villain's days as well as saint's days, and a wide variety of scatological and misogynist verse: "The blood beginneth now to rise," *Poor Robin* observed in the spring of 1666, "Which maketh some maids to scratch their Thighs."[11] As late as 1815, the ongoing American successor to Winstanley's almanac, *Old Poor Robin,* was printing bawdy dialogues between Robin and his spouse that echo the monetary conflict between Richard and Bridget Saunders that Franklin employs in the first prefaces to his own almanac series.

By comparison with *Poor Robin*'s licentious voice, however, Franklin's use of bawdy humor is remarkably restrained. *Poor Richard* prints some verses of erotic advice for May 1734, for example, that seem quite prim beside the hankerings of Winstanley's "maids":

> Astrologers say,
> This is a good Day
> To make love in May.

Franklin follows these lines with what amounts to a clerical homily:

> Who pleasure gives,
> Shall Joy receive.

Poor Richard's aphorisms and verse epigraph for the entire month of May 1734 form a continuum from Franklin's affirmation of joyful giving at one extreme to the more worldly sentiments expressed in the last of the month's proverbs: "Neither a Fortress nor a Maidenhead will hold out long after they begin to parly." As Poor Richard's name suggests, he has some sympathies with the subversive sexual energy represented by the tradition of *Poor Robin,* but he stops far short of the vulgarity to which his English predecessor routinely descends. Important personal forces unite Franklin to the traditional relationship between almanacs and the dispensing of marital or erotic advice, but he almost never takes Winstanley's lascivious tone or adopts the coldly "professional" position of the original Richard Saunders, who once suggested improving the human race by coordinating all procreation with favorable astrological signs, just as farmers customarily did with their planting and their livestock.[12]

An anonymous compiler producing *The Woman's Almanac* for 1694 under the pseudonym "Dorothy Partidge" recommends "a lusty, squab, fat bedfellow very good physic" for the chilly month of January—advice that the Franklins may have taken in good part, since both of their children appear to have been conceived between mid-December and early February. Franklin's January entries in his early almanacs likewise tend to follow the folk custom of prescribing sexual activity for the winter months and, on occasion, proscribing it for the so-called dog days of July and August—but seldom in either case with the frank sensuality of Dorothy Partridge. *Poor Richard* in 1733 begins the month of January with six lines of verse on realistic expectations in marital partnership that ridicule the fastidious attitude of "Old Batchelor," who would order "a Maiden for his Bed" like a commodity.

The third of the month's aphorisms offers some suggestive but at the same time sentimental domestic advice that appears well designed to

chasten still further both the coldly acquisitive temperament of Old Batchelor and the more fervent but equally reductive passions represented by
The Woman's Almanac: "A house without woman and Firelight, is like a
body without Soul or Sprite." The terms of the analogy form a complex
surprise for readers disposed to see "woman" as a domestic convenience
and for those disposed to view sex as "good physic." A more complete humanity consistently marks Poor Richard's treatment of his sexual themes, a
completeness that Franklin emphasizes in the first month of his first almanac by making his aphorisms and his verse epigraphs dramatically cohere.

The title page of *Poor Richard* for 1733 takes a similarly mixed approach
to the chronologies that Winstanley customarily prints on issues of *The
Protestant Almanac,* positioning the current year in relationship to epochal
events in religious history. *The Protestant Almanac* for 1690, for example,
advertises itself as appearing 5696 years since the creation of the world,
1690 years since the incarnation of Jesus Christ, 1500 years since England
received the Christian faith, 174 years since Martin Luther wrote against
the pope, and so on until the recent "miraculous Deliverance from Popery, by K. William" two years since.[13] Franklin's title page chronology for
Poor Richard, on the other hand, dispenses with the adversarial certainties
of Winstanley's practice, recording five different figures for the age of the
Earth since the creation, calculated by the Eastern Greeks, the "Latin
Church," Roman chronology, "the Jewish Rabbies," and one "W.W.," or
William Winstanley, Franklin's only direct reference to the zealous pro-
genitor of *Poor Robin* and *The Protestant Almanac.* These choices quietly
insist that human accounts of the creation are anything but authoritative.
The subversive intelligence of Poor Richard is not necessarily less pious
but simply less militant than that of his English forebear.

The most important of the distinctions in generic identity that came to
set *Poor Richard* apart from its peers and predecessors involves the way in
which Franklin modifies Isaac Bickerstaff's famous hoax, the attack on
John Partridge's notorious Whig almanacs in the first decades of the eighteenth century. Jonathan Swift's treatment of Partridge is quite perfunctory
in the initial *Predictions for the Year 1708.* Partridge himself did not particularly invite gentle consideration; he was a fiercely partisan figure who
had been compelled to flee the country when James II came to the throne.
He returned to England after the Glorious Revolution, to become the
preeminent almanac maker of his day. Continuing to mock the exiled
Stuarts through the turn of the century, Partridge in his almanacs refers to
the Old Pretender as "King James the T-rd" and so outraged English

Tories that he drew threats of assassination.[14] Under the circumstances, Swift treats him with considerable restraint: "My first Prediction is but a Trifle," Bickerstaff writes. "It relates to *Partridge* the Almanack-Maker; I have consulted the Star of his Nativity by my own Rules; and find he will infallibly die upon the 29th of March next, about eleven at Night, of a raging Fever: Therefore I advise him to consider of it, and settle his Affairs in Time."[15]

Later in the year, Swift returns to the hoax by publishing a brief "letter" from an anonymous gentleman purporting to describe Partridge's actual death, along with his deathbed confession that astrology is a "Deceit" that he only took up for profit, "having a Wife to maintain, and no other Way to get my Bread." Bickerstaff, the letter concludes, was off by nearly four hours in the prediction of Partridge's time of death. In 1709, Swift took up Partridge one last time in order to defend Bickerstaff's astrological accuracy and to maintain that, despite Partridge's protests and insults, he was indeed dead, the tedium and folly of his current almanac amply showing that "no Man alive" could have written it.[16]

Unlike Swift's relatively compressed treatment, Franklin stretches the device of Titan Leeds' untimely death across the first seven years of *Poor Richard's* existence, touching on Leeds' fate in the prefaces to five almanacs, including one (*Poor Richard* for 1740) that records a visit from Leeds' spirit a year after he had, in fact, died in 1738. Entering Saunders' left nostril, ascending to his brain, and taking control of his senses, the ghostly Leeds writes a letter in Saunders' hand, predicting that one of Franklin's surviving competitors, John Jerman, will convert to Catholicism in the coming year: "As I can see much clearer into Futurity, since I got free from the dark Prison of Flesh, in which I was continually molested and almost blinded with Fogs arising from Tiff, and the Smoke of burnt Drams; I shall in kindness to you, frequently give you informations of things to come, for the Improvement of your Almanack: Being Dear *Dick, Your affectionate Friend, T. Leeds*" (*Writings*, 1216).[17]

The Bickerstaff hoax is more concentrated, more relentless, far less humane, and at the same time less effective than *Poor Richard's* treatment of Titan Leeds. Astrology is never the serious irritant to Franklin that it is to Swift. As Poor Richard presents the case, in fact, he and Leeds are affectionate colleagues, together wrestling with the precise date and hour of Leeds' demise "these 9 Years past," until Leeds at length "is inclinable to agree with my judgment."[18] Franklin even fuses in Richard Saunders the roles of Bickerstaff and that of the solicitous, unnamed gentleman who visits Partridge on his deathbed, though in Swift's text the visit is more out of curiosity than concern.

By contrast, the warmth of the relationship that Franklin asserts between Saunders and Leeds sharply distinguishes *Poor Richard*'s tone from the cool prurience of Swift's narrator..Indeed, Poor Richard's economic plight at one point identifies him directly with the pathetic Partridge, as Swift mockingly presents him, confessing to the sad necessity of supporting Mrs. Partridge by some means more lucrative than shoe mending. Poor Richard writes out of similar economic necessity. In Franklin's Rabelaisian preface to the 1740 almanac, Saunders and Leeds even share the same body, if not the same snuff-taking and dram-drinking habits. The dramatic negotiations that Franklin creates in these first prefaces are openly indebted to Swift's invention at the same time that they are richer and more sophisticated in their execution. Franklin clearly invites the comparison with Bickerstaff's performance because he is convinced that he will not suffer by it.

The comparison, in fact, is more complicated and far-reaching than this contrast in hoaxes suggests. Swift's *Miscellanies* include, along with the *Predictions for the Year 1708*, three of Swift's most important, early essays on the prospects and strategies for moral reform in the last years of Queen Anne's reign. In particular, Swift was deeply committed to preserving the sacramental Test Act, which required that all English officeholders be communicants of the Church of England as a formal guarantee of their loyalty to the national constitution. The requirement was considerably softened by the widespread practice of "occasional conformity," taking the Anglican sacraments once or twice a year, only, as a nominal satisfaction of the act's demands, a strategy to which Swift does not explicitly object.

But in the three essays roughly contemporary with the Partridge hoax—"The Sentiments of a Church of England Man" (1708), "An Argument [against] the Abolishing of Christianity" (1708), "A Project for the Advancement of Religion" (1709)—Swift makes clear his alarm at the factional extremism, moral "Degeneracy," and general "Depravity" of the day. True Christian charity has long since been "laid aside by general Consent, as utterly inconsistent with our present Schemes of Wealth and Power." [19] The best reformation one could hope for in such a social and spiritual climate, Swift reasons, is a nominal conformity to church ceremonies and church attendance, coupled with toleration for existing sects. Indeed, in "A Project for the Advancement of Religion" Swift suggests a court-mandated system of ecclesiastical requirements for government employment and promotion that would virtually ensure widespread hypocrisy in the public service.[20]

The temptations to deceit, or to purely interested expressions of expedient "faith," inherent in such sacramental "tests" do not deeply trouble Swift. Hypocrisy "wears the Livery of Religion": "And I believe it is often with Religion as it is with Love; which, by much dissembling, at last grows real."[21] In some respects as reductive as Mandeville in his view of the pervasive effects of self-love and pride, Swift nevertheless remains, in these essays, a religious idealist of a peculiarly dark cast, driven to the extreme position of embracing state-enforced hypocrisy as the preparatory medium for genuine spiritual change. In the mid-seventeenth century, Blaise Pascal wrote in his social and religious meditations that "it is superstitious to put one's hopes in formalities, but arrogant to refuse to submit to them." With respect to the pure formality of England's sacramental test, Swift's position, both in its skepticism and in its resignation, is virtually identical to (though far more cynical than) Pascal's.[22]

The resulting mix is a kind of grimly conservative religious "enthusiasm" unlikely to please either committed Whigs, opposed to all sacramental "tests" as preconditions to public service, or Tories, who were no more amenable than their opponents to a strict policing of their outward behavior by moral "censors" of the court. Under the circumstances, it is surprising that in some London circles Swift was briefly credited with the authorship of Shaftesbury's *Letter concerning Enthusiasm*, which appeared anonymously in the same year as "The Sentiments of a Church-of-England Man."[23] Swift's tone, even in that most moderate of the three essays, is strikingly different from the generosity with which Shaftesbury surveys all sectarian enthusiasms from his perspective of good-humored toleration. When religion becomes entangled with "Wrath, Fury, and Revenge," Shaftesbury argues, it is a result of the projection of human passions upon divine character: "it would be well for us, if before we ascended into the higher Regions of *Divinity*, we would vouchsafe to descend a little into *ourselves*, and bestow some poor Thoughts upon plain honest *Morals*. . . . We might then understand how to *love*, and *praise*, when we had acquired some consistent Notion of what was *laudable* or *lovely*" (*CMM*, 1:41).

Shaftesbury's attraction to the spiritual heroism of Socrates leads him to advocate "this plain home-spun Philosophy of looking into ourselves . . . in rectifying our Errors in Religion." Swift, on the other hand, though he asserts his freedom from religious bigotry, is equally quick to proclaim his loyalty to the ceremonies of the established church and his suspicion of the disestablished sects: "When a *Schism* is once spread in a Nation . . . it is certain, that in the Sense of the Law, the *Schism* lies on that side which opposeth itself to the Religion of the State. . . . And I think it clear, that any great Separation from the established Worship, although to a new one that is more pure and perfect, may be an occasion of endangering the publick Peace."[24] Give the sectarians "ease" from the fear of criminal prosecution, Swift cautioned, but give them "little Power."

Franklin's almanac, like Swift's essays in the *Miscellanies* and Shaftesbury's letter, reflects this contemporary preoccupation with strategies of moral reform, but the genial figure of Poor Richard is much more in sympathy with Shaftesbury's "home-spun" model of ethical and spiritual self-examination than with Swift's expedient embrace of institutional authority. In "A Project for the Advancement of Religion," Swift proposes "that something parallel to the Office of Censors antiently in Rome" might prove useful as a means of policing the "Morals and Religion" of office-holders more effectively than law.[25] By contrast, Franklin begins his own systematic inquiries into the problem of public reform three years before the appearance of *Poor Richard* by creating, in the figure of the Busy-Body, a comic version of Swift's grimly authoritarian Censor. The Busy-Body papers purport to serve as "a Terror to Evil-Doers, as well as a Praise to them that do well," by carrying out the Busy-Body's self-appointed "Province as CENSOR" to promote "a sudden and general Amendment" of all vices in Pennsylvania (*Writings*, 104–5).

To this end, the Busy-Body announces "an Act of general Oblivion"— a kind of anti–Test Act—for all offenses and crimes committed between 1681 and the date of the first Busy-Body paper, but he promises at the same time to seek out new offenders with the assistance of one of his correspondents, who claims to be a descendant of John Bunyan, gifted with "Second Sight." The Busy-Body conceals the name of this clairvoyant for fear of assassination, the fate of his beloved pet monkey, Pugg, who was "barbarously stabbed and mangled in a Thousand places" once the rumor grew current that Pugg "snarl'd by instinct at every Female who had lost her virginity" (*Writings*, 107). "Titan Pleiades," however, writes to the Busy-Body suggesting that his second-sighted correspondent be put to work uncovering buried treasure, a proposal that Franklin employs as an introduction to his initial reflections on the usefulness of paper money and the differences between real and imaginary "treasure."

To a surprising degree, the Busy-Body serves as a vehicle for Franklin's first experiments in transforming Swift's social and ethical posture into the personal Socratic exercise of Shaftesbury's *Letter concerning Enthusiasm.* In his comic role of "CENSOR Morum, Esq.," the Busy-Body partly endorses Swift's portrait of the degeneracy of the times as well as his expedient of reviving an ancient Roman office to address the contemporary crisis, but he does so without Swift's disturbing loyalty to the police power of an established church. Shaftesbury's belief in the therapeutic effect of good humor shapes Franklin's tone, testing the efficacy of earnest laughter rather than ridicule. "Titan Pleiades" is Franklin's preliminary sketch for the more complete application of Bickerstaffian tactics in the preface to *Poor Richard* three years later. But just as in the case of Titan Leeds and the almanac, Franklin is less interested in targeting individual instances of "Folly and Madness" and more interested in forming a composite portrait of human character that modulates gradually from what Shaftesbury terms the "plain-looked" virtues to the shining ones.

The Busy-Body presents "Cato" as an allegory of the shining virtues, but Franklin never seriously expects the common reader to respond to such a saintly figure as a realistic model. In *Soliloquy; or, Advice to an Author,* Shaftesbury observes that the "natural capacity" of common men invariably predisposes them to be "rude, undisciplined, headstrong" creatures. Through the *"magical Glasses"* of philosophic dialogue, however, it is possible gradually to discover a second set of human capacities for moral and spiritual heroism. Such dialogues form the basis for the internal "soliloquy" of self-inspection—an internal dialogue between the "self" and a personal *censor morum*—that Shaftesbury recommends as moral discipline for any author who aspires to reform the manners of the age. The key to this internal discipline, as well as to the external philosophic dialogues of Plato upon which it is based, is drama: "'Twas not enough that these Pieces treated fundamentally of *Morals,* and in consequence pointed out *real Characters* and *Manners,*" Shaftesbury writes of the Platonic dialogues. "They exhibited 'em *alive,* and set the Countenances and Complexions of Men plainly in view. And by this means they not only taught us to know *Others;* but what was principal and of highest virtue in 'em, they taught us to know *Our-selves*" (*CMM,* 1:194).

What requires living exhibition in the magical glass—or, as Shaftesbury calls it, the *Pocket-Mirrour*—of philosophical dialogue is not a morality completely purified into prescriptive maxims but a picture of the full range of human ethical capacity that he so admires in the figure of Socrates, conversing amid the scenes of common life. Maxims in and of themselves are nothing more than a tactical formality, something like an aphoristic version of the sacramental test act. They readily lend themselves to a ritual of memorization and repetition that quickly becomes merely ceremonial or, worse still, deadening—as Father Abraham's extraordinary litany of proverbial wisdom threatens to do, with wonderful seriocomic results, in Franklin's last almanac. Without some more effective means of encouraging them to take root in one's character and to influence one's behavior, proverbs or moral aphorisms become simply verbal conveniences that are easily uttered and seldom followed—precisely the dramatic conditions that prevail in the case of "The Way to Wealth." "Know Thyself" is a classic instance of how the complexity and extension of dramatic action hardens into a formula.

Swift, Shaftesbury, and Franklin are alike in their conviction that simply prescribing or legislating moral reform is invariably useless. In the *Autobiography,* Franklin explains how he comes to place his own faith not in ethical knowledge alone but also in the constrictive power of habit. Despite his fervent support of the legalistic mechanism of the Test Act, Swift is equally skeptical of formalistic strategies: "Laws against Immorality have not been executed," he complains, "and Proclamations occasionally issued out to enforce them, are wholly unregarded as Things of Form. Religious Societies, although begun with excellent Intention, and by Persons of true Piety, are said, I know not whether truly or no, to have dwindled into factious Clubs." [26] The device of the extended "test act" that Swift recommends in his "Project for the Advancement of Religion" represents a way of internalizing virtuous habits through the characteristically negative means of fatigue. The practice of "long continued Disguise," he believes, is "too great a Constraint upon human Nature, especially an *English* Disposition. Men would leave off their Vices out of meer Weariness, rather than undergo the Toil and Hazard, and perhaps Expense of practising them perpetually in Private." Swift expects, in other words, not a conversion of the soul but a compliance of the body. Hypocritical disguises will fall into disuse, but the result will scarcely be a recovery of public or private virtue.

John Locke observes in *Some Thoughts concerning Education* that children do not learn manners prescriptively, through rules or lectures, but through the living exhibition of example: "We are all a sort of chameleons, that still take a tincture from things near us: nor is it to be wondered at in children, who better understand what they see than what they hear."[27] Accordingly, for Locke the choice of a tutor for one's children is as crucial a decision in life as the choice of a spouse. Character can be formed only by character, not by academic discipline. Tutors can teach, in the last analysis, only what they are, not what they know. Out of this broad critique of education by maxim or memorization, Swift and Franklin draw radically different conclusions: Swift, in the *Miscellanies,* favoring the renovation of habit through the imposed constraint of hypocrisy; Franklin favoring the gradual, tutorial strategy of what would become his almanac. A commitment to the complex narrative intersections of aphorism and anniversary, which the almanac provides, is Franklin's means of exhibiting "alive" the ethical capacities and incapacities of his readers, of forming a pocket mirror of what Shaftesbury calls the "heroic, the simple, the tragic, and the comic" fusions of character (*CMM,* 1:194).[28]

Poor Richard's Almanac does not, initially at least, seem to possess such grand social and ethical ambitions. But that apparent modesty is itself a familiar element of the traditions of authorial self-effacement, which suggest that great ends can most effectively be served by humble rhetorical means. Franklin indicates in the *Autobiography* that *Poor Richard* is not simply an opportunistic young printer's attempt to enter a lucrative market. It was from the beginning part of a larger design—a vocation that exceeded the traditional scope of a successful artisan's career, just as the almanac's first issue exceeded the dramatic and moral scope of Franklin's competitors and predecessors. The degree of self-exposure evident in the 1733 almanac's autobiographical verses, in Richard Saunders' (and Francis Folger's) significant nativities, and in Franklin's quasi-confessional preface suggests that the inquiry into character and common life in *Poor Richard's* pages is anything but superficial. The contrast with Swift's example clarifies Franklin's purposes and exposes the continuity between the Busy-Body and Richard Saunders. But the *Autobiography* suggests still more clearly the extent of Franklin's artistic investment in the almanac form.

He describes the commencement of *Poor Richard* in a single paragraph early in part 3, emphasizing its utility "as a proper Vehicle for conveying Instruction among the common People," an explanation of his intentions that is curiously narrow and seemingly calculated to provoke misunderstanding and resentment. The typographic appearance of almanacs in general, however, is clearly the source from which Franklin drew, sometime in 1733, the design for his private booklet of thirteen virtues and mottoes. Each page of this booklet is ruled like an almanac month, with the motto at the top and a column for each day of the week to mark Franklin's lapses from Temperance, Silence, Industry, or Cleanliness. He reproduces a sample page in the *Autobiography* to make the physical parallel with the almanac inescapable. *Poor Richard*, in other words, does not spring from an elitist philosopher's condescending attitude toward the productive habits of the "common People" but from Franklin's private determination to pursue a vision of moral heroism culminating in the admonition to imitate Jesus and Socrates.

Poor Richard's readers in 1733, of course, had no access to Franklin's pocket book of virtues with its inventory of daily lapses. Nor could they have known of the grand, moral vision of his Society of the Free and Easy, which Franklin intended to promote as an international "sect" of virtuous young men, pledged to self-reform and to one another's mutual advancement toward positions of influence in life. But together, these enterprises suggest the range of expectation with which Franklin approached the almanac. The Society of the Free and Easy was, effectively, part of the earnest critique of history that he undertook in the spring of 1731, ceremonially dating his conclusions much as the almanac invited its reader to reflect on the varied significances of ceremonial dates.

Human affairs are governed by factions, Franklin concludes in his library memorandum, but factions deteriorate into self-interested "Divisions," individual ambitions, and "Confusion." Principles of benevolence and virtue are adopted only as hypocritical pretenses in public affairs (*Writings*, 1395). Jonathan Swift could not have put the social and cultural diagnosis more bluntly. Franklin's *Autobiography* makes evident that the almanacs, as well as the *Pennsylvania Gazette,* represent part of Franklin's response to this sense of pervasive disorder: a profusion of hypocritical pretense and self-interested disguise in which civic life begins to resemble the disorienting experience of the public masquerades that began to seize the imagination of London society during Franklin's brief residence there in 1725 and 1726.[29]

As early as 1733, however, *Poor Richard's* readers could readily have detected Franklin's determination to link the aphoristic morality of the almanac to the personal disorders of his own moral history—to give a living exhibition of ethical struggle in the inclusive spirit of Shaftesbury's ideals, rather than simply presenting a narrow and reductive model of commercial prudence. Franklin's countenance and complexion plainly mingle with that of Richard Saunders, as Shaftesbury suggests they should, if the ethical dialogue of character is to be honestly and usefully explored.

Moreover, the drama of the calendar offers Franklin frequent opportunities to position the almanac's moralizing voice in the religious, political, and social year as well as in the personal circumstances of the compiler.

The 1733 almanac's juxtaposition of King Charles' fate with the seemingly derisive comment, "Kings and Bears often worry their Keepers," suggests how anniversaries and aphorisms might complicate one another. The comparison that Franklin employs can be purely derisive only if it is detached from history. Charles was, indeed, notoriously difficult to "keep," either as a monarch or as a prisoner, but it is the failures of the "keepers," too, that the aphorism plainly addresses. If Charles Stuart is not a martyr in Franklin's calendar, neither does he appear as an agent of conspiratorial Catholicism whose death becomes an unqualified cause for annual commemoration. "Worry" takes on much greater prominence, and the aphorism becomes more psychologically penetrating, once Franklin positions it in the context of the almanac's anniversaries.

In the month that follows, "Love well, whip well" is an unusually stern parental homily for Franklin to have employed, but it falls on the third Sunday in Lent, as "Light purse, heavy heart" (also from February 1733) roughly coincides with Ash Wednesday, while "Hunger never saw bad bread" is printed opposite Easter Week in the following March. The time of year significantly broadens and enriches the suggestive range of all three aphorisms. "Love well, whip well" becomes a colloquial intensification of God's proverbial chastisement of those whom he loves—fixing a host of local stories of punishment and love in the mythic context of the season—as well as a reminder that Lent is a time of stern self-discipline, reenacting a momentous religious drama.

Franklin's "light purse" on Ash Wednesday appears, superficially at least, to be the worldly cause of a "heavy heart," but in the religious calendar Ash Wednesday inaugurates a period of heaviness, or mourning, for deficiencies that have very little to do with spending money. A light purse, then, may suggest the misused or misplaced "talents" for which the heavy heart quite earnestly and soberly grieves. Probably it would have pleased Franklin to have his reader immediately sympathize with the effects of ordinary economic anxiety only to discover that, in the setting of the almanac, such anxiety abruptly loses significance in the face of the spiritual resonance of the larger narrative that subsumes it. If, as Franklin observes during Easter Week, "Hunger never saw bad bread," then perhaps the hunger of a post-Lenten feast should consider more closely the nature of the appetite that it satisfies.[30] In each instance, the site of the proverb within the almanac effectively reconstructs elements of a larger story to which its merely local meaning becomes subservient.

Reading a group of aphorisms in this way, as participants in a moral dialogue with the calendar, amounts to superimposing the meditative purposes of Franklin's "Articles of Belief" upon his almanac, the document that seems in some respects most closely associated with his secular interests. The almanac is inevitably more heterogeneous than this comparison suggests, but its composite nature is part of the ethical vision that it serves. In addition to the religious dimension of its Lenten proverbs, for example, *Poor Richard* for February 1733 also includes the rather blunt worldly advice, "Ne'er take a wife till thou hast a house (and a fire) to put her in," an aphorism whose syntax enacts the confusion that can occur when one gets things out of order. But the almanac as a whole, like the year that it documents, lends itself to abrupt and incongruous juxtapositions, the most vivid of which is the annual conjunction of Easter with All Fool's Day, a blending of sacred festival and burlesque release that is many centuries old.[31] Almanacs, in fact, are a kind of peddlers' genre, available for sale at print shops (as *Poor Richard* was) but also distributed in the streets, or at markets and fairs, by hawkers. Franklin traditionally printed the dates of local fairs, court sessions, and Quaker meetings in *Poor Richard* because those were all market days as well, times and places where large numbers of potential customers could be expected to gather with (ideally) heavy purses and light hearts.

Poor Richard was unquestionably shaped by marketing concerns that identify the almanac with the purely secular and festive economic energies of the public fair, but at points in the calendar where a reader might expect the full indulgence of the almanac's carnivalesque affinities, Franklin often grows surprisingly earnest, as he does in April 1733, when he prints opposite the All Fool's anniversary of April 1, "Great Talkers, little Doers." Human folly of a serious sort engages Franklin's attention in this month, a failing of will that is central to the general moral purposes of the almanac. With some of Swift's instinct for relentless pursuit, Franklin fills most of the aphorism column for this April with one of his longest proverbs, extending and intensifying his negative assessment of the disparity between profession and action: "Relation without friendship, friendship without power, power without will, will without effect, effect without profit, and profit without vertue, are not worth a farto" (*Papers,* 1:296). The vulgar license of the Feast of Fools erupts at the close of this succession of phrases, but Franklin's contempt seems as deep as it is (in a comic sense) low. The possession of will without effect sums up the nature of "Great Talkers" who do little, but the linkages extending from "relation" at one extreme to "vertue" at the other suggest that empty intentions, or hypocritical pretense, belong to a family of betrayals far more comprehensive than the first of the month's aphorisms suggests.

Franklin's contention is that the presence of substance beneath appearance, of doing beneath talking, must include all of these varied partnerships: relation with friendship, friendship with power, and so on through profit with virtue. Far from uncritically participating in the spirit of a fool's holiday, then, Franklin elects instead to strip away social costumes in search of the fundamental condition of virtuous character that must sustain all the varied activity of human relation. In one respect, it is perverse to force such a serious subject on the reader's attention at this moment in the almanac's implicit, psychological calendar; Franklin ends the aphorism on a note of verbal perversity as if to signal his awareness of the incongruities involved. But moral, or even devotional, literature of a kind much more formal and imposing than the almanac did not hesitate to express contempt in memorably physical terms in Franklin's day. William Law, in his *Serious Call to a Devout and Holy Life* (1728), gives the name "Flatus" to one of the many reprobate characters whom he sketches in that sober and influential book.[32]

Moreover, April is itself a month of incongruities, beginning with All Fools' Day and ending with the anniversary of the sack of Troy (as Franklin's calendar notes), followed in 1733 by Rogation Sunday, marking the Sabbath celebration that precedes the traditional anniversary of Christ's ascension to Heaven, forty days after Easter. "A rich rogue, is like a fat hog," Poor Richard prints for the middle of April 1733, "who never does good 'til as dead as a log." Such a sentiment seems entirely in harmony with the secular pleasures of misrule, but it, too, contains the month's incongruities in comic suspension. Resurrection and ascension, particularly as metaphors for spiritual fitness of the highest kind, are unlikely existential outcomes for rich rogues or dead hogs, whose interments are, literally, inanimate events. The sense of festive escape in April is most meaningful if one reads it as Franklin's aphorisms appear to recommend: as an opportunity to put aside the empty costumes of the flesh.

Death is a recurrent and traditional subject for almanacs, whose ephemeral nature as texts corresponds perfectly to the ephemeral nature of human life. "Death is a Fisherman, the world we see / His Fish-pond is, and we the Fishes be," Poor Richard duly notes at the head of his page for September 1733. Franklin's famous epitaph comparing his body to a cast-off book is drawn from a 1681 almanac epitaph composed to memorialize the death of John Foster, an almanac maker in seventeenth-century Boston:

> Thy body, which no activeness did lack
> Now's laid aside like an old Almanack
> But for the present only's out of date
> 'Twill have at length a far more active State.[33]

Over the first decade of *Poor Richard's* existence, birth and death played roles in Franklin's life that inevitably sharpened his sense of the almanac's mortal analogy. Francis Folger's birth begins this process of personal identification. Three years later, Franklin's brother James died in Newport, leaving to Franklin the responsibility for training James' son to assume his father's business, while Ann Franklin, James' widow, managed the family press and the family almanac. In the next year, on November 21, 1736, Francis Folger Franklin died of smallpox, a loss that Franklin deals with more openly in his almanac than in any other surviving records of his life, turning it into a kind of hidden anniversary in the almanac's calendar.

James Sappenfield first suggested the relationship between this date and the almanac text but turns to the wrong almanac to detect its literary effects.[34] *Poor Richard* for 1737 was advertised for sale on November 11, 1736, which indicates that it was almost certainly compiled and printed before the child's fatal illness began. Indeed, Franklin was customarily engaged in preparing the next year's almanac for publication on or about his son's birthday, October 20, a month before what would become the anniversary of his death. The annual writing and printing of *Poor Richard* clearly coincides with the memory of Francis Folger Franklin's death beginning with the almanac for 1738, where Bridget Saunders, likewise for the first time, stands in for her husband in the text's opening pages.

Poor Richard, she writes, has taken a trip to "see about a little Place for us to settle and end our Days on." Suspecting that he has been "flinging some of his old Skitts" at her in his new almanac preface, Bridget replaces Richard's introduction with her own:

> What a peasecods! cannot I have a little Fault or two, but all the Country must see it in print! They have already been told, at one time that I am proud, another time that I am loud, and that I have got a new Petticoat,

and abundance of such kind of stuff; and now, forsooth! all the World must know, that Poor Dick's Wife has lately taken a fancy to drink a little Tea now and then. A mighty matter, truly, to make a Song of! 'Tis true, I had a little Tea of a Present from the Printer last Year; and what, must a body throw it away? In short, I thought the Preface was not worth a print-ing, and so I fairly scratch'd it all out, and I believe you'll like our Alma-nack never the worse for it. (*Papers,* 2:191)

Finding too much bad weather in Richard's text, Bridget scratches that out as well, inserting "some *fair, pleasant, sunshiny,* &c. for the Good-Women to dry their Clothes in," but she has to give up her intention "to make some other Corrections": "I have just now unluckily broke my Spectacles; which obliges me to give it you as it is, and conclude Your lov-ing Friend, Bridget Saunders."

Perhaps the most conspicuous indication of the complex dramatic bur-den in this preface is the unusual warmth with which Bridget signs her name. Richard is customarily the reader's "friend and servant" in the al-manacs that precede this one, but Bridget's interposition in the year fol-lowing the death of Francis Folger signals a change that extends even to the reappearance of Richard in 1739 as the reader's "Affectionate friend." Bridget makes some acknowledgments of gifts and goodwill over the past year, changes what she can in her husband's forecasts for the year to come, but expresses her inability to make more substantive "Corrections," ac-cepting what cannot be changed.

Beginning on a note of comic resignation to death, Bridget indirectly acknowledges the inevitable publicity of grief ("all the Country must see it") as well as the role of friends and neighbors, and of trivial symbolic gifts, in the process of mourning. A year after Francis Folger's death, speaking through Deborah's fictive counterpart, Franklin expresses their gratitude, reclaims the family's privacy, and asserts their readiness to make, as well as to greet, a fairer future. The lines of verse that follow this preface, like the reflexive prophecies that celebrate their son's birth in *Poor Richard* for 1733, address the diminished but still mutually supportive bond in which the Franklins find themselves:

Lo as a Giant strong, the lusty Sun
Multiply'd Rounds in one great Round doth run.
Twofold his Course, yet constant his Career
Changing the Day and finishing the Year.
Again when his descending Orb retires

And Earth perceives the Absence of his Fires
The Moon affords us her alternate Ray,
And with kind Beams distributes fainter Day.
   (*Papers*, 2:191)

In Diogenes Laertius's *Lives of the Eminent Philosophers*—a handbook of exemplary biography familiar to Franklin and his contemporaries—the stories of Anaxagoras, Socrates' teacher, and of Xenophon, his pupil, record the quiet stoicism of each when learning of the death of their sons: "I knew my son was mortal," Xenophon is reported to have said.[35] What Franklin undertakes to mirror in the almanac for 1738 differs in important ways from such proverbial resignation.

Grief does not strive toward homiletic resolution in Franklin's ethical world. It is, instead, a continuing story, an ongoing and complex entanglement of past and present commemorated in the vivid experience of anniversaries. In the absence of his young son's living fires, Franklin offers, a year after the boy's death, a picture of parental grief in its contained rather than its acute phase: the "fainter Day" of Earth and moon, after the "Sun's" descent, to which his lines of poetry allude. He notes in the first of the aphorisms for October of this year—the month in which Francis Folger would have turned six years old—that "Time is an herb that cures all Diseases." But like the verse epigraph for that month, which Franklin titles "A Doubtful Meaning," this consolatory reliance on time looks forward to doubtful meanings, to death as much as to a state of restored health. Some diseases last as long as life, having periods of remission and periods of active suffering. These the almanac represents to Franklin during the painful anniversaries of its annual publication, and these he incorporates with great delicacy into its pages.

Less personal events inevitably intersect with the almanac in Franklin's biography, providing the means of recognizing dramatic purpose in the prefaces and aphorisms that is otherwise easy to miss. *Poor Richard* begins in the midst of Franklin's withdrawal from Jedidiah Andrews' Presbyterian congregation, in "disgust" at the doctrinaire preaching he encounters there, and his commencement of a private system of ethical self-discipline using his pocket booklet of thirteen virtues to record his lapses. "Great Talkers, little Doers" perfectly expresses Benjamin Franklin's disappointment in the narrow list of sectarian admonitions that Andrews drew out of a biblical passage from which Franklin expected more sublime incitements to virtue.

In a similar fashion, the almanac for 1736 appeared for sale in early December 1735, just a few weeks after Franklin's impassioned public defense of Samuel Hemphill in his conflict with the Presbyterian Synod over Hemphill's vigorous (and partly plagiarized) advocacy of good works.[36] In his pamphlet defense of Hemphill, Franklin ignores the embarrassing issue of Hemphill's plagiarism, but the preface to *Poor Richard* for 1736 does not. Assuring his "Loving Readers" that the envy and malice of "Ill-willers" will never discourage him from preparing his annual almanac, Saunders addresses those critics who have sought to "father" his "Offspring" on his hapless printer, and to cast doubt on Saunders' existence, with the following "publick and serious Declaration": "That what I have written heretofore, and do now write, neither was nor is written by any other Man or Men, Person or Persons whatsoever."

Like many of the pamphlets opposing Hemphill, Franklin's pamphlet defenses are (on the surface at least) anonymous, but through the comic sincerity of Richard Saunders' oath of authorship, Franklin can acknowledge the embarrassment of Hemphill's exposure and even share in the public amusement that the discovery must have created, while at the same time asserting that he stands by what he has said in defense of the doctrine that Hemphill preached. The voice of Richard Saunders, however, is several weeks removed from the heat of conflict; he offers an opportunity for a degree of reconciliation, mediated by the comic design of the almanac's 1736 preface: "My Performance for this Year follows; it submits itself, Kind Reader, to thy Censure, but hopes for thy Candor, to forgive its Faults. It devotes itself entirely to thy Service, and will serve thee faithfully: And if it has the good Fortune to please its Master, 'tis Gratification enough for the Labour of Poor R. Saunders" (*Papers*, 2:136). The performances that Franklin's language calls to mind include Hemphill's plagiarized (but ably performed) sermons, Franklin's own dramatic pamphlets and dialogues on the case, as well as Richard Saunders' modest almanac for 1736. This submission to the reader's kindness and candor is on behalf of all three performers, seeking to please (through the stubbornly undoctrinaire medium of "Service") a "Master" whose example of forgiveness forms a point of common spiritual ground shared by all of Philadelphia's theological camps. The almanac is a forum in which Franklin can begin the process of putting aside the old year's sectarian animosities.

After George Whitefield's arrival in Philadelphia in November 1739, Poor Richard's verses and aphorisms address themselves to a climate of spiritual self-scrutiny and revival rhetoric to which Franklin is partly attracted at the same time that he preserves a careful, intellectual distance. The example of Samuel Hemphill suggests the dangers of too close an affinity between theater and worship. It is difficult not to see Franklin's account of Whitefield's vocal powers in the *Autobiography* as an enactment of his mixed response to the substance of Whitefield's sermons. Franklin joins the crowd listening to Whitefield preach one evening from the Courthouse steps but gradually backs away from the speaker, down Market Street, out of curiosity to estimate the size of the audience. The resulting conclusions "reconcile" Franklin to newspaper accounts of Whitefield's vast congregations, at the same time that the picture of his slow retreat from the speaker suggests a less than satisfactory reconciliation with doctrine and language (*Writings*, 1409).

Whitefield, Franklin emphasizes in the *Autobiography*, is an itinerant preacher. In some respects, Richard Saunders too is an itinerant presence in his readers' lives, emerging from seclusion once a year to utter his preface, take up old controversies from last year's almanac, and present a new collection of aphorisms for the upcoming year. In the preface to the almanac for 1742, Franklin makes the analogy explicit by subjecting Poor Richard to the same suspicions with which skeptics must have frequently greeted the itinerant revivalist: "*Who knows him?* they cry: *Where does he live?*" (*Papers*, 2:332). But unlike Whitefield, Richard Saunders is a secret resident and not a traveler who is free to polish his rhetorical performances on audience after audience until the slightest modulations of voice take on (as Franklin notes in his memoir) the qualities of excellent music.

Moreover, the almanac is a year-long companion rather than an occasional text or rare performance. It is a pocket mirror, which must wear well on prolonged exposure. Accordingly, though the moral purposes of the almanac and the revivalist are suggestively similar, Poor Richard is suspicious of the theatrical professionalism that a religious revival can represent. Writing in the aphorisms for February 1741, he says:

Best is the Tongue that feels the rein;
He that talks much, must talk in vain;
We from the wordy Torrent fly;
Who listens to the chattering Pye?

The magpie's suggestively clerical plumage traditionally made it a favorite image of the verbally officious preacher, though Poor Richard targets all "chattering," not just the sort that drove Franklin out of the Presbyterian Church. In the two aphorisms that follow these couplets, Franklin seems intent on modeling brevity in moral admonition. "Think Cato sees thee," is the first of the two; and the month concludes with an acknowledgment that sometimes the most solid counsel can have a rugged, unappealing exterior: "No Wood without Bark."

Though moral self-scrutiny and spiritual earnestness play a part in *Poor Richard* from the beginning of the series, particularly after Francis Folger's death in 1736, the almanacs examine the awakened conscience more frequently—not in a burlesque of piety, however, but as a modification of its anxieties. To live as if Cato saw you is a serious ethical challenge but not a source of religious terror. "Enjoy the present hour," Poor Richard advises in 1741, "be mindful of the Past; / And neither fear nor wish the Approaches of the last" (*Papers,* 2:292). In the same almanac, once more in the otherwise festive month of April, Franklin warns: "E'er you remark another's Sin, / Bid your own Conscience look within." *Poor Richard* for 1741 concludes with an unusually formal benediction, by Franklin's standards, at the end of December: "Let no Pleasure tempt thee, no Profit allure thee, no Ambition corrupt thee, no Example sway thee, no Persuasion move thee, to do anything which thou knowest to be Evil; So shalt thou always live jollily: for a good Conscience is a continual Christmas. Adieu." These are sentiments so distinct from the judgmental world of revival rhetoric that it is difficult to imagine that Franklin was unaware of the contrast.

A more characteristic conclusion at the end of *Poor Richard* for 1742 equates the almanac with the year's mixture of uncertainties and disappointments. The verse epigraph for December 1742 describes the persistent religious contentions of the Protestant awakening:

> Among the Divines there has been much Debate,
> Concerning the World in its ancient Estate;
> Some say 'twas once good, but now is grown bad,
> Some say 'tis reform'd of the Faults it once had:
> I say, 'tis the best World, this that we now live in,
> Either to lend, or to spend, or to give in;
> But to borrow, to beg, or to get a Man's own,
> It is the worst World that ever was known.
> (*Papers,* 2:338)

The world, in other words, is at once generous and ungenerous, reformed and damned, full of spokesmen whose messages conflict. The continual Christmas that Poor Richard genially envisions at the end of the previous year gives way to a mixture of affirmation and resignation. The year's concluding resolution for 1742 is a couplet that urges the reader to make the "old Almanack" a repository for the year's "old Vices," taking up a clean spiritual slate with the new pocket calendar. Poor Richard, in effect, identifies his public booklet of anniversaries and advice with the private inventory of virtues that Franklin continued to use and reuse in his equally fruitless search for moral perfection.

Unlike the episodic experience of a great revival or a particularly potent sermon by a famous itinerant, the almanac was inherently a nagging conscience, an insistent voice in the day's dialogue. It was not for great occasions only. The aphorisms and epigraphs mingled typographically with the days of the week, historical anniversaries, holidays, tides, and the phases of the moon. From a reformer's point of view, it did not lend itself to the evasions of "occasional conformity," as England's Test Act did. More frequently, it became a diary, and as such was not cast off every year (as Poor Richard urged) but preserved with the individual notations of its owner, forming part of the extraordinarily mixed portrait of life in its pages. The tendency of the almanac as a source of guidance or advice, then, is to make daily admonitory demands—much as William Law (in *A Serious Call to a Devout and Holy Life*) argues that Christianity does. The New Testament, Law observes, does not prescribe church attendance and does not break life down into formally distinct spheres of sacred and secular activity. All of life, from the smallest features of daily routine and habit to the most consequential acts, is intended to be "worship." Only a life lived without reliance upon the purely formal disguises of prayer or churchly ritual can be truly Christian.[37]

William Law almost certainly came to Franklin's attention during his London months in 1725 and 1726, when Law accompanied Francis Hutcheson in the counterattack upon Bernard Mandeville. In 1726, Law also published an attack on "Stage Entertainments" and a manual of Christian conduct that was the forerunner to *A Serious Call* two years later. By the early 1740s, Deborah Franklin owned copies both of Law's *A Practical Treatise on Christian Perfection* (1726)—a likely source for the whimsical "title" of Franklin's "bold and arduous Project" for attaining perfection— and *A Serious Call*. Franklin had clearly read the second of these as early as 1735, when he paraphrases part of Law's passionate objections to Christian formalists in his defense of Samuel Hemphill's irregular sermons.

In the pages of the almanac, however, Franklin is interested not in the higher flights of religious rhetoric but in the least conspicuous moments of existence—in routine—where his sense of human psychology teaches him that the contest between vice and virtue is really waged. "There is no little enemy," Poor Richard observes in September 1733, one of dozens of aphorisms that invite a modern reader's misunderstanding. Franklin's contemporaries, steeped in the psychologically acute reform literature of the day, would have recognized (as William Law did) that the processes of rationalization and self-temptation invariably commence in small things:

> When, therefore, you are guilty of any folly, or extravagance, or indulge any vain temper, do not consider it as a small matter, because it may seem so if compared to some other sins; but consider it, as it is acting contrary to your nature, and then you will see that there is nothing small that is unreasonable; because all unreasonable ways are contrary to the nature of all rational beings, whether men or Angels: neither of which can be any longer agreeable to God, than so far as they act according to the reason and excellence of their nature.[38]

In the almanac, Franklin characteristically sharpens this insight into a form that expresses a posture of nearly militant vigilance over the self. He makes Law's doctrine assume a dramatic life that the unwary or unschooled reader might easily mistake for a partisan vindictiveness. But the corollary insight to "There is no little enemy" is, There are no insignificant victories. The ability to subject one small sphere of life to devotional discipline would have an expansive, regenerative effect. In *A Serious Call*, William Law likewise singles out eating as the most conspicuous daily evidence of animal nature in human beings. The "smallest rule" of religious self-denial applied to such a ubiquitous feature of physical existence would bring "a sense of religion into the ordinary actions of our common life."[39] Just such a redemption of the ordinary is Law's goal; in many respects, it is Poor Richard's goal as well.

Law's devotional handbook, however, and religious exhortations like it were unlikely to find an audience comparable in size and diversity to the audience of *Poor Richard*. The almanac is almost by definition the text of common life. In Franklin's hands, particularly, it becomes a complete portrait of the full range of human hungers, including the insistent hunger of the imagination that would become Samuel Johnson's chief literary theme. Franklin quotes several lines from "The Vanity of Human Wishes" in *Poor Richard* for 1750, published in Philadelphia less than a year after Johnson's poem appeared in London. Passages from Edward Young's *Night Thoughts,* as well as his *Satires on Fame,* and from the progressively expanded and revised versions of James Thomson's *The Seasons* also appear with some frequency in *Poor Richard*.

The poetic epigraph for the entire almanac of 1736—the year in which Richard Saunders' preface addressed the scandals and the intemperate passions of the Hemphill controversy—is drawn from Pope's *Essay on Man*, in print for just a little over a year when Franklin incorporates it into his complex summary of the lessons of religious conflict in Philadelphia:

> Presumptuous Man! the Reason wouldst thou find
> Why form'd so weak, so little, and so blind?
> First, if thou canst, the harder reason guess
> Why form'd no weaker, blinder, and no less?
> Ask of thy Mother Earth why Oaks are made,
> Taller or stronger than the Weeds they shade?
> Or ask of yonder argent Fields above,
> Why JOVE's Satellites are less than JOVE?

From such sublime poetic heights, it is true, Poor Richard abruptly descends, within a page, to "Fish and Visitors stink in 3 days."

The dizziness of such a descent is just the point. Man presumes and falls; we are not oaks, but weeds. Our "common" nature, however, can be a kind of presumption in masquerade—a disorderly disguise for genuine meanings that are precisely the opposite of appearances. "Fish and Visitors" appears in January, a month that opens with the Feast of the Epiphany and closes with the anniversary of the execution of Charles I. Fish may indeed spoil with notorious speed, but they also form part of a sacramental feast that Franklin's readers might readily recall in the closing days of the Christmas season. Epiphany itself is a commemoration of momentous, kingly visitors, whose submission to a higher power is the bright antitype to Charles' darkly typic fate. Three days is anything but an arbitrary interval to name in association with the process of flesh's decay. Franklin's application of the almanac's capacity for drama—a mingling of voices that enacts the simultaneous ascents and descents of human nature—here as elsewhere accounts for the living completeness of *Poor Richard*.

Chapter Four

The Theater of Science

Franklin's didactic journalism over the first twenty years of his Philadelphia career is rooted in the generous moral psychology of Shaftesbury, Addison, Hutcheson, and Locke—work in which he had steeped himself since his apprenticeship in Boston. The Busy-Body papers, the pamphlets in defense of Samuel Hemphill, and the almanacs all reflect not an arid and prescriptive ethics of thrift but a dynamic and disorderly vision of human character, patterned upon dialogue rather than commandment, on the evolution of internal soliloquy rather than the anguished preparation for an experience of ineffable grace. It is, moreover, a vision of character perfectly suited to the demands of Franklin's large, vocational design: the containment of the divisive energies that propel history toward confusion. The compound character of *Poor Richard* is Franklin's most extended effort at creating a portrait that might serve as a textual substitute for narrower expressions of the collective interest, first in Philadelphia, then in the wider colonial audience that the almanac reached.

As it evolves through personal crises, local religious controversies, and the shifting intellectual circumstances of its creator, the almanac strives to represent religious principle divested of sectarian rhetoric, learning divested of presumption, virtue divested of shallow formalism. It becomes, in some respects, an accessible and intimate successor to the iconic image of Cato in the Busy-Body: a figural embodiment of integrative claims that Franklin playfully invites his readers to associate with the traditional

Christomimetic doctrine of the king's two bodies.[1] Ernst Kantorowicz begins his definitive account of the development of this theological convention of medieval politics by examining its role in the central scenes of Shakespeare's *Richard II,* the pageant of "uncrowning" that begins on the Welsh coast and ends at Westminster, when Richard shatters the mirror in which he beholds the paradoxes of his own shattered being.

Franklin's Poor Richard is a singularly unlikely subject to be juxtaposed to Shakespeare's extraordinary creation if we consider him only in the first of his fictive bodies: that of the beleaguered stargazer who makes the almanac. But the final pages of *Poor Richard* for 1733 designate its imaginary compiler as "an American Prince without Subjects," listed among the reigning monarchs of Europe but uncrowned, just as Shakespeare's hero is when he comes to epitomize the mystery of uncrowned humanity, descending within the space of a brief exchange between the Duke and Duchess of York from "King Richard" to "poor Richard" (5.2.6–22). Franklin's figurative claims for his almanac portrait, conditioned as they are by popular comic convention and diffused over a twenty-five-year series of "ephemerae," cannot hope to match the sublime concentration of Shakespeare's stage, but sacramental and political mysteries mingle in the almanac's strategically "common" pages much as they do in the uncommon lines that form the heart of Shakespeare's play. King Richard, too, in his final scene, becomes a student of the moral aphorism whose words would not be out of place in Franklin's proverbial calendar: "I wasted time, and now doth time waste me" (5.5.49).

When he turned to the experimental study of electricity shortly before his retirement from his printing business, much of Franklin's excitement derived from the exhilaration he felt at discovering a demonstrably physical force that seemed to confirm the same integrative claims he attempts to represent in his journalistic portraits. Indeed, one of Franklin's most elaborate contrivances for illustrating the properties of an electrical charge was a portrait of the king, meticulously reconfigured to disguise a primitive battery, which the experimental virtuoso then used to dramatize his mysterious immunity to the superstitious perils of removing a crown.[2]

On the surface, at least, Franklin's interest in experimental science after 1746 seems a complete departure from his earlier career. The distinction between the two kinds of activity—that of popular moralist and that of physical investigator—is reflected in a similar division of interest among modern students of Franklin's work, very few of whom insist upon reading both aspects of Franklin's intellectual life in relationship to one another.[3]

But as Alfred Owen Aldridge observes, Franklin chose to describe his experimental output through the traditional form of semipublic letters to personal friends.[4] Early scientific societies regularly conducted their inquiries as an extension of the private correspondence of their members. Letters played a similarly dominant role in the structure of the *Spectator* essays. Silence Dogood's diagnoses of social conditions in Boston are framed as letters to the *New England Courant,* much as the Busy-Body papers later will be in Philadelphia and as Shaftesbury does with his *Letter concerning Enthusiasm* and the fictive correspondence that constitutes *The Moralists.* In a generic sense, then, Franklin's science is closely identified with his readerly experience and with his own long-standing literary practice.

More important than this formal resemblance, however, is the conceptual relationship that Franklin—like many of his contemporaries—came to recognize between vast natural systems of physical balance or imbalance, on the one hand, and human character and institutions, on the other. The relationship between the two was not simply an attractive analogy in Enlightenment thought. The critical seventeenth- and eighteenth-century term that natural philosophers applied to this pervasive relationship between a natural and a moral architecture was not *analogy* but *design.* The physical design of the natural universe and the moral design of its creatures were works of the same Designer, expressions of an identical end in the inconceivably diverse medium of creation. Difference was inevitably unity in disguise, according to these philosophical and scientific assumptions, while unity was inevitably expressed and embodied in difference.

Two of Franklin's favorite terms for the electrical phenomena that so engaged his interest through the last full decade he would spend in America were *fluid* and *fire.* That in his mind electricity could assume both of these antagonistic physical natures suggests the integrative power of the scientific imagination in Franklin's day as well as the potentially revolutionary conclusions he was prepared to draw from the identification of culture with nature, which he and his scientific contemporaries had come to endorse. In this context, then, the populist science of *Poor Richard* directly anticipates the scientific sophistication of Franklin's *Experiments and Observations on Electricity.* The twin enterprises of popular moralist and physical investigator reflect a common interest in natural design—a double focus that is captured in the genealogy of the aphorism from the 1736 almanac, which seems simultaneously to endorse and to deflate Pope's resonant couplets.

The source of Poor Richard's reflections on fish and visitors calls attention to the intersection of interests in Franklin's life that the almanac indirectly embodies from its first issue and directly incorporates after its transformation into *Poor Richard Improved* in 1748. The genre of the almanac traditionally existed on the border of astrology and astronomy, superstition and complex mathematics. Particularly in Franklin's lifetime, as the English calendar fell increasingly behind the celestial equinoxes, the significance of the almanac's relationship to cosmological movement and sublime natural order became a commonplace of popular consciousness. In 1752, *Poor Richard's* preface explains in great historical and scientific detail Parliament's decision to drop eleven days from September in order to realign the English year with sidereal time. Even quite late in the eighteenth century David Rittenhouse's orrery—a working model of the movements of the solar system that was, in many respects, a kinetic almanac—had a degree of contemporary scientific prestige that would rank it with the most sophisticated modern satellite.[5]

Poor Richard's expanded format in the last decade that Franklin prepared it allowed him to treat the almanac increasingly like a scientific digest as well as a vehicle of moral education, fitting into its pages discussions of sound, astronomy, demography, time, and microscopy, as well as brief biographical accounts of the most celebrated scientific practitioners of the past: Copernicus, Bacon, Boyle, Newton, Locke ("the Newton of the microcosm," as Poor Richard calls him). *Poor Richard Improved* for 1750 includes a verse epigraph for September that makes this devotion to scientific inquiry a prominent part of the moral structure of the almanacs:

> Still be your darling Study Nature's Laws;
> And to its Fountain trace up every Cause.
> Explore, for such it is, this high Abode,
> And tread the Paths which Boyle and Newton trod.
> Lo, Earth smiles wide, and radiant Heav'n looks down,
> All fair, all gay, and urgent to be known!
> Attend, and here are sown Delights immense,
> For every Intellect, and every Sense.
> (*Papers,* 3:450)

This marked shift in the almanac's contents roughly coincides with Franklin's first electrical experiments in 1746, but it is misleading to view his scientific curiosity as the diversion of a retired printer. In some respects, the relationship ought to be reversed: Franklin became a printer, a publisher, and a moral aphorist as logical expressions of the expansive scientific consciousness of the late seventeenth century, to which Franklin responded powerfully in his earliest years. This peculiarly rich understanding of the scientific calling has an improbable but instructive relation to the propensity of fish and visitors to stink.

In 1670 John Ray, a nonjuring Anglican clergyman, published a collection of popular proverbs that includes a French saying, derived ultimately from Plautus: "Fresh fish and new-come guests smell by that they are three days old."[6] Franklin's application of Ray's text to the political and religious calendar of *Poor Richard* is consistent in many ways with the circumstances of John Ray's life. When Vladimir Nabokov gives Ray's name to the fictive psychologist who introduces *Lolita,* he is playfully commemorating Ray's work as an early expert in English lepidoptera, but Ray's scientific and religious reputation extended far beyond lovers of butterflies. In 1660 he gave up a prestigious fellowship at Cambridge University rather than sign a loyalty oath to Charles II and began a long and productive career as a natural philosopher—a collector and classifier of the phenomena of nature—with a particular interest in documenting and disclosing the providential design that he and his scientific contemporaries believed all of the natural world revealed.

The most influential result of this life-long study is Ray's book, *The Wisdom of God Manifested in the Works of the Creation* (1691), which was among the most popular of the numerous seventeenth- and eighteenth-century tributes to the religious import of the natural world.[7] Ray's account of providential design went through seventeen editions between 1691 and 1798, remaining familiar enough to nineteenth-century readers to earn a place among Herman Melville's cetological authorities in *Moby-Dick.*[8] The unusual durability of Ray's book springs in part from its application of traditional investigative means to untraditional ends.

In *The Advancement of Learning* (1605), Francis Bacon compares the three empirical disciplines of divine philosophy, natural philosophy, and human philosophy to beams of light, with the "radius reflexus," or the knowledge of man, engaging the bulk of his attention. The line of Bacon's philosophical descendants to which John Ray belongs, however, was drawn to what Bacon calls the "radius refractus," or the investigation of God through nature, an area that Bacon pronounces limited in scope and potential because of "the inequality of the medium" to the magnificence of the mediated Divinity. Bacon's successors in natural philosophy came to treat the radius refractus with increasing respect, as knowledge of the natural medium dramatically expanded over the course of the seventeenth century and as reverence for the institutional practitioners of the study of divinity declined.[9]

William Wollaston's *The Religion of Nature Delineated*—the book that prompted Franklin to write his *Dissertation on Liberty and Necessity* in 1725—belongs to this intellectual and spiritual tradition. The philosophic and literary implications of a commitment to scientific theology receive particularly vivid illustration in Shaftesbury's ambitious 1709 dialogue, *The Moralists*, where Theocles and Philocles, Shaftesbury's speakers, pursue the scientific vision of nature to enthusiastic excess. Theocles' celebration of universal light and heat, suggestively combined into a judgmental atmospheric fire, sums up the aesthetic and religious context within which fall Isaac Newton's *Optics* and Franklin's electrical researches:

> But whither shall we trace the Sources of *the* LIGHT? or in what Ocean comprehend the luminous Matter so wide diffus'd thro the immense Spaces which it fills? What Seats shall we assign to that fierce Element of Fire, too active to be confin'd within the Compass of the *Sun,* and not excluded even the Bowels of the heavy *Earth?* . . . It cherishes the cold dull Massy *Globe,* and warms it to its Center. It forms the Minerals; gives Life and Growth to Vegetables; kindles a soft, invisible, and vital *Flame* in the Breasts of living Creatures; frames, animates, and nurses all the various Forms; sparing, as well as imploying for their Use, those *sulphurous* and *combustible* Matters of which they are compos'd. Benign and gentle amidst all, it still maintains this happy Peace and Concord, according to its stated and peculiar Laws. But these once broken, the acquitted *Being* takes its Course unrul'd. It runs impetuous thro the fatal Breach, and breaking into visible and fierce *Flames,* passes triumphant o'er the yielding Forms, converting all into it-self, and dissolving now those Systems, which it-self before had form'd. (*CMM,* 2:379–80)

Nature, Francis Bacon cautions, can dramatize "the omnipotency and wisdom" of its Designer, but it cannot present "His image." Natural philosophers like Ray and Shaftesbury increasingly come to disagree. Shaftesbury's apocalyptic metaphors make particularly evident how bold the visionary claims of natural philosophy had become in contrast to Bacon's cautious beginnings. The elemental fire with which Shaftesbury begins his reflections in *The Moralists* is both a generative parent and a vindictively "acquitted Being" that punishes breaches of its law with annihilation. It is, in effect, the Deity's image as well as a dramatic enactment of traditional divine attributes.

In part, this enhanced confidence in the legibility and metaphoric significance of the first of God's great books—nature —was built upon the biblical foundation of the Psalms, particularly Psalm 104, a classic text of natural philosophy that seventeenth- and eighteenth-century scientific and religious writers frequently identify as an inspiration for their work. Franklin devotes most of *Poor Richard Improved* for 1753 and 1754 to a reprinting of James Burgh's *An Hymn to the Creator of the World. The Thoughts taken chiefly from Psal. civ* (1750). John Tillotson's most forthright defense of natural religion over institutional piety in the last decade of the seventeenth century takes Psalm 104 as its sermon text. John Ray's celebrated contemporary, Thomas Burnet, derives critical metaphorical evidence from Psalm 104 for his attempts to reconcile geology with the Mosaic account of the Deluge in *The Sacred Theory of the Earth* (1691), and Ray himself takes the title of *The Wisdom of God Manifested in the Works of the Creation* directly from Psalm 104:

> O Lord, how manifold are Thy works!
>   In wisdom hast thou made them all;
>   The earth is full of thy creatures.
> Yonder is the sea, great and wide,
>   Which teems with things innumerable,
>   Living things both small and great.
> There go the ships, and Leviathan which Thou
>   Did'st form to sport in it.[10]

When Cotton Mather compiles "the Best Discoveries in Nature with Religious Improvements" into *The Christian Philosopher* (1721), he invokes a long list of earlier investigators and collectors to establish in his reader's mind an image of a diverse scientific and theological movement. William Harvey, Thomas Browne, Henry More, Robert Boyle, William Derham, George Cheyne all produced books that reinforce Mather's religioscientific purposes or, like Boyle's *Christian Virtuoso* (1690), directly anticipate his title. In the latter half of *The Christian Philosopher*, however, Mather relies most heavily on the work of "our pious Ray," "the industrious Ray," "our valuable Ray," a "modern Pliny" whose words Mather sometimes directly transposes into his own text without attribution in his eagerness to draw on the resources of John Ray's formidable science.[11] *The*

Wisdom of God Manifested in the Works of the Creation was already a proverbial authority among learned readers in New England during the years that Benjamin Franklin was helping to prepare his brother's newspaper, borrowing books from fellow apprentices, and reading freely from the volumes in the "pretty" collection of the "ingenious" tradesman, Matthew Adams.

Ray's silencing by the Restoration's Acts of Conformity inevitably links his religious and scientific example to a contentious political world, but Ray himself is careful to preserve the appearance of a disinterested servant. In his book's introduction, he observes that writing, at least, remains open to him as a way of serving his church.[12] The services that he undertakes in *The Wisdom of God,* however, have little to do with sustaining the Anglican establishment and much more to do with glorifying the expansive, and egalitarian, empire of science. In this respect, Ray completely agrees with Francis Bacon's distinction, in his "Religious Meditations," between the institutional shell and the "kernal" it houses. Labor in God's works, Bacon writes, is as "a sweet ointment" and a good conscience: "But if thou follow after the mighty things of men, thou shalt work with disgust and reproach."[13] In Ray's judgment, it is a "gross piece of Ignorance and Rusticity" to treat the natural world as if it were subordinate to the spiritual and material needs of man. Nature offers sublime religious instruction, Ray concludes, but it is equally sublime in its indifference to the conceptual power of the human observer.[14]

Indeed, at the end of his book Ray adapts Pascal's extraordinary wager against nothingness to his own religious purposes, conceding that faith in providential design, even if it is in fact illusory, is at least a pleasant dream. Atheists can never hope to be free from the "poison" of suspicion and fear, Ray observes, since no one can decisively prove a negative. But even a deluded believer runs no risk of being awakened from delusion: "Death making a full end of him."[15] For a writer who sets out to celebrate the "Sovereign Wisdom" of an omnipresent Deity manifested in the natural world, this is an extraordinary spiritual destination, but Ray's willingness to break with formulas is one reason that his example as a natural philosopher retained its appeal long after Henry More's *Antidote to Atheism* had interest chiefly for the antiquarian.

The comparative religious independence in Ray's book aligns him with radical critics of the "Newtonian" consensus that had been recently institutionalized in the Boyle lectures. Margaret Jacob describes how scientific theology became an increasingly conservative political force through the early years of the eighteenth century.[16] John Ray draws conclusions from his study of the natural world that differ from the implicit affirmation of hierarchy in Newton's celestial mechanics. Nature, as Ray argues in *The Wisdom of God*, takes the form of a complex state of "mutual Subserviency . . . conspiring to promote and carry on the publick Good." Its design is as much civic and political as religious or scientific, and the Deity whose voice Ray mimics in a remarkable passage from his book charges the natural philosopher to explore the globe very much as an inquiring correspondent of the Royal Society might move through the developing provinces of America:

> I have placed thee in a spacious and well-furnished World; I have endued thee with an ability of understanding what is beautiful and proportionable. . . . I have provided thee with Materials whereon to exercise and employ thy Art and Strength. . . . I have made thee a sociable Creature . . . for the Improvement of thy Understanding by conference, and Communication of Observations and Experiments; for mutual help, assistance, and defence; build Thee large Towns and Cities with streight and well-paved Streets, and elegant rows of Houses, adorned with magnificent temples for my Honour and Worship, with beautiful Palaces for Thy Princes and Grandees, with stately halls for public meetings of the Citizens and their several Companies.[17]

The entire divine monologue occupies more than three pages. In it, Ray establishes shipbuilding and the skill of celestial navigation, among other things, as providential gifts that make possible the global extension of "philosophical" inquiry to all foreign places and peoples, urging the scientific traveler to note "their Government, their Manners, Laws, and Customs, their Diet and medicine, their trades and Manufactures, their Houses and Buildings." "Go thither," Ray's Deity ultimately commands, "and bring home what may be useful and beneficial to thy country in general, or thy self in particular." Thomas Jefferson's instructions to the Lewis and Clark expedition more than a century later directly incorporate the cultural imperatives of John Ray's remarkable commandments to the natural philosopher, as do Benjamin Franklin's diplomatic exemptions that sought to protect James Cook's scientific expedition from interference by ships of war during the American Revolution.

As a direct reflection of its importance in his own process of self-education, Franklin makes Ray's book part of the ideal curriculum that he describes in his *Proposals Relating to the Education of Youth in Pensilvania*

(1749). His "Articles of Belief" (1728) includes quasi-liturgical directions citing *The Wisdom of God,* along with other inspirational texts, as preambles to "some Minutes [of] serious Silence" just before he is to sing Milton's "Hymn to the Creator" (*Papers,* 1:105). Such invocations of Ray's work aim at more ambitious goals than the stimulation of a meditative mood. Just as Franklin's "Articles of Belief" emphasizes the identification of works with worship, so John Ray's natural piety expresses itself as a divine endorsement for the energies of an active assembly of "Citizens" in "their several Companies," building and maintaining the "stately halls" of government. What makes Ray's text particularly significant to a reader interested in assessing its place in Franklin's early career is how closely Ray's natural philosophy identifies with the social practices of conference, communication, mutual assistance, and public meetings as well as with scientific collection and experimentation.

Ray's deific charge to the natural philosopher reads like a prophetic summary of the intellectual and political activities that occupied Benjamin Franklin between 1729, when he began publishing the *Pennsylvania Gazette,* and 1757, the beginning of his diplomatic career. If the natural science of America inevitably began as a provincial extension of the Royal Society of London, seeking its significance in a deferential relation to the European scientific community, it contained at the outset imperatives to intellectual and political self-determination as well—imperatives that may have influenced Cotton Mather in his selection of John Ray over Isaac Newton or Robert Boyle as the modern Pliny who presided over his scientific imagination.

Franklin's earliest demonstration of scientific ambition is marked by the political assumptions contained in Ray's exemplary book. In the *Autobiography,* Franklin records his sale to Hans Sloane of an asbestos purse that he had brought from America as an instance of the natural curiosities of the New World. Sloane heard of the purse because Franklin wrote him early in June 1725, proposing certain natural objects for sale and presenting himself in language that seems surprisingly grand for a nineteen-year-old printer's journeyman who found himself, six months earlier, unexpectedly stranded in London:

June 2, 1725

Sir

Having lately been in the Nothern Parts of America, I have brought from thence a Purse made of the Stone Asbestus, a Piece of the Stone, and a

Piece of Wood, the Pithy Part of which is of the same Nature, and call'd by the Inhabitants, Salamander Cotton. As you are noted to be a Lover of Curiosities, I have inform'd you of these; and if you have any Inclination to purchase them, or see 'em, let me know your Pleasure by a Line directed for me at the Golden Fan in Little Britain, and I will wait upon you with them. I am, Sir Your Most humble Servant

Benjamin   Franklin

P.S. I expect to be out of Town in 2 or 3 Days, and therefore beg an immediate Answer. (*Papers,* 1:54)

Franklin had clearly come to England on more than one errand. If his primary goal was the purchase of printing equipment on William Keith's credit, he had also taken the trouble before leaving Philadelphia to supply himself with a few "Curiosities" that might serve as a convenient introduction to London's "philosophical" circles. Franklin's goals appear to have included the opening of a scientific correspondence with members of the Royal Society similar to the one that Cotton Mather maintained from Boston during the years of Franklin's apprenticeship. Inevitably, the disappointment at Keith's empty promises delayed the execution of his intentions, but Franklin was apparently confident enough by June to unpack his specimens and address a letter to a future president of the Royal Society (Isaac Newton's successor in that role) and personal physician to the king.

The tone of Franklin's letter represents its youthful author very much as if he were a gentleman of leisure momentarily pausing in "Town" before continuing his travels. It is a social pose that Franklin could not reasonably have expected to maintain much beyond this brief note, but it is in some respects a perfectly appropriate message to be exchanged between "Citizens" in a common scientific community. Sloane moved most frequently among "Princes and Grandees," but the lessons of mutual subservience that John Ray finds inscribed in nature create unexpected democracies of knowledge that cut across the superficially wide gaps of social status and rank.

Franklin began to learn this lesson when his facility at writing earned him the praise and regard of his brother's circle of wits at the *New England Courant* and when the colonial governor of New York expressed a desire to meet the obscure young traveler from Boston, bound to Philadelphia with an impressive trunkful of books (*Writings,* 1336). The social utility of knowledge, particularly for a young man with few other visible assets, was as clear as the diplomatic efficacy of good manners. But the extension of metaphors of communal interdependence and the public good to the natural universe had implications for the exercise of colonial power that Franklin appears to have sensed at a very early stage in his career. The letter to Sloane is in many respects presumptuous, but what it presumes is a potential realignment of broad historical forces based on a common scientific culture.

The journal that Franklin kept of his voyage home to Philadelphia in 1726 is a more extensive experiment in the kind of self-projection represented by the letter to Sloane. When in part 1 of the *Autobiography* Franklin refers his son to the manuscript of this journal, forty-five years after it was written, he singles out for special attention the "Plan of Conduct" that must have formed part of the document's original text. Only a fragment of the plan survives, but Franklin's grandson, William Temple Franklin, transcribed and printed what appears to be a complete text of the voyage journal in the *Memoirs* of his grandfather published in London in 1817.[18] The journal is the reflective medium within which Franklin's formal plan takes shape. An account of how he occupies himself during the enforced idleness of the voyage, it is also a rich collection of incipient metaphors for the process of "planning," which spans the full range of Franklin's mature intellectual interests: from the careful, dispassionate observations of a natural scientist to the social and political generalizations of an instinctive reformer. Any journal is by nature a self-conscious document, but the sense of himself that emerges from Franklin's only surviving journal is more varied, suggestive, and playful than most. Although it culminates in a series of prudential rules, its structure from the outset is an exploration of the interchange between plan, or purposeful design, and chance—the crucial determinants of the seventeenth- and eighteenth-century debate on the significance of the natural world.[19]

In the process of conducting this inquiry, the journal becomes a vehicle for Franklin's increasingly ambitious experiments with the figurative intersection between science and politics. "Bring home what may be useful and beneficial to thy country in general, or thy self in particular," John Ray's deific voice urges. In some respects, Franklin undertakes to do just that. His letter to Hans Sloane is an amusing expression of neophyte ambition. The pages of the voyage journal, however, approach the question of Anglo-American scientific exchange on a broad historical and geographic scale, with disquieting and exhilarating results for the student of cultural design. The disintegrative tendencies of history were as evident to Franklin from the deck of his ship in 1726 as they would prove to be five years later when he drafted his library memorandum. To the eye of the natural philosopher, nature conspires in the succession of uncrownings, which the historical narrative records, but it simultaneously consoles and instructs an observer of that process. Mutual subserviency is the lesson John Ray detects throughout the Creator's works. Franklin's scientific career is dedicated to developing the implications of that lesson in the geopolitical design of the eighteenth century.

Franklin's ship, the *Berkshire,* descended the Thames from London on July 22, 1726, and after a considerable delay caused by adverse winds, finally sailed out of English waters for the first time on August 9. Franklin's melodramatic address to the "chalky cliffs of England" in his journal entry for July 24 ("Albion, farewell!") is a comic instance of how circumstances exercise an unpredictable influence over the grand exits and entrances with which human beings strive to punctuate their lives. He would remain very much in Albion's orbit, onshore and onboard ship, for the next sixteen days.

The voyage continued to be plagued by westerly winds off and on for two months. The *Berkshire* did not sight land until Sunday, October 9, and Franklin did not set foot in Philadelphia until October 11, when a pleasure boat of "young Philadelphians" gave him a lift upriver from the ship's last anchorage. It had been a "tedious and dangerous" voyage, according to the journal's concluding entry, leaving Franklin much weakened by the sea diet and lack of exercise, but it probably did not escape his notice that the "long-wished for sound, LAND! LAND!" heard from the *Berkshire*'s lookouts on October 9 coincided very closely with the anniversary of Christopher Columbus's first landfall—a fact often recorded in almanacs like the one that Franklin had consulted at sea when he sat up on September 30, 1726, to observe a predicted eclipse of the moon. In Franklin's youth, the New England festive calendar included the commemoration of Columbus's voyage, a fact duly exploited by that assiduous courter of eligible widows Samuel Sewall, who closed a note to Katherine Brattle Winthrop on October 11, 1720, with his wishes for a "joyful entrance upon the Two hundred and twenty-ninth year of Christopher Columbus his Discovery."[20]

If Franklin's exit from the Old World was marred by uncooperative weather, his return to the New was more auspicious than he could have hoped for. October 11 in the Old Style calendar, the last entry in Franklin's voyage journal, is effectively Columbus Day, a coincidence that one might expect the self-satisfied young correspondent of Sir Hans Sloane to celebrate. But Franklin handles anniversaries in the journal with a degree of restraint that makes their presence all the more conspicuous and interesting. They offer opportunities for taking social and cultural measurements of a sort that can suggest, to an heir of seventeenth-century natural philosophy, the providential design hidden in the drift of events.

The voyage journal's first entry, like its last, is marked by a chronological conjunction that will prove suggestive as Franklin's sequence of subjects unfolds. The *Berkshire* descended the Thames to Gravesend on July 22 and dropped anchor for the night opposite Tilbury Fort, which Franklin viewed the following morning from the top of Windmill Hill while his ship waited for a favorable tide. Tilbury was the vast showpiece of English coastal fortification in the early eighteenth century, with more than one hundred heavy guns capable of commanding the approaches to London for many miles. Daniel Defoe describes the fortress in admiring detail in his *Travels through the Whole Island of England and Scotland* (1725), where it becomes his standard for defensive potency.[21] But its significance extends deep into English political history. Tilbury Fort and its adjacent plain is the site where Leicester collected his troops to repel the anticipated Spanish landing in the summer of 1588. Elizabeth had addressed her soldiers at Tilbury Camp in early August of that year, shortly after Howard, Hawkins, Frobisher, and Drake had herded the Armada past the Isle of Wight in a series of engagements and maneuvers that took place between July 21 and July 28 (Old Style), the day when English fire ships finally drove the Spanish out of Calais toward the North Sea.

Bonfires often commemorated the anniversary of the famous chain of beacons that announced the sighting of the Spanish off Plymouth, a celebration that took on multiplied significance after the centennial year of 1688, when William of Orange ended a second Catholic threat to the English throne. Popular almanacs like *Poor Robin* frequently appeared with doggerel printed opposite the last days of July to remind the reader suffering through the summer doldrums of the larger significance of the time:

> In fifteen hundred eighty eight,
> The Spaniards thought in England strait
> To have arriv'd, but the proud Don
> Show'd but his Teeth, and so was gone.[22]

Like Guy Fawkes Day, the Armada defeat was an emblem of national success in the protracted struggle with "Romish" conspiracy and Catholic monarchs—a memorable sign of divine determination to safeguard the Reformation against Continental reaction.

But even an "agreeable" anniversary prospect of Tilbury Plain from Windmill Hill, along with "two or three reaches of the river with ships and boats sailing both up and down," left the young Franklin conspicuously silent on the subjects of English empire or English greatness. Over the next two weeks he would explore a number of landmarks and monuments touching on a range of notable events from English history as the *Berkshire* tried to make its way against the same prevailing westerlies that doomed the Spanish fleet. In the process of commenting on what he saw, Franklin constructed a picture of social metamorphosis for which the natural world was quietly providing models and signs. Much of what he recorded in his voyage journal suggests Franklin's implicit theme that a mature and formidable cultural "organism" was gradually yielding place to its New World successor. Gravesend, Tilbury, and Dover in late July form a configuration that evokes England's victorious past, against which Franklin projects an initial image of its reduced present in the form of the "*cursed biting*" commercial exploitation of "strangers" at Gravesend: "If you buy any thing of them, and give half what they ask, you pay twice as much as the thing is worth. Thank God we shall leave it to-morrow" (*Papers*, 1:72).

The impression of fallen grandeur grew as Franklin recorded visits to Portsmouth and Carisbrooke Castle on the Isle of Wight over the ensuing six days. The *Berkshire* took shelter from heavy west winds at Spithead, Cowes, and Yarmouth before finally making headway into the Atlantic in early August. At each port, Franklin and a few companions disembark for long, sightseeing walks, the first of which includes a survey of the fortifications at Portsmouth that reads like the report of a spy rather than the travel journal of an aspiring dry goods clerk. Franklin notes harbor facilities, trenches, walls, and gun emplacements very much as if he were making notes for a coastal raid similar to those he helped orchestrate from his diplomatic post in Paris more than fifty years later. The Portsmouth that he describes is an example of England's continuing maritime vigor, coupled with disquieting signs of the nation's vulnerability. Its wartime garrison of ten thousand men is strikingly reduced; "at present 'tis only manned by about 100 Invalids," Franklin observes. The harbor might hold a thousand ships and support three fleets at sea, but it contained at

Franklin's visit only a relatively small number of unrigged vessels "of 2nd, 3rd, and 4th rates . . . easily fitted out upon occasion" but currently out of service.

More significant than the state of the garrison or the fleet, however, was the state of the city's recent leadership. Even at age twenty, Franklin is interested in the immaterial expressions of power. On these less visible grounds, too, Portsmouth has lessons for a colonial observer. The people of the city told stories of the excesses of a recent military governor who kept soldiers in "a miserable dungeon by the towngate" for what the citizens viewed as "trifling misdemeanors . . . till they were almost starved to death." Franklin's private comments on this tyrannical policy indicate that he had not forgotten the extract from the *London Journal* on free speech and wicked governors that Silence Dogood sent to the *New England Courant* four years earlier:

> 'Tis a common maxim, that without severe discipline it is impossible to govern the licentious rabble of soldiery. I own indeed that if a commander finds he has not those qualities in him that will make him beloved by his people, he ought by all means to make use of such methods as will make them fear him, since one or the other (or both) is absolutely necessary; but Alexander and Caesar, those renowned generals, received more faithful service, and performed greater actions by means of the love their soldiers bore them, than they could possibly have done, if instead of being beloved and respected they had been hated and feared by those they commanded. (*Papers,* 1:74)

As revealing as the superiority of love to fear is the example that the Portsmouth anecdotes offer of the judgmental accuracy of popular memory. Two days later, at the end of a tour of Carisbrooke Castle, Franklin notes that the misdeeds of another recent military governor, however ably concealed in his lifetime, were well known even to "the silly old fellow" who guides him on his tour: "In short I believe it is impossible for a man, though he has all the cunning of a devil, to live and die a villain and yet conceal it so well as to carry the name of an honest fellow to the grave with him. . . . Truth and Sincerity have a certain distinguishing native luster about them which cannot be perfectly counterfeited, they are like fire and flame that cannot be painted" (*Papers,* 1:78). All the political cunning in the world cannot distort or disguise the natural "luster" of moral excellence, any more than the coercive discipline of the governor of Portsmouth can match the "attractive" agency of love. Franklin's youthful analyses subtly weave together traditional religious ethics, politics, and science in the emerging portrait of an England that is spiritually shrinking within its vast, defensive shell.

Between his visits to Portsmouth and Carisbrooke, Franklin records the first of the journal's two reflections on shipboard games and gamesmanship that serve as playful extensions of the atmosphere of imperial contest, which the observations at Portsmouth had begun to explore. Part of the time that the *Berkshire* lay in the harbor at Cowes on the Isle of Wight Franklin amused himself "at the draft board." The key to success at drafts, he notes, is a significant degree of indifference to the consequences of the game, particularly when large sums of money are at stake. Anxiety invariably confounds the judgment, Franklin concludes, leading him to propound an "infallible Rule" of play: "he that loves money most shall lose." A corollary rule projects the game of drafts as an analogy for contests between nations: "Courage is almost as requisite for the good conduct of this game as in a real battle; for if the player imagines himself opposed by one that is much his superior in skill, his mind is so intent on the defensive part that an advantage passes unobserved."

The voyage journal, even in its initial entries, presents its author as self-possessed in precisely the manner that Franklin recommends for the successful gambler at cards: engaged in making a series of calm observations, untroubled by excessive anxiety about the consequences of the "game," watchful for the inherent advantages that might be consistent even with relative weakness. If the commercial practices of Gravesend are any indication, England has developed a crippling devotion to gain, while an American contestant will do well to remember that the power and skill of his opponent may exist to a significant degree only in the challenger's imagination. Several strategies play a role in Franklin's discussion of the requirements for success at drafts, with the natural result that the voyage journal, too, takes on increasingly strategic qualities.

In his brief description of the "pretty prospect" of Newport on the Isle of Wight, Franklin claims that he "could not learn" the name of the "tall old-fashioned" church that distinguishes the town, but he has no difficulty in gathering from the inhabitants a detailed account of how they fatten oysters for the London markets. With this deft suggestion of the state of local priorities, Franklin introduces a lengthy account of his visit to Carisbrooke, a mile outside of Newport and the site of a castle, dating from Saxon times, that had served as one of the prisons of Charles I. The tombs and ancient monuments at Carisbrooke were constructed from a local stone "of such a soft crumbling nature that the inscriptions are none of them legible." The castle is slowly eroding, the debris from its walls nearly filling the ditch that originally surrounded them, and its grand rooms stripped bare of furnishings by the last military governor as a result of a commercial disagreement with his successor. The stairway from the lower to the upper castle is "so broken and decayed that I was almost afraid to come down again when I was up," but the view of the whole island from the upper battlements is rewarding. Franklin and his companions entertain themselves on these heights, and later in the lower castle, in a manner that suggests their peculiar freedom from the psychological burden of ruins:

> From the battlements of this upper castle (which they call the coop) you have a fine prospect of the greatest part of the island, of the sea on one side, of Cowes road at a distance, and of Newport as it were just below you. There is a well in the middle of the coop, which they called the bottomless well, because of its great depth; but it is now half filled up with stones and rubbish, and is covered with two or three loose planks; yet a stone, as we tried, is near a quarter of a minute in falling before you hear it strike. But the well that supplies the inhabitants at present with water is in the lower castle, and is thirty fathoms deep. They draw their water with a great wheel, and with a bucket that holds near a barrel. It makes a great sound if you speak in it, and echoed the flute we played over it very sweetly. (*Papers,* 1:77–78)

Franklin closes the entry by noting the poor condition of the castle's remaining ordnance and reproducing the one inscription in the soft stone of Carisbrooke that apparently is still readable: "1598/ E. R./ 40," a commemoration of the restoration and repairs completed by Elizabeth in the fortieth year of her reign.

By this point in the journal, nearly a week after the *Berkshire*'s departure from London, it is clear that Franklin's farewell to England is a more complex gesture than it may initially have seemed to be. Part of the knowledge that the natural philosopher gleans from travel, according to John Ray, is cultural. Franklin's philosophical observations accordingly begin to suggest a familiar cultural pattern of growth and decline, from the triumphal late years of Elizabeth's reign or the Civil War successes of the armies of Parliament to the deteriorating stone of Carisbrooke. His entry for July 30 underscores this jaundiced view of the state of English heroism by commenting on the vainglorious tomb of Sir Robert Holmes, a late seventeenth-century governor of the Isle of Wight, who seized upon some salvaged marble "designed by the French King for his palace at Versailles" to build a monument to himself, complete with eulogistic inscription. Franklin allows this chance association between the grand ambitions of Louis XIV and the petty ambitions of Robert Holmes to suggest its own conclusions to the student of individual or national aggrandizement on any scale.

Such a self-serving colonial interpretation of the current condition of the home island may have struck Franklin as unacceptably smug, for he follows these passages with an elaborate portrait of provincial ineptitude. On another long ramble through the Isle of Wight, he and his companions find themselves stranded by the refusal of a sleepy ferryman to carry them over a tidal estuary to Yarmouth. The resourceful tourists "design" to steal the ferryboat—possibly at the instigation of Franklin, who was proud of his aquatic skills—but the results are less spectacular than his swimming displays in the Thames. Franklin slips as he wades out to the mooring stake and "got up to my middle in mud" (*Papers,* 1:80). The ferry proves to be securely chained. After an hour of "fatigue and trouble," Franklin returns to shore and is preparing to spend the night with his companions in a haystack when one of them recalls that he picked up a horseshoe on their walk. Using the horseshoe as a tool, Franklin is successful on a second attempt at freeing the ferry from its chain, but the whole party are very shortly aground on a mud bank in midriver at ebb tide in a stolen boat: "It was hard to lie in an open boat all night exposed to the wind and weather; but it was worse to think how foolish we should look in the morning when the owner of the boat should catch us in that condition, where we must be exposed to the view of all the town."

In the end, they avoid embarrassing exposure, and perhaps prosecution, when Franklin and another equally amphibious member of the party strip off their clothes, lighten the boat by getting into the river, and drag the ferry off the mud bank "upon our knees near fifty yards into deeper water." The entry concludes on a note of whimsical relief—"thus ended our walk"—but its circumstances inevitably occur to the reader a few pages later when Franklin describes some tiny crab embryos that he studies as the *Berkshire* draws near American soundings. These creatures live on patches of gulfweed drifting in the ocean, where they reproduce in a peculiar vegetative way, developing out of eggs that resemble small, yellow berries fixed to the floating weed by gristly stalks. Taking a sample of the weed onboard, Franklin confirms the transformation of "this odd kind of fruit" into crabs, which he pronounces, half playfully, to be "native" to the gulfweed:

> I remember that the last calm we had, we took notice of a large crab upon the surface of the sea, swimming from one branch of weed to another, which he seemed to prey upon; and I likewise recollect that at Boston, in New England, I have often seen small crabs with a shell like a snail's upon their backs, crawling about in the salt water; and likewise at Portsmouth in England. It is likely nature has provided this hard shell to secure them till their own proper shell has acquired a sufficient hardness, which once perfected, they quit their old habitation and venture abroad safe in their own strength. The various changes that silk-worms, butterflies, and several other insects go through, make such alterations and metamorphoses not improbable. (*Papers*, 1:94)

Seventeenth- and eighteenth-century natural philosophers were intent on replacing sexual superstition with scientific descriptions of nature's reproductive processes. John Ray devotes the longest sustained discussion in *The Wisdom of God* to a celebration of the tenacious intercourse of frogs in order to heap ridicule on the idea of spontaneous generation. Far from being the by-products of heavy rainfall, frogs are energetically sexual creatures, capable of linking together "in complexu Venereo" for up to a month at a time. "What needs all this ado," Ray wonders, if nature alone can spontaneously generate living things?[23]

In his consideration of crab embryos, however, Franklin is less interested in the religious than in the political applications of reproductive biology. Weaker creatures understandably adapt to their limitations until they are able to "venture abroad safe in their own strength." The fatal predicament of the flying fish that Franklin also observes during the voyage derives from their inability to change course once they are airborne to avoid the dolphins, which simply pursue them until they drop back into the water. But alterations and metamorphoses like those of the gulfweed crab are the attributes of a successful design, enabling these creatures to "quit their old habitation," to thrive in the open sea, and to adapt to life as "natives" on both sides of the Atlantic, where their propensity for "crawling about in the salt water" bears an uncanny resemblance to the picture of Franklin and his aquatic companion crawling about on the tidal mud flats of Yarmouth.

Such apparently extravagant analogies were conventional practice in the work of contemporary natural philosophers, who were accustomed to suggesting the presence of vast metaphors for the state in the arrangements of the solar system or drawing instructive parallels between the human and natural worlds, as John Ray does when he compares the erotic life of frogs to that of human beings *in complexu Venereo.* Franklin conducts his experiment with the gulfweed crabs as the *Berkshire,* too, drifts about the ocean, in company with an emigrant ship bound for New York, at the mercy of unpredictable weather and adverse winds:

> There is really something strangely cheering to the spirits in the meeting of a ship at sea, containing a society of creatures of the same species and in the same circumstances with ourselves, after we had been long separated and excommunicated as it were from the rest of mankind. My heart fluttered in my breast with joy when I saw so many human countenances, and I could scarce refrain from that kind of laughter which proceeds from some degree of inward pleasure. When we have been for a considerable time tossing on the vast waters, far from the sight of any land or ships, or any mortal creature but ourselves (except a few fish and sea birds) the whole world, for aught we know, may be under a second deluge, and we (like Noah and his company in the Ark) the only surviving remnant of the human race. (*Papers,* 1:91)

As he draws near his Columbian arrival in Philadelphia—still more than two weeks away as he writes this passage—Franklin invokes the psychological and spiritual stresses of that pioneering voyage and anticipates the pleasure he will experience on his long-postponed return to America. When he plucks his curious sample of weed out of the ocean five days after this entry in the journal, he implicitly understands himself as a member of one drifting society of creatures encountering another. The loneliness and anxiety temporarily instilled by the "vast waters" briefly suggest to this native of Puritan Boston that he belongs to the "surviving remnant" of a second Deluge, a privileged member of the providential design.

There are limits, however, to the leveling impact of natural philosophy. Franklin and his fellow passengers on the *Berkshire* congratulate themselves that they are not forced to share ship's quarters with the indentured Irish servants who form the human cargo of their companion vessel: "We reckon ourselves in a kind of paradise, when we consider how they live, confined and stifled up with such a lousy stinking rabble in this sultry latitude." The community on the *Berkshire* are no rabble. They were on the open sea scarcely ten days before they formed themselves into a "Court of Justice," complete with a designated "Attorney General," to conduct a "trial in form" of an English passenger who had, "with a fraudulent design," marked the only two decks of cards onboard. The crime was witnessed more than two weeks earlier by a Dutch passenger while the ship still lay at anchor in Cowes, the offender imagining that because the Dutchman could not speak English he must be too stupid to recognize the preliminary acts of a card cheat. For reasons that the journal never makes explicit, Franklin and his companions wait until they are well at sea before convening their court, taking the Dutchman's testimony through an interpreter, and imposing a fine enforced by complete social ostracism until the sentence is satisfied.

The *Berkshire* passengers at sea are, to some extent, free of English jurisdiction as well as English prejudice. The evidence of the Dutch witness "was plain and positive," Franklin writes, despite the language barrier, and the ship's crew were available to help when the prisoner resisted being exposed for three hours in the roundtop as part of his punishment. These events suggest to Franklin some conclusions about the general need for conversation and communication among people, but the incidents illustrate more particular needs as well. The aggrieved passengers do not simply appeal to duly constituted authority when the original crime is committed in an English harbor. They delay until the opportunity is available to constitute "authority" in themselves, to form their own court of justice and to hand down their own sentences. Like the individual whom they punish, the *Berkshire* court has a design, one that distinguishes them both from the England they have left—their old habitation—and the "rabble" that they observe on the neighboring ship.

After five days of isolation, "our excommunicated ship-mate" paid his fine: "we have this morning received him into unity again" (*Papers*, 1:85). This sudden restoration of unity, after the potent rites of excommunication, suggests Franklin's youthful pleasure in the cultural tools with which the *Berkshire* community felt itself free to experiment in the social and geographical vacuum of the open sea. But that same geographical space is responsible for the second instance of shipboard justice that the voyage journal records. In accordance with maritime practice, the *Berkshire*'s steward is whipped before the entire ship's company for repeatedly using too much flour in his puddings "and for several other misdemeanors." Atlantic crossings were subject to long, unpredictable delays that could make an improvident use of ship's stores early in the trip a cause of starvation later on. Even so, the steward's punishment seems harsh—a reflection of the tensions raised onboard by persistent adverse winds.[24]

Franklin does not directly attempt to explain or mitigate this sentence, but later in the same hot day he notes the chance appearance of a large shark around the becalmed vessel that prevents him from taking a restorative swim. As with other "chance" encounters in the voyage journal, this one, too, suggests the instructive design behind accidental appearance:

> He seemed to be about five feet long, moves round the ship at some distance in a slow majestic manner, attended by near a dozen of those they call pilot-fish, of different sizes; the largest of them is not so big as a small mackerel, and the smallest not bigger than my little finger. Two of these diminutive pilots keep just before his nose, and he seems to govern himself in his motions by their direction; while the rest surround him on every side indifferently. A shark is never seen without a retinue of these, who are his purveyors, discovering and distinguishing his prey for him; while he in return gratefully protects them from the ravenous hungry dolphin. They are commonly counted a very greedy fish; yet this refuses to meddle with the bait we have thrown out for him. 'Tis likely he has lately made a full meal. (*Papers*, 1:90)

Like the voracious cod in the *Autobiography*, which teach Franklin the vanity of his meatless diet, this shark and its retinue evoke the contest of appetites out of which the natural universe is made: a compound of animal hunger and the cultural disguises that such hunger may adopt among human predators in human governments. It is both a menacing and a reassuring visitor, a signal that the fears of the *Berkshire*'s captain are not without foundation as well as a suggestion that even the law of the shark is governed by some degree of dependence upon weakness. Franklin is able to shape this entry, along with much of the journal from which it emerges, as a classic instance of the exposure of "design" in chance phenomena, an outcome in which the natural, political, and moral "sciences" of the eighteenth century increasingly placed their faith.

Twenty years separate the provisional investigation of natural design in the voyage journal from the commencement of Franklin's systematic study of electricity. Five additional years pass before Peter Collinson and John Fothergill prepare the first edition of *Experiments and Observations on Electricity* (1751), the book upon which Franklin's international scientific reputation is based. Between 1726 and 1746, his interest in science expresses itself largely in social forms, a direct result of Franklin's conviction that the pursuit of knowledge is a matter of organizing the increase of "the common stock." Ongoing, cooperative inquiry—not the sudden insights of a lonely investigator—is the intellectual model that influenced all of Franklin's public life in the years before his retirement from business liberated him to focus on the intriguing properties of "Muschenbroek's wonderful bottle," the Leyden jar. When he took over publication of the *Pennsylvania Gazette* from Samuel Keimer in 1729, the changes that he immediately made in the paper reflect his disposition to collect and synthesize the observations of others rather than to offer the public authoritative essays culled from Ephraim Chambers's *Cyclopedia*, as had been Keimer's practice.[25]

To mark the change in ownership and philosophy, Franklin announces his intention to publish the *Gazette* twice as often as Keimer had, at half its previous length, and invites the talents of his readers to play a major role in the paper's composition: "We ask Assistance, because we are fully sensible, that to publish a good News-Paper is not so easy an Undertaking as many People imagine it to be":

> The Author of a *Gazette* (in the Opinion of the Learned) ought to be qualified with an extensive Acquaintance with Languages, a great Easiness and Command of Writing and Relating Things cleanly and intelligibly, and in few Words; he should be able to speak of War both by Land and Sea; be well acquainted with Geography, with the History of the Time, with the several Interests of Princes and States, the Secrets of Courts, and the Manners and Customs of all Nations. Men thus accomplish'd are very rare in this remote Part of the World; and it would be well if the Writer of these Papers could make up among his Friends what is wanting in himself. (*Writings,* 137)

Such a range of accomplishments joined in a single individual would be rare in any part of the world. Franklin is in fact sketching an unattainable ideal in order to express a professional principle. Journalism, as he hoped to practice it, was a branch of learning to which he would offer his services as the secretary of a correspondence society. He played a similar role a few years later when he prepared the list of standing questions to give structure to the eclectic curiosity of the Junto, when he assisted his friend Joseph Breitnal as secretary of the Library Company, and later still when he proposed himself as the first secretary of the American Philosophical Society. All three organizations combined social, political, and scientific elements with different degrees of emphasis and reflected Franklin's increasingly expansive command of the intellectual synthesis that had already begun to predispose him toward cultural and political "unions" of a radical kind.

The 1743 broadside, "A Proposal for Promoting Useful Knowledge Among the British Plantations in America," is in some respects an auto-biographical sketch in which Franklin sums up the conclusions of his fif-teen-year career as an independent tradesman and publisher in Philadel-phia. In that proposal, Franklin presents the Philosophical Society as the political fulfillment of English colonization in the New World. The con-ditions that initially make such a scientific society attractive, in Franklin's view, are geographical and social as much as intellectual. The English settle-ments stretch from Nova Scotia to Georgia across a wide range of soils, re-sources, and climates; in this vast space, "The first Drudgery of Settling new Colonies . . . is now pretty well over" (*Writings*, 295). In fact, the drudgery of settlement had just begun. What has clearly ended, however, is the period of Franklin's single-minded attention to his printing business, which was so critical to his commercial success during the past decade.

He is generalizing from personal experience when he observes in the Philosophical Society "Proposal" that "there are many in every Province in Circumstances that set them at Ease, and afford Leisure to cultivate the finer Arts, and improve the common Stock of Knowledge." But the suc-cess of the Library Company confirmed Franklin's individual inclinations and played an equally influential role in convincing him that "Men of Speculation" existed throughout the colonies who might benefit from mutual contact. He was in a position to help promote such contact, hav-ing been appointed postmaster at Philadelphia in 1737.

The solution to what Franklin calls—in yet another tactical under-statement—the "Inconvenience" of America's size was centralization. His resolutions toward establishing a Philosophical Society emphasize that goal:

> That One Society be formed of Virtuosi or ingenious Men residing in the several Colonies, to be called *The American Philosophical Society;* who are to maintain a constant Correspondence.
>
> That *Philadelphia* being the City nearest the Centre of the Continent-Colonies, communicating with all of them northward and southward by Post, and with all the Islands by Sea, and having the Advantage of a good growing Library, be the Centre of the Society.
>
> That at *Philadelphia* there be always at least seven Members, *viz.* a Phy-sician, a Botanist, a Mathematician, a Chemist, a Mechanician, a Geog-

rapher, and a general Natural Philosopher, besides a President, Treasurer and Secretary.

That these Members meet once a Month, or oftner, at their own Expence, to communicate to each other their Observations, Experiments, etc. to receive, read and consider such Letters, Communication, or Queries as shall be sent from distant Members; to direct the Dispersing of Copies of such Communications as are valuable, to other distant Members, in order to procure their Sentiments thereupon. (*Writings*, 295)

Franklin drew the structure of these propositions from private life as much as from organizational logic. He proposed to manage the flow of letters and abstracts personally, to "methodize" the society's papers, and to keep the books.

Most of these features of intellectual self-government reflect the practice of the Royal Society of London, upon which Franklin and his colleagues were modeling their new institution. But the English Royal Society, despite its wide-ranging correspondence, identified itself closely with the urban capital in which it was founded.[26] The American Philosophical Society, on the other hand, addressed itself both to the promotion of scientific learning and to the collective identity of the "Continent-Colonies"—to the making of "One Society" out of widely dispersed correspondents who shared a common intellectual language. Within three or four years of the formation of his band of "Virtuosi," Franklin would be completely taken up with the study of a mysterious physical force that seemed equally rich in potential political implications.

The original scientific excitement that Franklin experienced as he began the research that would make him famous derived, in part, from the erroneous conception that electricity was a great unifier in the natural design: a single fluid universally distributed and circulating throughout all "common Matter." Franklin's physics have long since been supplanted by more sophisticated analyses of the subatomic basis of the electrical charge, but in some respects the obsolete nature of his science makes its metaphorical content all the more visible. The experimental "Opinions and Conjectures" that he lists for Peter Collinson in late July 1750, for example, come very close to serving as aphorisms on the relationship between political power and the common body of the state:

1. The Electrical Matter consists of Particles extreamly subtile, since it can permeate common Matter, even the densest Mettals, with such Ease and Freedom, as not to receive any perceptible Resistance.

2. If any one should doubt, whether the Electrical Matter passes thro' the Substance of Bodies, or only over and along their Surfaces, a Shock from an electrified large Glass Jar, taken thro' his own body, will probably convince him.

3. Electrical Matter differs from common Matter in this, That the Parts of the latter mutually attract, those of the former mutually repel each other; Hence the appearing Divergency in a Stream of Electrical Effluvia.

4. But tho' the Particles of Electrical Matter do repel each other, they are strongly attracted by all other Matter.

5. From these three Things . . . arises this Effect; That when a Quantity of Electrical Matter is apply'd to a Mass of common Matter . . . it is immediately and equally diffus'd thro' the Whole.

6. Thus common Matter is a Kind of a Spunge to the Electrical Fluid. (*Papers,* 4:9–10)

John Fothergill's preface to the first edition of Franklin's *Experiments and Observations on Electricity* (1751) draws on Franklin's account of universal electrical diffusion to point out the cataclysmic consequences of an "unequal distribution" of this "invisible, subtle matter."[27] Evenly "disseminated through all nature in various proportions," Fothergill observes, the electrical fluid itself is "inoffensive." But once an imbalance occurs—a concentration of charge "in one part of space . . . vacuity, or want, in another"—electricity instantly becomes "the most formidable and irresistible agent in the universe" (Cohen, 166). As Fothergill clearly recognizes, Franklin's electrical analysis does not in any sense subject lightning to the complacent management of secular science. The Philadelphia experiments simply make evident an unexpected richness and complexity in the operations of sublime force.

Common matter exists in an electrical plenum, as Franklin calls it, which ensures a global balance of Attraction and Repulsion, much as the *Dissertation on Liberty and Necessity,* a quarter of a century earlier, expresses Franklin's youthful conception of the universal plenum of Divine esteem.[28] In the 1750 "Opinions and Conjectures," he emphasizes the metaphysical significance of the prevailing state of electrical saturation in nature:

For had this globe we live on, as much [electricity] in proportion as we can give to a globe of iron, wood, or the like, the particles of dust and other light matters that get loose from it, would, by virtue of their separate electrical atmospheres, not only repel each other, but be repelled from the earth, and not easily be brought to unite with it again; whence our air would continually be more and more clogged with foreign matter, and grow unfit for respiration. This affords another occasion of adoring that Wisdom which has made all things by weight and measure! (Cohen, 215).

If the Divine weight and measure were too perfectly poised, however, the result would be not purity of atmosphere but complete stasis, a condition of stagnation. Disequilibrium, rather than balance, is the significant and exciting scientific phenomenon, with far-reaching explanatory power.

What made the electrical condenser, or Leyden jar, such an intriguing experimental tool for Franklin and his Philadelphia colleagues was its ability to bring states of radical disequilibrium into the workshop for study. Franklin applies a range of metaphors to these antagonistic conditions to supplement the scientifically dispassionate terminology of plus and minus, positive and negative, which represent his most durable contribution to electrical science. Once the condenser was charged, it was divided into what Franklin variously terms "wanting" and "abounding" states, with "giving" and "requiring" points of contact where equilibrium could be restored (Cohen, 188). Electricity is a "matter," a "fluid," and a "fire" almost interchangeably in Franklin's letters, as if it united three of the four primal elements of creation and, under some conditions, would temporarily attach itself to particles of air as well. This fusion of terms was common to many of Franklin's contemporaries and predecessors in electrical study, but Franklin indulges himself from time to time in acts of verbal condensation that make his experimental propositions read like forerunners of Blake's "Proverbs from Hell." He presents Peter Collinson with an illustration of this love of natural paradox in an initial investigation of "thundergusts": "Electrical fire loves water, is strongly attracted by it, and they can subsist together" (Cohen, 201).

The Leyden jar was a perfect emblem of these exhilarating physical riddles. John Fothergill's rearrangement of the order of Franklin's original letters for the 1751 collection of his scientific work appropriately emphasizes the critical role of this piece of experimental apparatus by beginning the text of *Experiments and Observations* with Franklin's most deeply felt hymn to the "bottle":

So wonderfully are these two states of Electricity, the *plus* and *minus*, combined and balanced in this miraculous bottle! situated and related to each other in a manner that I can by no means comprehend! If it were possible that a bottle should in one part contain a quantity of air strongly comprest, and in another part a perfect vacuum, we know the equilibrium would be instantly restored *within*. But here we have a bottle containing at the same time a plenum of electrical fire, and a *vacuum* of the same fire; and yet the equilibrium cannot be restored between them but by a communication *without!* though the *plenum* presses violently to expand, and the hungry vacuum seems to attract as violently in order to be filled. (Cohen, 181)

The physical mechanisms by which such phenomena are produced might be incomprehensible to Franklin's science, but the metaphorical potential of these electrical mysteries is almost immediately evident. His conceptual intoxication with Muschenbroek's condenser does not prevent Franklin from introducing a collection of additional apparatus to investigate the nature of "charging" and "discharging," conduction, and insulation. He and his companions modified the design of the bottle by filling it with granulated lead instead of water—in which condition, Franklin sometimes refers to the bottle as "armed" (Cohen, 183). Musket balls decorated with feathers or thread play interesting roles in the restoration of electrical equilibrium in Franklin's experiments. In a rushed description of what he provocatively terms "American Electricity" near the close of an early letter to Collinson, Franklin reports lighting candles and igniting spirits with an electrical charge, running a current through the gilt flowers on a plate of china, charging his companions and having them exchange sparks through an "electrical kiss" (Cohen, 176). The Royal Society may have adopted its initially dismissive attitude toward Franklin's reports partly because his experiments incorporate such significant elements of the ridiculous or the playful. But the experiments could also take potentially serious and subversive turns.

On a number of occasions Franklin reports to Collinson a gleefully Faustian display of conductivity produced by passing a strong current of electricity through the ornamental gold inlay on the binding of a book. The most elaborate of these demonstrations appears in the letter that Fothergill printed first in the *Experiments and Observations*. Properly executed, the procedure results in a "strong spark and stroke" before the whole line of gold appears as a "vivid flame, like the sharpest lightning." For the best effects, Franklin advises, the room should be dark: "If you would have the whole filleting round the cover appear in fire at once, let the bottle and wire touch the gold in the diagonally opposite corners" (Cohen, 186).

A demonstration designed by Ebenezer Kinnersley was still more elaborately and suggestively staged. Franklin and his colleagues called this experiment "the magical picture" and used it to show how panes of glass could collect an electrical charge much as the Leyden jar did. English scientists preceded the Americans in this discovery, Franklin concedes in his letter, but he repeats the Philadelphia version to Collinson because "we tried the experiment differently...and, as far as we hitherto know have carried it farther" (Cohen, 193). The experimental "advances" that Franklin describes, however, are almost entirely theatrical. It is not difficult to see why an English experimenter demonstrating his procedures before the Royal Society would not have channeled the electrical fire in quite this way:

> Having a large metzotinto with a frame and glass, suppose of the KING (God preserve him) take out the print, and cut a pannel out of it near two inches distant from the frame all round. If the cut is through the picture it is not the worse. With thin paste, or gum water, fix the border that is cut off on the inside of the glass, pressing it smooth and close; then fill up the vacancy by gilding the glass well with leaf gold or brass. Gild likewise the inner edge of the back of the frame all round, except the top part, and form a communication between that gilding and the gilding behind the glass: then put in the board, and that side is finished. Turn up the glass, and gild the fore side exactly over the back gilding, and when it is dry, cover it, by pasting on the pannel of the picture that hath been cut out, observing to bring the correspondent parts of the border and picture together, by which the picture will appear of a piece, as at first, only part is behind the glass, and part before. Hold the picture horizontally by the top, and place a little moveable gilt crown on the king's head. If now the picture be moderately electrified, and another person take hold of the frame with one hand, so that his fingers touch its inside gilding, and with the other hand endeavour to take off the crown, he will receive a terrible blow, and fail in the attempt. If the picture were highly charged, the consequence might perhaps be as fatal as that of high treason.... The operator, who holds the picture by the upper end, where the inside of the frame is not gilt, to prevent its falling, feels nothing of the shock, and may touch the face of the picture without danger, which he pretends is a test of his loyalty. If a ring of persons take the shock among them, the experiment is called, *The Conspirators*. (Cohen, 194)

By comparison with some instances of European experimentation on human beings, the magical picture—or "The Conspirators"—is a modest practical joke. In France, the Abbe Nollet once entertained the court of Louis XV by administering a simultaneous shock to a line of seven hundred monks linked together by bits of iron wire (Cohen, 48).

What distinguishes Kinnersley's design is the elaborate preparation of its apparatus and Franklin's cool indifference to the prospect of defacing the king's portrait. Real power in this little parable from Philadelphia is associated neither with the king's image nor with the conspiratorial "ring" but with the bland "operator" who holds the frame, understands the technical principles of its construction, and is careful to leave the crown in place, not because of any electrical danger but as part of the pretense of loyalty. When he edited Franklin's correspondence for publication, John Fothergill was sufficiently sensitive to the implications of this experiment to alter the text of the original letter to Collinson, in which Franklin reports that the operator may touch the crown itself with no risk. Franklin, too, later adds a comical emendation to his description to verify the deadly nature of the magical picture's shock: "We have since found it fatal to small animals, but 'tis not strong enough to kill large ones. The biggest we have killed is a hen." Like Fothergill, he seems to sense the necessity of restoring, as well as disordering, the rhetorical equilibrium of his "science," keeping his language free of too marked a degree of subversive intent without completely blunting its antiroyalist edge. The king's grandiose fire is reduced to the ignoble work of killing chickens.[29]

Franklin designed another illustration of the movement of an electrical charge that incorporates a celebrated metaphor from the religious awakening with which his early scientific work coincided. The Abbe Nollet's seven hundred leaping monks may have been a related response to the eighteenth century's renewed awareness that religious enthusiasm produced dramatic bodily effects: "strong, high, exalted exercises of the heart," Jonathan Edwards calls them in *Some Thoughts Concerning the Present Revival of Religion* (1742), as well as "involuntary motions of the fluids and solids of men's bodies."[30] Edwards' clinical language seems out of place in the context of what amounts to a religious history, but scientifically inclined clergymen in the tradition of John Ray were among the most notable pioneers of eighteenth-century research. Stephen Hales, who made sophisticated hydraulic studies of the movement of the fluids and solids of animal bodies, was chaplain to George II. Ebenezer Kinnersley, one of Franklin's electrical colleagues, had been a Baptist minister in

Philadelphia until his public criticism of George Whitefield's revival techniques led his aroused congregation to expel him.

Electricity, like religious conversion, could produce involuntary motions and strong exercises. Both phenomena involve the concentration, intensification, and discharge of invisible force, moving across space with no apparent medium and capable of passing through a limitless chain of human as well as nonhuman conductors. Under the circumstances, Franklin's commitment to this branch of physical science was not by any means a clear indication of the secular nature of his intelligence, but his adaptation of Jonathan Edwards' portrait of human depravity to an electrical procedure indicates the degree to which he encouraged scientific knowledge to illuminate faith as well as politics.

Edwards' *Sinners in the Hands of an Angry God* was printed in Boston in 1741, the year that Edwards first delivered the sermon at Enfield, Connecticut, and two years before Franklin recommends Edwards' history of the revival in a letter to his sister, Jane Mecom. The simile to which Edwards' sermon owes much of its fame is distributed over several vivid paragraphs in the "Application" portion of the text, mingled with images of whirlwinds, great waters of judgmental wrath, and the bent bow of an outraged Deity: "Your wickedness," Edwards tells his congregation, "makes you as it were heavy as lead, and to tend downwards with great weight and pressure towards hell . . . and all your righteousness, would have no more influence to uphold you and keep you out of hell, than a spider's web would have to stop a fallen rock." God holds you over the pit, Edwards concludes, "much as one holds a spider or some loathsome insect over the fire."[31]

Six years later, Franklin seems to have neglected no detail of this scenario in his construction of what he terms a "counterfeit spider" to illustrate the restoration of electrical equilibrium between a charged phial and a piece of wire planted in a tabletop:

> We suspend by fine silk thread a counterfeit spider, made of a small piece of burnt cork, with legs of linnen thread, and a grain or two of lead stuck in him, to give him more weight. Upon the table, over which he hangs, we stick a wire upright, as high as the phial and wire, four or five inches from the spider; then we animate him, by setting the electrified phial at the same distance on the other side of him; he will immediately fly to the wire of the phial, bend his legs in touching it; then spring off, and fly to the wire in the table; thence again to the wire of the phial, playing with his

legs against both, in a very entertaining manner, appearing perfectly alive to persons unacquainted. He will continue this motion an hour or more in dry weather. (Cohen, 177)

Peter Collinson, the English recipient of this letter, was probably not in a position to appreciate the full entertainment value of Franklin's vigorous little puppet, but his Philadelphia companions could scarcely have missed both the parody of revival rhetoric and the allusion to the role of good weather in sustaining the spiritual exertions of open-air preachers like George Whitefield.[32]

A judgmental Diety charged with wrath has very little in common with Franklin's conception of the wisdom that had made all things by weight and measure, but his counterfeit spider is "animated" by a very real, omnipresent force in nature, capable of extraordinarily delicate as well as devastating displays. It took very little in the way of laboratory equipment to disclose the potency of this force, its ability to inhabit the frailest of vessels. "A thin glass bubble," Franklin writes Collinson in 1749, "about an inch in diameter, weighing only six grains, being half filled with water, partly gilt on the outside, and furnished with a wire hook, gives, when electrified, as great a shock as a man can well bear" (Cohen, 197). This little bubble is a diminutive world as well as a formidable condenser of electrical "fire." The physical disparities it illustrates could have been represented in any number of ways, but only this particular object would have suggested the global analogies that were beginning to occur to Franklin's imagination.

Charged balls of cork or lead shot could be made to collect little atmospheres of rosin smoke, which seem to Franklin "proportionable" and beautiful, "like some of the figures in *Burnet's* or *Whiston's* Theory of the Earth" (Cohen, 173). The light of the sun does not destroy the repellency that creates these miniaturized and simplified planets, as firelight seems to do. At the same time that he was investigating the properties of pointed conductors, Franklin was also building and electrifying tiny globes, following an experimental model that led to areas of speculation that engaged much more of his attention than the development of lightning rods.

His apparently inexplicable delays in recording and reporting the kite experiment suggest Franklin's comparative indifference to the study of lightning. Only the excited demands of his European correspondents encouraged him to elaborate on it. The dramatic demonstration of lightning's electrical nature, with which he became popularly associated, interested him as an investigator far less than the inconspicuous role electrical charges might play in the suspension of fresh water in the atmosphere, leading to the release of rain over land, where it might benefit living things. The fifty-six propositions that compose the fourth letter in *Experiments and Observations on Electricity* (1751) contain the first of Franklin's allusions to lightning in this subordinate role. Beginning with an initial observation that charged bodies communicate their surplus electricity "by a snap" when uncharged bodies approach them, Franklin outlines the operation of a global water cycle that unites his simplified molecular understanding of evaporation with the circulation of the Earth's atmosphere in stratified layers from the tropics to the polar regions:

38. It is a common thing to see clouds at different heights passing different ways, which shews different currents of air one under the other. As the air between the tropics is rarified by the sun, it rises, the denser northern and southern air pressing into its place. The air so rarified and forced up, passes northward and southward, and must descend in the polar regions, if it has no opportunity before, that the circulation may be carried on.

39. As currents of air, with the clouds therein, pass different ways, 'tis easy to conceive how the clouds, passing over each other, may attract each other, and so come near enough for the electrical stroke. And also how electrical clouds may be carried within land very far from the sea, before they have an opportunity to strike. . . .

41. When there is great heat on the land, in a particular region (the sun having shone on it perhaps several days, while the surrounding countries have been screened by clouds) the lower air is rarified and rises, the cooler denser air above descends; the clouds in that air meet from all sides, and join over the heated place; and if some are electrified, others not, lightning and thunder succeed, and showers fall. (Cohen, 208–9)

Electrical "fire," Franklin reasons, is in some respects a form of heat, with effects analogous to the heat of the sun upon physical substances. At different points in his life, this analogy would lead Franklin to a consideration of tornados and waterspouts, formed by descending and ascending columns of air along a thermal gradient, as well as to simple demonstrations of the thermal properties of colored cloth distributed in swatches over a sunlit snowbank. The movement of currents of heated air in the chambers of an iron stove engaged Franklin's interest nearly a decade before he began his electrical experiments, but he includes reports and letters on all these varied phenomena in later editions of *Experiments and Observations* in some measure because of their underlying unity as well as their superficial variety.[33]

Looking back over his entire course of research in 1762, Franklin draws attention to the prominence of heat and fire as its common conceptual elements, thinking perhaps of the renewed examples of explosive passion that his diplomatic experience is beginning to provide. The most intense geopolitical conflicts of his lifetime are still ahead of him when he addresses these lines to his old scientific colleague Ebenezer Kinnersley, but Franklin's earlier colonial years were full of instances confirming the universal diffusion of the "inflammable principle":

> How many ways there are of kindling fire, or producing heat in bodies! By the sun's rays, by collision, by friction, by hammering, by putrefaction, by fermentation, by mixtures of fluids, by mixtures of solids with fluids, and by electricity. And yet the fire when produced, though in different bodies it may differ in circumstances, as in colour, vehemence, etc. yet in the same bodies is generally the same. Does not this seem to indicate that the fire existed in the body, though in a quiescent state, before it was by any of these means excited, disengaged, and brought forth to action and to view? May it not constitute part, and even a principal part, of the solid substance of bodies? If this should be the case, kindling fire in a body would be nothing more than developing this inflammable principle, and setting it at liberty to act in separating the parts of that body, which then exhibits the appearances of scorching, melting, burning, etc. When a man lights an hundred candles from the flame of one, without diminishing that flame, can it be properly said to have communicated all that fire? When a single spark from a flint, applied to a magazine of gunpowder, is immediately attended with this consequence, that the whole is in flame, exploding with immense violence, could all this fire exist first in the spark? We cannot conceive it. (Cohen, 371)

Physics almost effortlessly blends into psychology, politics, and religion in such a passage; it is Franklin's most direct application of the rhapsodic tradition that Shaftesbury so effectively applies to the ubiquitous "Element of Fire" in *The Moralists* over half a century earlier. The rhetorical mixture is not simply fortuitous or figurative. We live in the midst of fire, Franklin asserts, not quite as Jonathan Edwards envisions us, helplessly suspended over the burning pit, but sustained as well as menaced by omnipresent force.

Over its successive editions, *Experiments and Observations* gradually became what I. Bernard Cohen calls a "miscellany of American science" of the eighteenth century, but its contents are not entirely miscellaneous. The Leyden jar and the "terraqueous globe" are, as Franklin comes to recognize, versions of one another. The circulating states of balance and imbalance, hunger and repletion, heat and cold occur in conformity with identical laws in each system and even extend their principles to Franklin's understanding of the human body. As early as 1734, in a sketch from the *Pennsylvania Gazette* on "The Death of Infants," he marvels at the mechanical intricacy of the circulatory and nervous systems. In letters to Cadwallader Colden, Franklin wonders about the possible effects of ventricular suction on circulation and about the application of Stephen Hales' "statical" studies to the understanding of perspiration.

By 1757, on the eve of his departure for England, Franklin's physiological interest embraced metabolic energy as well. Where does the living animal obtain its internal fire, Franklin wonders, if not from "a kind of fermentation in the juices of the body" analogous to distillation (Cohen, 343). Like the ubiquitous electrical fire, blood is a circulating fluid involved in the grand thermal design of nature. And like electricity, it shows very little respect for the boundaries of individual identity or for worldly pride. "All blood is alike ancient," Poor Richard observes in 1745, shortly after Franklin purchased his first collection of electrical apparatus from an itinerant scientific exhibitor, along with a glass model of the circulatory system.[34]

Six years later the almanac elaborates on Poor Richard's earlier aphorism by calculating the demographic impossibility of "Purity of Blood in ancient Families." Such noble pretension "is a mere joke," Poor Richard declares. The great lesson of fluid dynamics in eighteenth-century science is mixture and movement, "rendering all the People related by Blood, and, as it were, of one Family" (*Papers,* 4:98). If within nations such coherence is the inevitable outcome of the local disequilibria of blood and power, then across the borders of nations and races similar dynamic principles will have a similar, unifying result. Franklin's scientific metaphors move inevitably toward a radical vision of human community founded upon, rather than imperiled by, the complex, restless circulation of fire.

Chapter Five

A Vast Demand, a Glorious Market

Between 1747 and 1754, Franklin's attention was increasingly occupied by political affairs associated with the intensifying imperial conflict between England and France. The last of his substantive letters to Peter Collinson on electricity is dated from Philadelphia in September 1753, the year in which the Royal Society of London awarded him the Copley Medal. By that time, Franklin had been serving as a regular member of the Pennsylvania Assembly for nearly two years and had recently added to his political responsibilities the duties of deputy postmaster general for North America. Though his interest in natural philosophy and scientific experiments remained strong, his energies inevitably became engrossed by public affairs.

In these years, Franklin produced a series of documents that address the challenges presented by the necessity for civil union in a pluralistic community, where urgent common interests compete for public influence with equally compelling regional, cultural, religious, and political differences. By comparison with the civic commotions that engaged Silence Dogood in 1722, the colonial and imperial predicament that Franklin faced in midcentury was much more complex, but its fundamental nature was quite similar to the partisan passions that characterized the Boston of Franklin's youth.

Indeed, the portrait that Franklin paints of the eleven colonies that participated in drafting the Albany Plan of Union in 1754 suggests that, in his view, differences of political scale were less significant than the psychological and moral diseases that invariably erupt when reason ceases to govern appetite either in individual or in legislative bodies. The experience of the Albany Congress vividly confirmed the larger patterns of history that Franklin had discerned more than twenty years earlier: general designs for the common good at best achieve only a temporary ascendancy over the claims of private interest; principles of benevolence alone almost never decisively shape public affairs. Franklin's relationship to contemporary events, however, had developed into that of a participant rather than a disinterested observer of the progress of the historical narrative in a library reading room. His representational task had acquired practical as well as literary dimensions, which are reflected in the unusual figurative complexity of his prose.

In 1754, at the urging of Thomas Pownall, an informal agent of the British Board of Trade, Franklin prepared extensive annotations on the structure of the Albany Plan, including a substantial account of the motives for drafting it. The eleven colonies whose agents met at Albany that summer resembled, in Franklin's view, a quarrelsome neighborhood or small city in their collective jealousies and opportunism. Provincial assemblies more often than not were at odds with governors or councils, "and the several branches of the government not on terms of doing business with each other" (*Papers,* 5:399). Internal dissension crippled the efforts of the individual colonies to act together against a joint menace. When Virginia appealed to seven of its neighbors for help against the French on its western frontiers, Franklin notes, only one responded. Instead, "selfish views" or "particular whims and prejudices" prevailed in colonial government: "one assembly waiting to see what another will do, being afraid of doing more than its share, or desirous of doing less; or refusing to do anything, because its country is not at present so much exposed as others, or because another will reap more immediate advantage."

These disintegrative forces affect relations with the government of England as well, though Franklin quickly recognizes that geographical separation makes the problem of accommodating colonial interests with those of "the government at home" quite different from that of pooling colonial resources to address a specifically North American need. Just as human individuals are specimens of a "compound kind," in Shaftesbury's moral psychology, so human communities are inevitably and irreducibly heterogeneous. To govern such entities requires a recognition of their diverse collective energies and an application of ingenuity to channel rather than to repress or eradicate them. Franklin's most ambitious consideration of the challenges facing human government, his 1751 essay "Observations Concerning the Increase of Mankind," falls into the middle of this period of literary production. In its pages he examines the operations of human partiality in the broadest possible framework. Once the terms of that examination are clear, Franklin's rhetorical purposes in *Plain Truth,* his strategic hopes for the Albany Plan of Union, and his final almanacs complete the account of his civic and moral vision on the point of his 1757 departure for England.

To comment on a series of documents and events in this fashion is, invariably, to separate phenomena that are, in many respects, concurrent in Franklin's experience. Almanacs, pamphlets, and scientific experiments do not reflect distinct phases of a changing career but the mingled activities of a single vocation addressed to the sense of "great Occasion" that Franklin associated with the many-faceted "Project" of a United Party for Virtue. His days throughout this period, even after the delegation of much of the responsibility for his printing business to David Hall, continued to involve some form of the private religious exercises and daily self-examination that he outlines in the "Articles of Belief" of 1728 and in the daily schedule reproduced in part 2 of the *Autobiography.* Franklin's adaptation of scientific language to political and religious discourse is, likewise, a reflection both of the vital intellectual traditions of natural philosophy and of his simultaneous involvement in the discrete activities of science, politics, and religion—the three expressions of the human intellect that frame his redemptive design. While in one respect his body of work, before the *Autobiography,* is a heterogeneous collection of brief public and private documents, in this larger sense it is a compound whole in its own right. The process of intellectual convergence becomes more evident through a close look at the nature of Franklin's most important work in the years immediately before his second transatlantic voyage.

Franklin's science emphasizes inclusive physical systems: the single fluids whose movements could explain the accumulation of an electrical charge in a glass condenser, the circulation of water and fire in the atmosphere, the common familial bond of human blood. But in 1751, the year that Poor Richard mocks the aristocratic fiction of genealogical purity, Franklin also wrote "Observations Concerning the Increase of Mankind," a series of twenty-four propositions in which he appears to endorse the vision of a purely English empire of unblemished Anglo-Saxon complexion in

North America, "where we have so fair an Opportunity, by excluding all Blacks and Tawneys, of increasing the lovely White and Red" (*Writings,* 374). The inclusive physicist seems capable of expressing the convictions of an exclusionary racist, convictions that Franklin also appears to court in the pamphlet *Plain Truth* (1747), which seeks to arouse the citizens of Philadelphia to defend themselves against the lust of Spanish pirates and their African crews.

The recognition of terrible inconsistencies in human character was a fundamental insight of eighteenth-century moralists, but the spectacle of such inconsistencies lodged in the moralist himself is uniquely disturbing. Franklin seems to have fully appreciated the unsettling implications of his text. Though he wrote the "Observations" in 1751 and sent copies to a number of correspondents in the following year, he did not agree to its publication until 1754. It appears only once in unexcised form, as an anonymous appendix to a report by William Clarke on French encroachments in British North America (1755). Reprints of the "Observations" as a separate essay in 1755, 1756, 1760, and 1761, identifying Franklin's authorship, delete the final proposition, which includes his remarks on "Scouring" the continent's "face" of nonwhite races. The version of the essay that Franklin adds to the fourth edition of *Experiments and Observations on Electricity* (1769) is similarly excised.[1]

This degree of sensitivity to the reception of his text is as inconsistent with the profile of a xenophobic racist as such attitudes are inconsistent with the balance of Franklin's intellectual life. Peter Collinson, the recipient of Franklin's original letters on electricity, was also the first to receive an unexcised copy of "Observations Concerning the Increase of Mankind." A lifelong pacifist and advocate for the rights of Indians, as well as a dedicated horticultural pioneer, Collinson was precisely the wrong audience for a brief essay endorsing racial imperialism in North America, but he was ideally qualified to appreciate the complicated scientific, social, and literary texture of Franklin's remarks on colonial population.[2] Collinson's response to the "Observations" is instructive. He writes Franklin late in the summer of 1752 that he is "greatly Entertain'd" by the piece, to which Franklin responds at length the following spring with a letter elaborating on the challenges presented by the stubborn resistance to cultural assimilation displayed by Pennsylvania's German immigrants and Indian neighbors. Franklin closes his reply to Collinson with an admonitory citation from *Paradise Lost* on the decay of liberty among nations, warning his friend that it is in Britain's interest "to secure freedom to her children; they may be able one day to assist her in defending her own" (*Writings*, 474).

Behind this exchange are indications that Franklin's true subject in his 1751 essay is assimilation rather than exclusion. But he does not underestimate the obstacles to its attainment. The extraordinary human increase that he foresaw in North America—the vast demand for British manufactures and the glorious market for her merchants, which he hoped would ensure Anglo-American union—were jointly dependent upon the English ability to overcome cultural and political assumptions of superiority to colonial communities and the colonists' own ability to overcome the natural "Partiality" of mankind for one's native language, religion, and customs.

In his 1753 correspondence with Peter Collinson, Franklin freely confessed to his own partiality for all things English. National culture is the matrix through which the universal forces of attraction and repulsion express themselves in "Observations Concerning the Increase of Mankind." The essay's closing propositions, however, dramatize these forces in such a way that their blindness proves to be at least as conspicuous as their emotional authority. In that mixture of blindness and insight, Franklin risks losing his reader. It is easy to mistake his subtle critique of partisan passion for its opposite: a particularly coarse endorsement of ethnocentric bigotry. The risk is worth running, however, because the forces against which Franklin hopes to contend will never yield to direct opposition. The lessons of personal conversation gleaned from his early years suggested that only the dramatic tactics of indirection and disguise could hope to supplant the entrenched appeal of national identity.

Franklin both invoked and challenged that appeal as he drew near the critical conclusion of his essay. The twenty-second of Franklin's twenty-four sections closes with a series of exclamatory celebrations of English imperial growth. The accelerated doubling of the colonial population that he confidently predicts in the main body of the "Observations" already entailed a mixture of exhilarating and disquieting results that corresponds closely to the cultural comparisons implicit in Franklin's 1726 voyage journal. "What an Accession of Power to the *British* Empire by Sea as well as Land!" Franklin exults as he surveys colonial growth over the first half of the eighteenth century. "What Increase of Trade and Navigation! What Numbers of Ships and Seamen! We have been here but little more than 100 Years, and yet the Force of our Privateers in the late War, united, was greater, both in Men and Guns, than that of the whole *British* Navy in Queen *Elizabeth*'s Time" (*Writings*, 373). This language implies that some colonial observers already viewed themselves as an "Accession" on the verge of achieving parity with its national "parent" and becoming a "united" ally; the power that Franklin celebrates may be British, but the privateers are "ours."[3] Let Britain be all the more "careful," Franklin concludes, to secure favorable borders "between her Colonies and the *French.*" Population increase and the wealth that it can create depends upon room, but it also depends upon the negotiated equilibrium between jealousy and mutual interest, which Franklin's cautionary language evokes.

The occasion for writing "Observations Concerning the Increase of Mankind" was Parliament's enactment of a law restraining the development of colonial ironworks.[4] Very few signs of this specific provocation remain in Franklin's finished text. He instead moves abruptly from a single instance of ill-conceived mercantile policy to a broad consideration of the well-being of "Mankind" as a whole. In the course of doing so, Franklin inevitably subjects all narrower definitions of the collective human interest to ridicule, a strategy that becomes most evident in the metaphor for national growth with which he chooses to open the essay's twenty-third proposition: "In fine, A Nation well regulated is like a Polypus; take away a Limb, its Place is soon supply'd; cut it in two, and each deficient Part shall speedily grow out of the Part remaining. Thus if you have Room and Subsistence enough, as you may by dividing, make ten Polypes out of one, you may of one make ten Nations, equally populous and powerful; or rather, increase a Nation ten fold in Numbers and Strength" (*Writings,* 374). The implications of the analogy subtly and whimsically invert its terms: a well-regulated nation ought to strive to be as little like a polyp as possible if its desire is, in fact, to consolidate rather than to diminish its strength.

Franklin describes in some detail the regenerative and digestive habits of the polyp in his 1751 almanac, where it forms part of an extensive account of the wonders disclosed by the microscope. Found in the bottom of ditches or in standing water, the polyps reproduce by buds and branches ("They do not seem to be of different sexes"), can live and feed even when turned inside out, and are capable of miraculous recoveries from infestations of "Vermin" that sometimes devour their heads.[5] It is difficult not to see in the almanac's polyp a delightful miniaturization of the Stuart monarchy—a traditional target of almanac makers and whose miraculous regeneration of a missing head was commemorated in Franklin's calendar on May 29, the birthday of Charles II and the anniversary of the Restoration. But the larger role of this resilient microorganism in

"Observations" is to prepare for the more elaborate mockery of national vanity that swiftly follows.

Why (Franklin abruptly inquires) "should the *Palatine Boors* be suffered to swarm into our Settlements . . . a Colony of *Aliens,* who will shortly be so numerous as to Germanize us instead of our Anglifying them, and will never adopt our Language or Customs any more than they can acquire our Complexion?" Surely, he contends, the natural increase of "Detachments of *English* from *Britain*" would alone be adequate to populate the American colonies (*Writings,* 374). Like the playfully inverted analogy to polyps, this is the sort of rhetorical gambit that eighteenth-century readers were more equipped to handle than their twentieth-century successors. Most of Franklin's contemporaries could readily recall the cultural anxieties aroused by the filling of the English throne with a succession of non-English-speaking monarchs in the years following the flight of James II. In "The True-Born Englishman" (1701), Daniel Defoe scored his first great literary success by satirizing such anxieties, exposing the complex genetic heritage of the English population with a savage gusto characteristic of the time:

> Thus from a Mixture of all Kinds began,
> That Het'rogeneous Thing, an *Englishman:*
> In eager Rapes, and furious Lust begot,
> Betwixt a painted *Britton* and a *Scot:*
> Whose gend'ring Offspring quickly learnt to bow
> And yoke their Heifers to the *Roman* Plough:
> From whence a Mongrel half-breed Race there came,
> With neither Name nor Nation, Speech or Fame,
> In whose hot Veins new Mixtures quickly ran,
> Infus'd betwixt a *Saxon* and a *Dane.*
> While their rank Daughters, to their Parents just,
> Receiv'd all Nations with Promiscuous Lust.
> This Nauseous Brood directly did contain
> The well-extracted Blood of *Englishmen.*[6]

This is the sort of furious assault on public sensibility that Franklin's early experience had taught him to avoid. Instead, his strategy of indirection chooses the risks of covert utterance.

The text of the "Observations" moves with bewildering speed from the apparently dispassionate introduction of the polypus metaphor to a subtle dramatic parody of human bigotry, with its nightmarish vision of invading swarms and colonies of microscopic "aliens." In effect, Franklin chooses to illustrate, all too vividly, what it is like when people begin to react like polyps instead of to reflect like human beings. The swiftness with which he inhabits his metaphor is part of its dramatic meaning, a formal equivalent for the speed with which passion is capable of eclipsing reason, spilling over into the caricature of xenophobic suspicion that comprises the essay's final proposition:

> Which leads me to add one Remark: That the Number of purely white People in the World is proportionably very small. All *Africa* is black or tawny. *Asia* chiefly tawny. *America* (exclusive of the new Comers) wholly so. And in *Europe*, the *Spaniards, Italians, French, Russians* and *Swedes*, are generally of what we call a swarthy Complexion; as are the *Germans* also, the *Saxons* only excepted, who with the *English*, make the principal Body of White People on the Face of the Earth. I could wish their Numbers were increased. And while we are, as I may call it, *Scouring* our Planet, by clearing *America* of Woods, and so making this Side of our Globe reflect a brighter Light to the Eyes of Inhabitants in *Mars* or *Venus*, why should we in the Sight of Superior Beings, darken its People? why increase the Sons of *Africa*, by Planting them in *America*, where we have so fair an Opportunity, by excluding all Blacks and Tawneys, of increasing the lovely White and Red? But perhaps I am partial to the Complexion of my Country, for such Kind of Partiality is natural to Mankind. (*Writings*, 374)

This closing remark represents a rhetorical increase of several kinds over the sum of Franklin's prior "Observations." The effects of race and nationality compound with one another in this paragraph until the "swarthy" peoples of the world appear to embrace everyone from the Italians to the Swedes, the Spanish to the Chinese.

Such a planet will require considerable scouring before the inhabitants of Mars and Venus—Wrath and Lust—will be able to take much satisfaction in the brilliance of its appearance. The "Superior Beings" whom Franklin purports to associate with this ridiculous spectacle invariably suggest not neighboring planets but human appetites, which are the source of a genuinely terrifying darkness in the people of Earth. These are no more than the natural partialities of man in action, Franklin suggests, and their indulgence will invariably result in a North American outbreak of the "Plague of Heroism," which the "Observations" scornfully alludes to a few sentences earlier in its survey of the warlike nations of Europe.

The faint suggestion, in this final proposition, of the delusions of a mad gardener who confuses human communities with flower beds extends an analogy between plants and people with which Franklin introduces the most sweeping imperial predictions of the "Observations." The relationship between emptiness and growth that occupies him throughout the essay is not simply a study in demographic pressures. It draws together ethical, religious, and civic concerns that preoccupied Franklin throughout his journalistic career.

In a century, Franklin predicts, "the greatest Number of *Englishmen* will be on this Side the Water," a deduction he bases largely upon informal statistical projections but that he introduces with a curious and disturbing image of the revivification of a "vacant" Earth: "There is in short, no bound to the prolific Nature of Plants or Animals, but what is made by their crowding and interfering with each others Means of Subsistence. Was the Face of the Earth vacant of other Plants, it might be gradually sowed and overspread with one Kind only; as, for Instance, with Fennel; and were it empty of other Inhabitants, it might in a few Ages be replenish'd from one Nation only; as, for Instance, with *Englishmen*" (*Writings*, 373). Just such a replenishment, he observes, is already taking place in North America, though as Franklin is well aware, the continent was anything but vacant upon its discovery, nor could it in any realistic future hope to be composed exclusively of "Englishmen"—whatever that term might be taken to mean after Defoe's withering assault. The full effect of Franklin's passage hinges on the significance that a reader of the "Observations" is likely to attach to the prospect of a planet sown in fennel.

In the allegorical herbarium, fennel is an emblem of jealousy and flattery, a traditional association that explains why the mad Ophelia offers fennel to Claudius in the fourth act of *Hamlet* and why Milton's disguised Satan alludes to the serpent's proverbial love of fennel when he describes for Eve the wonder with which he professes to view the beautiful fruits of Paradise:

> Empress of this fair World, resplendent *Eve*,
> Easy to mee it is to tell thee all
> What thou command'st and right thou should'st be obey'd:
> I was at first as other Beasts that graze
> The trodden Herb, of abject thoughts and low,
> As was my food, nor aught but food discern'd
> Or Sex, and apprehended nothing high:
> Till on a day roving the field, I chanc'd

A goodly Tree far distant to behold
Loaden with fruit of fairest colors mixt,
Ruddy and Gold: I nearer drew to gaze;
When from the boughs a savory odor blown,
Grateful to appetite, more pleas'd my sense
Than smell of sweetest Fennel, or the Teats
Of Ewe or Goat dropping with Milk at Ev'n,
Unsuckt of Lamb or Kid, that tend thir play.[7]

Franklin's allusion to book 12 of *Paradise Lost* in his 1753 letter to Peter Collinson is some indication that Milton was on his mind in connection with his analysis of the conditions necessary to human increase. Collinson's initially favorable response to "Observations Concerning the Increase of Mankind" apparently grew a bit tentative in subsequent letters, which are missing from the correspondence. Franklin's extraordinary appeal to the complex ethnic and social circumstances of Pennsylvania concludes by referring Collinson to the point in Milton's poem where both sides to the emerging Anglo-American division might find their strengths and weaknesses painfully exposed.

Adam, expressing outrage at the growth of earthly tyranny foretold by the archangel Michael, affirms that God has "human left from human free"—a radical ideal of individual liberty, which Michael reminds Adam no longer applies to a fallen world, where "inordinate desires / And upstart Passions catch the Government / From Reason."[8] This disordered internal government is reflected in the external rule of "violent Lords" and in the curse of racial servitude, which taints both the master and the slave with collective, earthly iniquity.

If Franklin intends Collinson to take a warning from the suggestions of English decline in these lines, he does so in such a way that invites an equally stern warning for American slave masters. Just as the Germans' stubborn refusal to "Anglify" and to participate in the common defense against the French alarms Franklin, so also the presence of slaves in America strikes him as incompatible with colonial growth. Deprived of any interest in the fruits of labor, the slave is "by *Nature* a Thief," an economic and, ultimately, a moral drain on the community. But in the "Observations," Franklin proposes no direct solution to the problem of slavery. He closes his letter to Collinson with an acknowledgment that England and America have a joint predicament to address rather than a grievance to adjudicate: "O let not Britain seek to oppress us, but like an affectionate parent endeavour to secure freedom to her children." The double-edged nature of this complaint becomes apparent when Franklin cautions his friend that "a Mortification begun in the Foot may spread upwards to the destruction of the Nobler parts of the Body" (*Writings*, 474). Not English decline but colonial disease is the menace here, an iniquity peculiar to the American extremity of the political body.

Even without the suggestive interplay of his correspondence with Collinson, Franklin's interest in what the text of the "Observations" refers to as "*generative Laws*" establishes the Miltonic resonance and scope of Franklin's imperial views. A long passage from *Paradise Lost* celebrating the generative energy of the universe is a centerpiece of Franklin's daily recitations in the "Articles of Belief." In a "Reply to a Piece of Advice" from the *Pennsylvania Gazette* (1735), he cites Milton's hymn to wedded love from book 4 of *Paradise Lost,* along with a passage from Thomson's *Seasons,* as decisive endorsements of marriage and familial increase from "the two best English Poets that ever were." The sublime heights to which "Polly Baker" rises in her 1747 defense of procreation are nearly inexplicable without an appreciation for Franklin's long-standing familiarity with and admiration for Milton's impassioned verse:

> If mine, then, is a religious Offence, leave it, Gentlemen, to religious Punishments. You have already excluded me from all the Comforts of your Church Communion: Is not that sufficient? You believe I have offended Heaven, and must suffer eternal Fire: Will not that be sufficient? What need is there, then, of your additional Fines and Whippings? . . . But how can it be believed, that Heaven is angry at my having Children, when, to the little done by me towards it, God has been pleased to add his divine Skill and admirable Workmanship in the Formation of their Bodies, and crown'd it by furnishing them with rational and immortal souls? (*Writings,* 307)

It seems evident that Franklin intends a reader of the "Observations" to bring to the text some appreciation for the traditional significance that English letters associate with the subject of mankind's increase. As Milton's satanic address to Eve implies, an Earth sown with fennel could only be a serpent's Paradise, superficially homogeneous but in fact the product and the nursery of jealousy rather than a prolific garden capable of doubling its human occupants every twenty-five years.[9]

The genuine fruits of Paradise, as Satan himself obliquely acknowledges in his address to Eve, are "of fairest colors mixt," a condition that

Franklin seeks to promote in the human fruits of British America, provided that certain preconditions of the assimilation can be met and preserved. Among those preconditions he clearly includes a general acceptance of English as the common language of public life. Franklin complains to Peter Collinson in 1753 about the inconveniences of bilingual commercial and legal practices in Philadelphia, fearing that the stubborn loyalty of German immigrants to their native language could, within a few years, make interpreters necessary in the colonial Assembly "to tell one half of our Legislators what the other half say" (*Writings*, 473). Franklin himself, however, was the publisher of the first German-language newspaper in North America, an indication that the concerns he expresses to Collinson were founded upon the desire to promote a common political language for the colony rather than to ensure a completely homogeneous culture.[10]

As critical to Franklin's vision of Pennsylvania's future as a common language were the common values of industry and frugality, along with a commitment to free labor, all of which tend to encourage early marriage, population growth, and the development of trade. The opening paragraph of the *Autobiography* creates the misleading impression that Franklin's interest in personal virtue ends with the achievement of personal affluence. Instead, the ethical prescriptions of the "Observations" reflect an emphasis on the relationship between private habit and public growth, which unites all of Franklin's literary output—a unity he derives in part from his determination to revise the prescriptions for national prosperity that Bernard Mandeville made notorious in *The Fable of the Bees*.

For most of his professional life in Philadelphia between 1729 and 1757, Franklin was composing rules by which a small colony might develop into a great empire. His vision of colonial growth in the "Observations" sums up this lifelong reply to the conception of imperial glory, which forms the central subject of the extensive prose commentaries and appendixes to Mandeville's 1705 poem. Bernard Mandeville was the beguiling serpent in Franklin's garden, and it is to Mandeville's assertion of the interrelationship between growth and vice that much of Franklin's seemingly unrelated civic activity over his twenty-five year domestic career is addressed.

The lengthy description of Franklin's colonial accomplishments, which forms the third part of the *Autobiography* (1788), responds directly to Mandeville's most concise account of his thesis. But Franklin's 1729 pamphlet on paper currency had already established the connection between colonial "increase" and revolutionary politics that informed "Observations Concerning the Increase of Mankind" twenty-two years later. The idea of increase was the great theme of Franklin's public life. As the literary texture of the "Observations" indicates, it was not strictly a material end that he had in mind, but the full scope of Franklin's joint commitment to virtue and growth drew upon quite pragmatic as well as exalted sources.

In the preface to *The Fable of the Bees* (1714), Mandeville makes his purposes clear: "the main Design of the Fable is to shew the Impossibility of enjoying all the most elegant Comforts of Life that are to be met with in an industrious, wealthy and powerful Nation, and at the same time be bless'd with all the Virtue and Innocence that can be wish'd for in a Golden Age" (*Fable,* 6). Virtue can build a stagnant village, but only vice can build a great empire. The analogies Mandeville proposes—to the human body and to the streets of London—display the gift for vivid fallacy that so infuriated his opponents. Just as the human anatomy is composed of "small trifling films and little Pipes" that are as necesary to life as bone, muscle, or skin, so man's "vilest and most hateful Qualities" are indispensable to sustaining "the happiest and most flourishing Societies" (*Fable,* 4). The streets of London, Mandeville agrees, are full of filth, but such "Nastiness" is the inescapable by-product of "the Plenty, great Traffick and Oppulency of that mighty City." It would be more pleasant to stroll in a fragrant garden or country grove rather than "the stinking streets of London," he concedes, but the stench is a condition of London's "Felicity" as well as a source of employment to shoeblacks and scavengers.

The pride Franklin took in the role that he played in paving, lighting, and cleaning the streets of Philadelphia reflects his grasp of Mandeville's economic analysis as well as his subtle critique of the reductive principles upon which Mandeville grounds his social psychology. In the *Autobiography,* Franklin describes at some length the circumstances that led him to propose to John Fothergill a systematic method of street cleaning in London. In the course of this description, he calls attention to his own apparent willingness to exploit a destitute old woman to illustrate the feasibility of his idea—a gesture reminiscent of Mandeville's dismissive attitude toward the "scavengers" who lived off of London's filth. Franklin's account is carefully framed, however, not to outrage the reader of the *Autobiography* but to dramatize a number of Franklin's long-standing objections to Mandeville's economy of vice and empire. In so doing, he deftly exposes his reader's vulnerability to the hidden relationship between vanity and sympathy.

In 1757, fresh from the public relations success of the newly paved and regularly cleaned Philadelphia market, Franklin, upon taking up residence in England, notes the inconvenience and "Annoyance" produced by the accumulating "Slush" and mud of London's streets. Coming out of his Craven Street lodgings one morning, he finds a poor woman with a birch broom sweeping in front of his door:

> She appeared very pale & feeble as just come out of a Fit of Sickness. I ask'd who employ'd her to sweep there. She said, "Nobody; but I am very poor and in Distress, and I sweeps before Gentlefolkeses Doors, and hopes they will give me something." I bid her sweep the whole Street clean and I would give her a Shilling. This was at 9 aClock. At 12 she came for the Shilling. From the slowness I saw at first in her Working, I could scarce believe that the Work was done so soon, and sent my Servant to examine it, who reported that the whole Street was swept perfectly clean, and all the dust plac'd in the Gutter which was in the Middle. And the next Rain wash'd it quite away so that the Pavement & even the Kennel were perfectly clean. (*Writings*, 1427)

Reasoning from this instance that a force of strong, active men might have a considerable impact on public sanitation, Franklin proposes organizing, equipping, and paying such a force on a regular basis.

What reads at first like the bloodless speculation of a social engineer is in fact a carefully considered rebuke to a city that relies for an essential element of its civic health on the unpredictable, inconsistent charity of "Gentlefolkeses." Franklin goes out of his way to portray himself as Dives to the old woman's Lazarus in part to invite the reader's sentimental participation in the indulgent pleasures of benevolence. He essentially agrees with Mandeville that reflexive feelings of generosity or pity are no more than singularly gratifying disguises for self-love—gratifying, in the long run, at very little real expense to the self. As Mandeville memorably puts it in his essay "On Charity and Charity-Schools," "Pride and Vanity have built more Hospitals than all the Virtues together" (*Fable*, 261).

Franklin could easily have indulged his own pride and vanity in this portion of the *Autobiography*, casting himself in a much more sympathetic light than he chooses to in his dealings with the sweeping woman, but the results would have been less instructive and less interesting. Instead, he adopts the less common course of exposing a system that prefers to indulge the capricious generosity of the upper classes rather than to make arrangements that would secure regular, remunerative work without the degradation of begging. His brief account confers an unsentimental dignity on the sweeping woman's labor and on her language, which is completely foreign to the kind of icy scorn with which Mandeville frequently describes the relentless necessity for menial work in a society that aspires to his conception of civil greatness:

> The whole Earth being Curs'd and no Bread to be had but what we eat in the sweat of our Brows, vast Toil must be undergone before Man can provide himself with Necessaries for his Sustenance and the bare Support of his corrupt and defective Nature as he is a single Creature; but infinitely more to make Life comfortable in a Civil society, where Men are become taught Animals, and great Numbers of them have by mutual compact framed themselves into a Body Politick. . . . It is impossible that a Society can long subsist, and suffer many of its Members to live in Idleness, and enjoy all the Ease and Pleasure they can invent, without having at the same time great Multitudes of People that to make good this Defect will condescend to be quite the reverse, and by use and patience inure their Bodies to work for others and themselves besides. . . . From what has been said it is manifest, that in a free Nation where Slaves are not allow'd of, the surest Wealth consists in a Multitude of laborious Poor; for besides that they are the never-failing Nursery of Fleets and Armies, without them there could be no Enjoyment, and no Product of any Country could be valuable. To make the Society happy and People easy under the meanest Circumstances, it is requisite that great Numbers of them should be Ignorant as well as Poor. . . . No Creatures submit contentedly to their Equals, and should a Horse know as much as a Man, I should not desire to be his Rider. (*Fable*, 287-90)

These passages from "On Charity and Charity Schools" embody the dark side to the coffeehouse wit whom Franklin encountered in London in 1725. They represent the grimmest conclusions that Mandeville drew from what he viewed as his psychological and political realism.

In portions of his alphabetical commentary on the *Fable*, Mandeville seems to approach Franklin's more generous position that the labor of the people is the only real "treasure" of a nation, a position that both he and Franklin derive from the work of Thomas Hobbes and William Petty. The central assumptions of *The Fable of the Bees*, however, remain identical to those that characterize Satan's temptation of Eve in *Paradise Lost:* fertile soil, abundant land, a "happy" climate, and mild government can only generate what Mandeville dismisses as a society of "slothful Ease and stupid Innocence," totally devoid of Arts or Sciences, a "lumpish Machine" resembling "a huge Wind-mill without a breath of Air" (*Fable,* 184). Passion is the source of all meaningful cultural energy, in Mandeville's analysis; it is the wind that brings the cumbersome machine to life:

> Would you render a Society of Men strong and powerful, you must touch their Passions. Divide the Land, tho' there be never so much to spare, and their Possessions will make them Covetous: Rouse them, tho' but in Jest, from their Idleness with Praises, and Pride will set them to work in earnest: Teach them Trades and Handicrafts, and you'll bring Envy and Emulation among them.... Let Property be inviolably secured, and Privileges equal to all Men; Suffer no body to act but what is lawful, and every body to think what he pleases.... Then promote Navigation, cherish the Merchant, and encourage Trade in every Branch of it; this will bring Riches, and where they are, Arts and Sciences will soon follow, and by the Help of what I have named and good Management, it is that Politicians can make a People potent, renown'd and flourishing. (*Fable,* 184-85)

In his disparagement of the social conditions of stupid innocence and cultural inertia, Mandeville could well be thinking of the proverbially fertile soil, abundant land, and mild government of the American colonies. His emphasis on the security of property and on equal "Privileges" to all men reflects Mandeville's admiration for the legislative practice of the Dutch Republic, where liberty of conscience helped ensure the undisturbed operations of commerce.[11] At various points in his life, Franklin repeatedly endorsed both of these attitudes. Like Mandeville, his aim in writing many of his economic and civic proposals was the "Cause of advancing this Province in Trade and Riches." Maintaining a perpetual state of bucolic peace in eighteenth-century Pennsylvania was not Franklin's idea of the best way of advancing the larger interests of England.

But Mandeville's analysis of the utility of vice in producing a "potent" people runs directly counter to Franklin's metaphysical convictions as well as his practical experience. Avarice, in Franklin's view, is not only repellent, it is also an impediment to the development of just the sort of flourishing, commercial nation that he and Mandeville both prize. Key elements of this rejoinder to Mandeville emerge in Franklin's work within a few years of his return from London to Philadelphia. In particular, the opening pages of his "Modest Enquiry into the Nature and Necessity of a Paper-Currency" (1729) present Franklin's case for concluding that a restricted money supply favors only lenders, who wish to preserve a high interest rate, along with lawyers, speculators, and their political "Dependents." It discourages anyone who needs to borrow for the purposes of developing land or opening a small shop or manufacturing business.

The result of such a tight money supply is the sacrifice of economic diversity and population growth in favor of short-lived profits for a privileged few. A policy crafted by the "Covetous," in other words, produces a desert. The modesty of Franklin's 1729 title, along with his apparent humility in offering to the public his thoughts on this "abstruse and intricate" subject, does not prevent him from speculating about the motives behind the proprietary opposition to paper currency. Either the "Gentlemen of Trade in *England*" simply misunderstand colonial needs, or their actions reflect the determination of the "Government at Home" to impoverish Pennsylvania, a policy directly contrary to the long-term interest of England as a whole, so that the greed of a few large creditors might be satisfied (*Writings*, 125). In any event, the proprietors and their advisers, Franklin observes, fail to appreciate the distinction between money as merchandise and money as currency, the "running Cash" of the community.

An adequate supply of such running cash secures the growth of the colonial population and the vigor of its commercial activity, which in turn sustains or gradually increases the value of colonial land, which in turn secures the paper bills of credit—the "coined Land," as Franklin calls it—that form the circulating medium of the colony. "We, who are the best Judges of our own Necessities," Franklin argues, understand America as an independent commercial organism—nearly half a century before political independence and twenty-two years before the "Observations Concerning the Increase of Mankind" points out the growing potency of the North American accessions.

Franklin closes the "Modest Enquiry" with language that belies his youth and looks forward with uncanny accuracy to the oppositional themes of the Declaration of Independence:

> As this Essay is wrote and published in Haste, and the Subject in it self intricate, I hope I shall be censured with Candour, if for want of Time carefully to revise what I have written, in some Places I should appear to have express'd my self too obscurely. . . . I sincerely desire to be acquainted with the Truth, and on that Account shall think my self obliged to any one, who will take the Pains to shew me, or the Publick, where I am mistaken in my Conclusions, And as we all know there are among us several Gen-

tlemen of acute Parts and profound Learning, who are very much against any Addition to our Money, it were to be wished that they would favour the Country with their Sentiments on this Head in Print. . . . But as those ingenious Gentlemen have not yet (and I doubt never will) think it worth their Concern to enlighten the Minds of their erring Countrymen in this Particular, I think it would be highly commendable in every one of us, more fully to bend our Minds to the Study of *What is the true Interest of PENNSYLVANIA;* whereby we may be enabled, not only to reason pertinently with one another; but, if Occasion requires, to transmit Home such clear Representations, as must inevitably convince our Superiors of the Reasonableness and Integrity of our Designs. (*Writings,* 134–35)

This passage outlines a far-reaching political program for colonial "Representations" that already envisions the evolution of American diplomacy that preceded American independence. In effect, Franklin is previewing his entire public career at the age of twenty-three, seven years before he accepted his first public appointment of any kind and nearly twenty years before he was first elected to public office.

Even a contemporary reader disinclined to share Franklin's enthusiasm for a discussion of the money supply would have found the political implications of the "Modest Enquiry" anything but obscure or puzzling. John Trenchard warns a few years earlier, in *Cato's Letters* (1722), that in the normal "Course of Human Affairs" colonies eventually strive to gain their independence. America's northern colonies, in particular, seem to him destined to increase in population "and in less than a Century must become powerful States," a prediction that Franklin's estimates forcefully confirm in the 1751 "Observations." It is in the British interest, Trenchard concludes, to keep these colonists contented, "for it is much to be feared, if we do not find Employment for them, they may find it for us."[12] Trenchard, however, also recognizes that the powerful "Interests of a few private Gentlemen" in England were thwarting the prudent management necessary to prevent the outbreak of political "Mischief."

Franklin's acquaintance with *Cato's Letters* began in Boston, when Silence Dogood quotes Trenchard's collaborator, Thomas Gordon, in her correspondence with the *New England Courant.* In "A Modest Enquiry into the Nature and Necessity of a Paper-Currency" seven years later, Franklin's analysis of the destructive influence of private interests upon public policy conforms perfectly with Trenchard's warnings, but the emphasis that Franklin places upon the desirability of "increase" and his understanding of the social means to its promotion derive most directly from Richard Steele and William Petty, a seventeenth-century polymath and founding member of the Royal Society, whose work also found a place in the eclectic reading of Silence Dogood.

In the third volume of the *Spectator*—Franklin's composition manual—Steele takes up the relationship between population and national wealth that Petty describes in his posthumously published *Political Arithmetick* (1690). Steele is extending some observations of "Philarithmus" in *Spectator* #180 concerning the self-defeating nature of military conquest, which depletes population and interferes with domestic life to such an extent that it never repays its costs. People, through their work and through their consumption in great commercial cities, generate the revenue of the prince and the power of the state. This insight so exhilarates Steele that he briefly succumbs to a vision of England's utopian future:

> When I was got into this way of thinking, I presently grew conceited of the Argument, and was just preparing to write a letter of Advice to a Member of Parliament, for opening the Freedom of our Towns and Trades, for taking away all manner of distinctions between the Natives and Foreigners, for repealing our Laws of Parish Settlements, and removing every other Obstacle to the Increase of the People. But as soon as I had recollected with what inimitable Eloquence my Fellow labourers had exaggerated the Mischiefs of selling the Birth-right of *Britons* for a Shilling, of spoiling the pure *British* Blood with foreign Mixtures, of introducing a Confusion of Languages and Religions, and of letting in Strangers to eat the Bread out of the Mouths of our own People, I became so humble as to let my Project fall to the Ground, and leave my Country to encrease by the ordinary way of Generation. (*Spectator*, 3:119–20)

Falling back upon the methods of ordinary generation represents Steele's reluctant concession to the xenophobic fears of his countrymen, fears that had already begun to produce what Joyce Appleby describes as the increasingly reactionary economic policy of England between 1696 and 1713.[13] The *Spectator*'s rhetorical strategy in the face of English protectionism is similar to the more elaborate attack that Franklin later adopts in "Observations Concerning the Increase of Mankind." Both writers derive from William Petty an appreciation for the role that the incorporation of "Foreigners" played in the economic success of the Dutch Republic.[14]

Steele draws particular attention in the *Spectator* to what Petty calls his "jocular" proposition "that if all the *moveables* and People of *Ireland*, and of the Highlands of *Scotland,* were transported into the rest of *Great Brittain;* that then the King and his Subjects would thereby become more *Rich* and *Strong,* both *offensively* and *defensively,* than now they are."[15] Petty fully recognizes (when he writes this prediction—as Steele does when he quotes it) that it would horrify a large proportion of his readership, who view the Highland Scots and the subjugated Irish in much the same light that many of Franklin's contemporaries did American Indians and that many in Richard Steele's audience did the foreign "Mixtures" that threatened the purity of British blood. Nevertheless, Steele suggests, Petty is merely confirming a paradox from Hesiod: that "Half is more than the Whole." The father of ten children benefits his country more than "he who has added to it 10000 Acres of Land and no People" (*Spectator,* 3:122). This pronouncement must have delighted the youngest son, and the seventh of ten children, born to Josiah Franklin and Abiah Folger. Franklin's 1757 epitaph for his parents, commemorating the prolific nature of their marriage, assumes that its informed reader will recognize that the claims of these two obscure people upon the gratitude of the community are much more than simply sentimental.

But the Franklins of Boston increased exclusively by ordinary generation. The Dutch, whom William Petty, Bernard Mandeville, and Benjamin Franklin all admired, increased the more rapidly (according to Petty) by naturalizing strangers through informal domestic means, by marriage and by birth, rather than by the fictions of law. Petty recommends just such a strategy in the case of Ireland, where he concludes that the interest of "these poorer Irish" lay first in the "reform" of their housing so that English women might be content to marry them and smooth their gradual transformation into a civil and free people.[16]

His declared intention in *Political Arithmetick* is to demonstrate that, even after enduring plague, fire, and the ravages of civil war, England remains more than a match for its great rival, France, despite the disparity in size between the two nations. The example of the Dutch forms the basis of Petty's case. A small country might equal or exceed the wealth and power of a larger one provided that it nurtures carefully its chief resource: people. Large quantities of vacant land, Petty believes, actually hamper the increase of wealth by diverting too much labor and ingenuity to subsistence agriculture. The key to national growth is a diverse, centralized commercial economy and a fluid money supply along the lines of that created and sustained by the Dutch banking system. It might even be advisable, Petty thought, to sell England's surplus land to foreigners and use the capital for domestic investment—exactly the principle of coined land that Franklin later adopts in his argument for the usefulness of a paper currency in Pennsylvania.

The bodily metaphor for the money supply that Petty prefers is "fat" rather than "blood," or circulating currency, but his emphasis is similar to Franklin's: as fat lubricates, nourishes, and beautifies the body, he reasons, "so doth Money in the State quicken its Action." But too much money, Petty writes in *Verbum Sapienti* (1691), will hinder the "Agility" of the "Body Politick," just as too little will make it sick.[17] Finding and maintaining the ideal medium is important—and easier to accomplish in a compact island nation close to potential foreign investors than in an inchoate, expanding colony thousands of miles from European capital. Once a healthy balance of money and trade is achieved, however, the nation might turn its attention to what Petty considers the proper objects of the human mind: "Ratiocinations upon the Works and Will of God, to be supported not only by the indolency, but also by the pleasure of the Body; and not only by the tranquility, but serenity of the mind; and this Exercise is the natural end of man in this world, and that which best disposeth him for his spiritual happiness in that other which is to come."[18]

Great industry leads to leisure and leisure to intellectual serenity, in mature nations as in mature individuals. Petty's "Ratiocinations" sound very much like the program of "Philosophical Studies and Amusements" that Franklin projects for his own indolent and pleasurable retirement, but it will require many decades of agile trading, Franklin realizes, before Pennsylvania or America as a whole will attain the contemplative balance that Petty envisions for the mature commercial community.

If population density and industry—guided by what Petty calls in *Verbum Sapienti* the "Facilitations of Art"—are the necessary ingredients of a flourishing nation, then other aspects of public policy that he explores in his treatises might help accelerate America's development into a philosophical utopia. Petty advocates the English adoption of measures that encourage the steady, domestic assimilation of foreign immigrants. To this end, religious toleration is essential. Dissenters ought to be willing to pay for the privilege of being excused from enforced conformity, just as members of the established church pay for the support of their clergy. Toleration fees might even be proportioned to the scope of the "dissent" in particular cases—or to the magnitude of the individual heresy. Radical materialists, who deny the existence of the human soul, seem to Petty too dangerous for any society to admit without constraints on their liberty that amount to virtual slavery. But he does not anticipate encountering large numbers of citizens who will stubbornly deny all distinctions between men and animals.

Petty steadfastly opposes any form of persecution intended to coerce religious dissenters. Even the punishing of unbelievers only penalizes the state by depriving it of the labor of a traditionally ingenious portion of its people and by discouraging immigration. Moreover, the government's interest in religion will be more consistently and usefully served if it addresses religious heterodoxy by fining the shepherds of the established church as well as their strayed sheep. We pay our clergy for inspiring and persuasive examples of personal holiness, Petty contends, not for sermons. Heresy can only grow where inspiration by personal example is in short supply; the market for "bare Pulpit-discourses" is already glutted. Franklin's receptive attitude to Samuel Hemphill's recycled sermons in 1735 reflects William Petty's disparaging application of the ideas of supply and demand to preaching, just as his critique of narrow human "Partialities," in "Observations Concerning the Increase of Mankind," extends Petty's emphasis on the relation between toleration and growth.[19]

In his economic masterpiece, *A Treatise of Taxes and Contributions* (1662), Petty extends his analysis of finance to address the widest definition of the "Publick Charges" of government. Full employment is the primary obligation of the state, in Petty's view. Indigent members of the population who are able to work ought to be employed on extensive public improvement projects: highways, bridges, mines, reforestation "for timber, delight, and fruit," the maintenance and extension of navigable rivers. Those too old or too sick to work should be cared for at public expense to prevent the demoralizing and degrading effects of begging, "for the permitting of any to beg is a more chargeable way of maintaining them whom the law of Nature will not suffer to starve, where food may possibly be had."

All orphans and abandoned children should be raised at public expense and educated to the point where their skills and gifts might make them valuable citizens: "it were probable that one in twenty of them might be of excellent wit and towardness." Such wards of the state "might afford the King the fittest Instruments for all kinde of his Affairs, and be as firmly obliged to be his faithful servants as his own natural Children."[20] The contrast with Mandeville's complacent account of the necessity for a "Multitude of laborious Poor" is striking. Petty does not build his case for public education on moral or religious grounds, but the outcome of his delineation of useful economic policies is the portrait of a charitable state.

When Franklin drafted his proposals for educating the "youth" of Pennsylvania, he was in part following Petty's model, suggesting that the members of the founding corporation "look on the Students as in some Sort their Children." Franklin envisions extending this parental oversight to the establishment of academy graduates in business or marriage. Petty believes that universities, too, should be supported as a public charge, with their students chosen impartially on the basis of ability. Parents and influential friends should play no role in admission; they are the "Crows that think their own Birds ever Fairest," sentiments that Silence Dogood later paraphrases in her scrutiny of the student body of Harvard College.

Petty's social vision derives in large measure from personal circumstances as well as from his analysis of the success of the Dutch. His life is a prototype of Franklin's autobiography, a feature of his influence on Franklin's thought that is elusive but critical to the placement of Franklin's work in its full context. Petty was born to a poor clothier in 1623, and although he rose to some prominence as a physician, he had amused himself as a child by studying the skills of various craftsmen until, as John Aubrey records, he "could have worked at any of their trades." Aubrey's famous account of Petty's life remained in manuscript in the Ashmolean Museum until 1813, but legends about Petty's rise from obscurity and poverty circulated as freely as his treatises throughout the eighteenth century. In a letter of "Advice" that Petty wrote to Samuel Hartlib, published in the 1745 *Harleian Miscellany,* he comments on the eagerness with which children often watch skilled workmen and experiment with their tools. Anthony Wood draws directly on Aubrey's description of Petty's childhood fascination with "artificers" in the biographical sketch of Petty that he includes in *Athenae Oxonienses* (1691), a reference work popular enough to be reprinted in 1721, a few years before Franklin's first arrival in London, and important enough even to colonial readers to be included among the collections of the Library Company of Philadelphia by 1741.[21]

Such details from Petty's background may have recurred to Franklin when he describes his father's practice of allowing him to watch "Joiners, Bricklayers, Turners, Braziers &c. at their Work" until he had acquired enough facility with tools to do "little Jobs" about the house or "to construct little Machines for my Experiments" (*Writings,* 1317). Petty's haphazard education eventually led to the study of medicine at Leyden and Paris, under Thomas Hobbes, and to a fellowship at Brasenose College, largely as a result of his good fortune in attracting the notice of some French Jesuits through his knowledge of Latin. He was among the one in twenty poor children whose education more than repaid its costs, but Petty's gifts could easily have been wasted if he had not been injured while working as a ship's boy in the English Channel and put ashore to fend for himself on the Normandy coast. Petty fulfilled in fact Franklin's boyhood dream of going to sea, and like Franklin nearly a century later he was abandoned in a foreign country and forced to live by his wits.[22] Such biographical parallels would almost certainly have attracted the interest of a writer who enjoyed reminding his son of the uncanny resemblance between himself and an uncle who had died four years before Franklin was born (*Writings*, 1310).

In addition to his economic writings and his medical practice, Petty was distinguished as a professor of music and a minor inventor, an aspect of his varied career that (as Garry Wills points out) attracted the attention of Thomas Jefferson, much as his economic essays attracted Benjamin Franklin.[23] Petty designed a double-writing machine for making copies, which may have inspired Jefferson's similar efforts a century later, and produced several versions of a double-bottomed boat, or catamaran, christened the "Experiment," which Jefferson also emulated in the name of the collapsible boat frame that he urged upon Meriwether Lewis for his expedition up the Missouri River. The liberal proposals for public education that Jefferson outlines in *Notes on the State of Virginia* are similarly indebted to Petty's *Treatise on Taxes*.[24] But Petty's full educational legacy to America—along with the legacy of the revolutionary context from which Petty's thinking emerged—is more clearly evident in the pamphlet that Franklin composed in 1749 to awaken public interest in forming an academy in Philadelphia.

Petty's name does not appear among the list of direct sources that Franklin identifies in *Proposals Relating to the Education of Youth in Pensilvania*[25] Nor does the Academy, as Franklin and his colleagues conceived it, envision admitting all "youth," regardless of ability to pay, as a public charge. The original tuition appears to have been four pounds a year.[26] But the organization of instruction that Franklin outlines in his paper, like the parental obligations he attaches to the school's governing board, suggests the pervasive influence of Petty's conception of generative laws in a small nation that hopes to flourish amid more established and more powerful neighbors. At the same time, Franklin clearly adapts the royalist posture that marked the last decades of Petty's life, along with most of his writing, to the political necessities of an increasingly antiroyalist and anticolonial America.

An important purpose of "Seminaries of Learning," Franklin observes in the preamble to his *Proposals,* was to "supply the succeeding Age with Men qualified to serve the Publick with Honour to themselves, and to their Country" (*Writings,* 324). William Petty urges the education of all abandoned and orphaned children as one means of providing "fit Instruments" for the king's affairs, and Charles Rollin, one of Franklin's pedagogical authorities, sums up the case for a civic education (derived from Quintillian) by asking "Is it not evident that youth are as the nursery of the state?"[27] Franklin offers his own educational "Hints" as one means of avoiding "the mischievous Consequences that would attend a general Ignorance among us," but at the same time the proposals incorporate a considerable measure of mischief in the curriculum.

The most conspicuous sign of Franklin's complex intention is the list of writers he suggests as models of English style. In the last year of his life, Franklin recalls that his interest in the Academy originally focused on the establishment of an "English" school rather than the traditional course of instruction in classical languages and civilization that influenced many other members of the Academy's original board of directors.[28] A primary object of vernacular education would be the promotion of correct grammar and clear, concise writing, which Franklin suggests the students might accomplish by sending letters to one another, making abstracts of their reading, or "writing the same Things in their own Words" (*Writings,* 352–53). In short, Franklin proposes a version of the literary self-discipline that he practiced during his apprentice years, as he abstracted and recast *Spectator* papers or exchanged arguments by letter with John Collins on the question of education for women.

The models of style that Franklin names for the Academy's more formal instruction include the familiar prose master of his youth, Joseph Addison, along with Tillotsen and Pope—names to which no midcentury gentleman of moderate politics would be likely to take exception. But Franklin's recommended "classicks" also include Trenchard and Gordon's *Cato's Letters* and the work of Algernon Sidney, the "British Cassius," as James Thomson describes him in *The Seasons,* "By ancient Learning to th' enlighten'd Love / Of ancient Freedom warm'd." Franklin quotes these lines from Thomson in the almanac for 1750, in which he memorializes Sidney's execution for treason on December 7, 1683. The only crime Sidney committed was the possession of his manuscript, *Discourses Concerning Government,* an extended reply to Filmer's *Patriarcha,* which (like Locke's more celebrated *Treatises on Government*) strenuously defends popular sovereignty and the right of revolution. A glance at the headings of the brief sections into which Sidney divides the *Discourses* indicates why Judge Jeffreys concluded that, from the strict royalist point of view, every page of Sidney's manuscript was treasonable: "To depend upon the will of man is slavery"; "God leaves to man the choice of forms in government"; "No man comes to command many, unless by consent or by force"; "All just magistratical power is from the people"; "The liberties of nations are from God, not from Kings"; "Unjust commands are not to be obeyed"; "The general revolt of a nation cannot be called a rebellion."[29]

Trenchard and Gordon in *Cato's Letters* defend the actions of Caesar's assassins, argue for liberty of speech, and oppose standing armies, but they maintain throughout a scrupulous tone of loyalty to the king. In a late paper on "Charity and Charity Schools," Trenchard borrows from Mandeville not only his title but his scornful attitude toward the education of "beggars" beyond their rightful station.[30] Algernon Sidney was the heir of a much more distinguished aristocratic lineage than the authors of *Cato's Letters,* but his passionate opposition to all government by privilege is expressed throughout the *Discourses* in language that Jonathan Scott persuasively compares to "the simple flight of a hand grenade."[31] The single-mindedness with which Sidney attacks virtually every clause of Filmer's defense of absolute monarchy is a measure of his tenacious resentment of authoritarian rule. "Those kings only are heads of the people," he declares, "who are good, wise, and seek to advance no interest but that of the publick."[32] The attributes of the legitimate monarch, in other words, are identical to the educational ends that Franklin proposes for the Philadelphia Academy. An English school that sets its students the task of studying Sidney's aphoristic and historical *Discourses* would inevitably educate a body of principled critics opposing both royal and parliamentary abuses of the public interest.

The subversive implications of Sidney's thinking, even half a century after his execution, are reflected in a curious bibliographic coincidence from these years. James Ralph, Franklin's companion on his first trip to London, published *Of the Use and Abuse of Parliaments* in 1744 and included as the first of the book's two "Historical Discourses" a manuscript letter by Algernon Sidney presenting "A General View of Government in Europe." In this thumbnail history, Sidney cites William Petty's "excellent

Memorials" as authorities for the sovereign stature of the people in "commons" over the nominally higher House of Lords.[33] Ralph's lengthy extension of Sidney's paper—to which Ralph did not sign his name—purports to be an anonymous "Detection" of recent parliamentary concessions to the king that had eroded Parliament's claims to legitimacy. The result, Ralph concludes, was the reversion of governmental prerogative to the people.

Franklin followed James Ralph's checkered literary career closely enough to note Pope's disparaging reference to his poetry in 1729 and Ralph's more successful attempts to succeed thereafter as a "pretty good Prose Writer." *Of the Use and Abuse of Parliaments,* like Sidney's *Discourses,* was in the collections of the Library Company of Philadelphia by 1757. It is impossible to confirm whether Franklin knew of Ralph's authorship of the parliamentary treatises before the two met again in London, but Ralph's book effectively emphasizes the political dangers inherent in Sidney's thought in the mid-eighteenth century.

Franklin's subsequent discussion of history at the core of his curricular proposal for the Academy makes plain that his educational intention is not limited to following Rollin's traditional prescription—that history is the school of morality—but extends to the exploration of Algernon Sidney's example: that history is the school of power. The mischievous consequences of ignorance that Franklin seeks to thwart through his *Proposals* stem from the excesses of the rulers and not from the ruled. A people educated in the obligations of popular sovereignty are fit to govern themselves and to resist all impositions on their rightful liberty.

The emphasis that the 1749 *Proposals* place on the study of the English language—as well as on drawing, bookkeeping, arithmetic, composition, and oratory—reflect Franklin's determination to fit the curriculum of the Academy to the needs of a community that conducts its business in English. But the reading of history, Franklin believes, provides the best mixture of pleasure with "useful Knowledge" (*Writings,* 335). In particular, history would disclose how "Modern Political Oratory" might apply the technology of the press to the business of "governing, turning, and leading great Bodies of Mankind." History is a library of "Civil Orders and Constitutions," where the student can study the advantages of liberty and the "first Principles of sound Politics," a phrase that Franklin annotates with a passage from Milton's *Of Education,* urging that students "be instructed in the Beginning, End and Reasons of political Societies; that they may not, in a dangerous Fit of the Commonwealth, be such poor, shaken, uncertain Reeds, of such a tottering Conscience, as many of our great Councellors have lately shewn themselves, but stedfast Pillars of the State." Franklin's curriculum is a training ground for consciences that will not totter in the most severe political storms. In addition to being a storehouse for the tools of statecraft, history teaches methods of adjudicating right and wrong—"the Art of Reasoning to *discover* Truth, and of Arguing to *defend* it"—and historical thinkers like Grotius and Puffendorf teach the related arts of war and peace, so that once a society has been properly "turned" it might be competent to defend itself.

Studying "the new *Universal History,*" Franklin argues, as well as classical, biblical, or national history, "would give a *connected* Idea of Human Affairs," to which the history "of these Colonies" could be attached, "accompanied with Observations on their Rise, Encrease, Use to *Great Britain,* Encouragements, Discouragements, &c. the Means to make them flourish, secure their Liberties." The Academy, then, might provide fit instruments to make the representations on America's behalf that, as early as 1729, Franklin thought might be necessary should the "Government at Home" continue to cripple rather than to nourish colonial life. The course of human affairs and the defense of liberty that Jefferson would weave into the Preamble of the Declaration of Independence twenty-six years later form the curriculum of Franklin's ideal school. It was an education for independence and for revolution that he hoped to institutionalize, after which he envisioned the necessity for renewed application to what *Proposals* calls "Histories of Nature," the improvement of medicine and agriculture, the study of commerce and mechanics. Out of these more pacific arts and sciences the greater republic of William Petty's vision might be built.

Franklin's closing encomium on the end of all learning springs from his personal "Articles of Belief," as well as from the rich religious heritage of his Boston upbringing, but it also looks forward to the subordination of human partialities that he will address in "Observations Concerning the Increase of Mankind" two years after writing the Academy *Proposals:* "The Idea of what is *true Merit,* should also be often presented to Youth, explain'd and impress'd on their Minds, as consisting in an *Inclination* join'd with an *Ability* to serve Mankind, one's Country, Friends and Family; which *Ability* is (with the Blessing of God) to be acquir'd or greatly encreas'd by *true Learning;* and should indeed be the great *Aim* and *End* of all Learning" (*Writings,* 342). Along with other accounts of his intellectual life that Franklin sent to Peter Collinson in these years, he included a copy

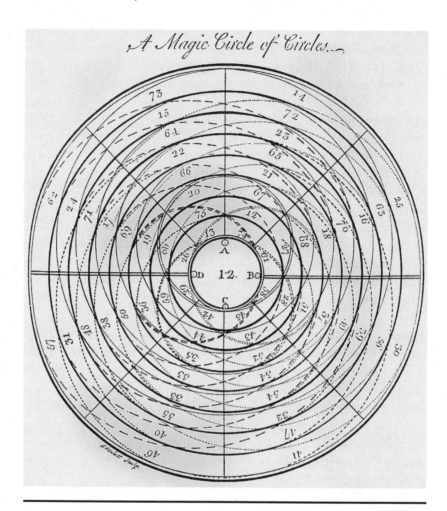

Franklin first described his Magic Circle of Circles in an undated letter to Peter Collinson, which the editors of the Yale Papers assign to 1752. It was first printed in a volume of tables and tracts by James Ferguson (London, 1767) and reprinted from Ferguson's book in the 1769 edition of Franklin's *Experiments and Observations on Electricity.* "These interwoven circles make so perplexed an appearance," Franklin wrote Collinson, "that it is not easy for the eye to trace every circle of numbers one would examine, through all the maze of circles intersected by it" (*Papers,* 4:400). But the viewer who employs a compass will find all the proper spaces by following "the moving foot." This playful disclosure of design within an apparent maze suggests the comprehensive ethical and religious principles that shaped Franklin's civic and religious practice.

of one of his numerical puzzles—a system of circles resembling an elaborate web filled with numbers that produced a bewildering consistency of sums yielding 180 or 360. "It may be observed," he notes, "that there is not one of the numbers but what belongs at least to two of the different circular spaces; some to three, some to four, some to five; and yet they are all so placed as never to break the required number 360, in any of the 28 circular spaces within the primitive circle" (*Writings*, 453).

For Franklin, this diagram might readily have embodied, in a curious and delightful way, the concept of a plural unity to which his civic and political experience in America necessarily led. *Proposals* reflects the same recurring design. Our most immediate and intimate connections form only the first of the social "sums" to which we contribute. Heeding exclusively the results of a single calculation is the natural limitation of human partiality. Within the circumference of the primitive circle, a single figure contributes to the formation of many required wholes. The aggregate calculation is mankind itself, the most inclusive expression of individual identity, containing all lesser expressions like the concentric and "excentric" interlocking rings on the "Magic Circle of Circles" with which Franklin half playfully inscribed his sense of order.[34]

Chapter Six

PLANS OF UNION

In the Academy *Proposals* of 1749 and the "Observations Concerning the Increase of Mankind" of 1751, Franklin addresses the intractable problem of human partiality on an imperial scale, drawing upon the full range of his reading to suggest the historical context of English colonial existence as well as the spiritual menaces that threatened it. The rich landscape of North America was ideally suited to human increase, provided its occupants were careful not to sow it in fennel–the emblem of an inflammable jealousy that could swiftly consume the continent's human potential. Education, as Franklin describes it in his English Academy, would replace aristocratic privilege with republican principle, cultivating servants of the people rather than servants of the king.

Both before and after writing these visionary documents, Franklin involved himself directly in specific contests between destructive partiality and the general welfare, in each case drafting specific responses to the challenge that these contests posed to prospects for a workable American union. The Association militia of 1747 in Pennsylvania and the 1754 Albany Plan of Union were the results of these two early experiments in forming governments that could "compound," or federate, in an effective social body reflecting a population more heterogeneous than any described in the histories that Franklin proposed for the instruction of his Academy students. The Association militia, which grew directly out of Franklin's 1747 pamphlet *Plain Truth,* was largely a colonial response to

Anglo-European political and military circumstances. The Albany Plan developed out of the efforts of the colonies to centralize and regulate, in some equitable way, their relations with the native tribes. Taken together, these two political and literary enterprises demonstrate Franklin's progressive adaptation to local demands of the ideals of toleration in which his reading had instructed him.

If Shaftesbury's strictures on enthusiasm and William Petty's idealization of the Dutch Republic guided Franklin's views on the spiritual and economic utility of toleration, John Locke offered a suggestive synthesis of their principles in imperial politics. Franklin included Locke's *Letters concerning Toleration* among the books he advertised for sale from his print shop in 1744, the year he published the most comprehensive list of the volumes that he stocked.[1] The opening letter of Locke's series, a translation of his *Epistola de Tolerantia* (1689), is a classic statement of the distinction between civil and religious authority as well as an impassioned argument for liberty of conscience. In the course of presenting his case, Locke sketches out the operations of "Christian" partiality in the settlement of the New World with a bluntness that must have struck his American readers with particular force. "Let us trace this matter to the bottom," Locke begins as he considers the rights of a native people to the same privileges of belief that he would accord all the contending faiths of Europe and the Near East:

Thus it is: an inconsiderable and weak number of Christians, destitute of every thing, arrive in a pagan country; these foreigners beseech the inhabitants, by the bowels of humanity, that they would succour them with the necessaries of life; those necessaries are given them, habitations are granted, and they all join together, and grow up into one body of people. The Christian religion by this means takes root in that country, and spreads itself; but does not suddenly grow the strongest. While things are in this condition, peace, friendship, faith, and equal justice, are preserved amongst them. At length the magistrate becomes a Christian, and by that means their party becomes the most powerful. Then immediately all compacts are to be broken, all civil rights to be violated, that idolatry may be extirpated: and unless these innocent pagans, strict observers of the rules of equity and the law of nature, and no ways offending against the laws of the society, I say unless they will forsake their ancient religion, and embrace a new and strange one, they are to be turned out of the lands and possessions of their forefathers, and perhaps deprived of life itself. Then at

last it appears what zeal for the church, joined with the desire of domin-
ion, is capable to produce: and how easily the pretence of religion, and of
the care of souls, serves for a cloke to covetousness, rapine, and ambition.[2]

Locke's grim account of the colonial experience is artificially simplified
in several respects in order to enhance its representative power, but his
strikingly inclusive vision of "one body of people," pagan and Christian,
European and "American," becomes the prelapsarian condition to which
Franklin's thinking and writing in these years strives to return. The effort
is not as quixotic as it sounds. Locke's summary does not purport to retell
a biblical fable so much as it projects a fabulous history—too simple to
have ever really occurred as he describes it but by no means as remote as
Edenic myth. In these crucial direct engagements with colonial government between 1747 and 1754, Franklin is attempting to reconstruct at
least a few of the elements of Locke's visionary historiography.

That reconstruction depends, to a significant degree, upon Franklin's
successful modification of the conditions set forth in Locke's historical fable. To the communities of Christian emigrants and pagan natives that
Locke invokes, Franklin adds the remote authority of European imperial
power: England and France, whose schemes of domination complicated
the diplomatic predicament of the North American colonies and their Indian neighbors. The roles of invader and invaded, emigrant and native,
could become unexpectedly fluid in mid-eighteenth-century Pennsylvania, particularly in the hands of a writer who is interested in the complex opportunities presented by shifting mythological identities in the
historical narrative.

Franklin manipulates those identities most conspicuously in the pages
of *Plain Truth*, in the effort to disclose common interests uniting the heterogeneous communities of North America. He weaves together the emblematic experiences of Israel and Rome in such a way as to make these familiar stories suggest the emergence of unfamiliar bonds among his
readers.[3] In Locke's parable, the common "bowels of humanity" break
down the distinction between foreign and native to permit the growth of
"one body of people." Franklin's historical circumstances require him to
find in *Plain Truth* a less figurative but equally effective equivalent for the
transformation of consciousness to which Locke points.

Very little in *Plain Truth* is plain. Its ostensible audience—the city of Philadelphia and the province of Pennsylvania—is in fact much less compact

and much more complex than these entities. The immediate military threat that Franklin addresses derives from the presence of Spanish and French privateers seizing commercial vessels in and around Delaware Bay. In mid-July 1747, a small party of these sailors looted two plantation houses some eighty miles downriver from Philadelphia. Occasional rumors and depositions from released captives suggested that this remote and comparatively minor incident indicated the enemy's intention to attack the city directly. But the menace remained largely prospective rather than actual: a matter of potential dangers only, the nature and scope of which were difficult to predict and which, in the end, failed to materialize.[4]

Pennsylvania was without a governor in the closing months of 1747; the current occupant of the office, George Thomas, had returned to England for his health. In his absence during the summer and fall of that year, as Gary Nash suggests, both the governor's Provincial Council and the Pennsylvania Assembly were influenced by ulterior motives as they considered how to respond to their defenseless circumstances.[5] The deadlock between the Council and the Assembly reflected long-standing debates over the financial obligations of the proprietor, Thomas Penn, to the colony as well as disagreements over the colony's obligations to the crown for supporting joint military expeditions against the French. Old monetary grievances were as important as perceived military threats to the audience that *Plain Truth* addresses. Franklin's literary motives, however, were both more involved and more opportunistic than those of his readers.

A preliminary disclosure of those motives occurs in the long quotation from Sallust's history of the Catiline conspiracy that Franklin prints in Latin on the title page of the first issue of *Plain Truth*. He provided a translation of the passage in the *Pennsylvania Gazette* two days after the pamphlet originally appeared, and the second edition includes this translation at the end of the text (*Papers,* 3:204). The words come from Sallust's rendering of a speech by Cato urging the Roman Senate to show no clemency to a handful of Catiline's accomplices currently in their custody. More important, Cato argues that the defense of the city against Catiline's approaching army seems utterly neglected while the Senate engages in feckless debate over the sentences of a handful of traitors seized within the city walls. The larger issue to which he directs the Senate's attention is the fate of the imperiled Republic, which depends on the active virtue of its citizens rather than the irresistible will of the gods.[6]

The parallel between Philadelphia in 1747 and Rome in the last years of the Republic is at best strained, but it offers Franklin an occasion to remind his readers of the same interesting fact that his allusion to the Book of Judges early in the body of his text also underscores: at the time of the publication of *Plain Truth,* and in several related senses, there are no "kings" in Pennsylvania. The quotation from Sallust is a celebration of "republican" rather than imperial spirit, attributed to one of the last heroes of preimperial Rome who, at the time, is replying to a speech by Julius Caesar advocating moderation in the punishment of Catiline's aristocratic henchmen.

The epigraph, in effect, functions as a dramatic analogy. As Cato is to Caesar, so the author of *Plain Truth* is to all temporizing spirits in Pennsylvania who are unwilling to assert a virtuous independence in defense of their community. If Franklin does not put the point quite so plainly as his epigraph implies, it is primarily because the larger purpose of his pamphlet is to encourage the formation of what he later calls ties and engagements of unity embracing the entire colonial community as well as the people of Pennsylvania. Moreover, the crisis that the colonies collectively face, as Franklin interprets it, is less from the aggression of the French, the Spanish, and their Indian allies than from the neglect or the indifference of the English government in London.

The absence of the proprietor's personal representative, Governor Thomas, at a time of such public concern is a minor inconvenience by comparison with the vast distance that separates America from the great European concentration of English power. Invoking the story of the destruction of Laish from Judges 18 early in the pages of *Plain Truth* allows Franklin to make the geographical conclusion explicit: in the event of genuine danger, Pennsylvania is far indeed from any potential British "Deliverer." The people of Laish may have been culpable in their carelessness, but they were also helpless against even a small invading force because of their distance from Zidon, or Sidon, the urban capital of their people.

In Pennsylvania, distance is exacerbated by the attributes of national character. Franklin opens *Plain Truth* by citing an Italian proverb that, like the passages from Sallust and Judges, has a double-edged significance for his audience: "The English *feel,* but they do not *see*" (*Papers,* 3:188). They respond to inconvenience or to danger only when it is too late for preventive measures: "After great Fires, they provide Buckets and Engines." Such "After-Wisdom," Franklin notes, brings to mind another proverbial commonplace: "When the Steed is stolen you shut the Stable Door." Imprudence of this sort is a temptation to more than one sort of thief. At this point in the pamphlet, as well as in Franklin's own consciousness, the English are still "our Nation," but under the stresses of imperial war the transatlantic bond is wearing thin. In *Plain Truth,* Franklin explores the increasing vulnerability of that bond to a revolutionary, republican spirit founded in the heroic ideals embodied by Cato and the "middling" people of America.

Franklin expresses his doubts about the intentions and the goodwill of the home government in his comments on the necessity for paper currency in Pennsylvania nearly twenty years earlier. He makes these doubts explicit once again in the preamble to the *Form of Association,* which he printed (as promised) a week after the appearance of *Plain Truth.* A preamble is necessary, he explains in the *Gazette,* because Pennsylvania's circumstances are so unusual. Perhaps nowhere else in the world does a government exist that, from "religious considerations," fails to provide for the protection of its people. This comment appears to be directed exclusively at the Quaker representatives in the Pennsylvania Assembly who refused on pacifist grounds to spend public money for military preparations, but *Plain Truth* extends the claim of governmental neglect directly to the "unseeing" and improvident English themselves. Delaware Bay, Franklin suggests, had been left as open as the proverbial stable door. A "boasted" land expedition to punish the marauding French and Indians to the north had been abruptly disbanded "by orders from the Crown," leaving the Indian allies of the English colonies filled with "Disgust at our Usage," exposed to their northern enemies, and open to the diplomatic artifice of French priests (*Papers,* 3:194).

The Quakers, Franklin observes, can at least plead conscience as a cause for their political deficiencies, but wealthy merchants of Philadelphia who simply balk at defense expenses, or officers of the crown who fail in their duty to protect shipping and settlers, can enter no comparable plea. The language of the Association's preamble makes this breach in the larger social fabric explicit:

> We whose Names are hereunto subscribed, Inhabitants of the Province of Pennsylvania in America, taking into serious Consideration, that Great Britain, to which we are subject, is now engag'd in a War with two powerful Nations: That it is become too well known to our enemies, that this Colony is in a naked, defenceless State . . . That we are at a great Distance from our Mother Country, and cannot, on any Emergency, receive Assistance from thence: That thro' the Multiplicity of other Affairs of greater Importance (as we presume) no particular Care hath hitherto been taken

by the Government at Home of our Protection . . . That being thus unprotected by the Government under which we live, against our foreign Enemies that may come to invade us, As we think it absolutely necessary, WE DO hereby, for our mutual Defence and Security, and for the Security of our Wives, Children and Estates, and the Preservation of the Persons and Estates of others, our Neighbours and Fellow Subjects, form ourselves into an ASSOCIATION, and, imploring the Blessing of Heaven on our Undertaking, do agree *solemnly* with each other in the Manner following. (*Papers*, 3:205–6)

In some respects, *Plain Truth* exists in order to justify this revolutionary preamble: to make the case for a neglect of governmental obligation that frees the "subject" to form new arrangements with his "Fellows" for the safety of the commonwealth.

These are, in practice, the radical "republican" sentiments for which Algernon Sidney was executed and which even fervent critics of public abuses like John Trenchard and Thomas Gordon are careful to disavow while, nevertheless, praising some elements of Sidney's work.[7] The association that Franklin proposes is intended to function precisely like a substitute government for Pennsylvania, with a written constitution, a system of elections, assemblies, laws, and taxes, all conducted and administered on a limited, voluntary basis but surprisingly complete in its design. This completeness is a reflection not only of the associators' obligations to their families and immediate neighbors but also of Pennsylvania's larger obligation to the emerging colonial neighborhood of North America.

In *Plain Truth*, Franklin emphasizes that Pennsylvania is indebted to adjacent colonies, not to the "Mother Country," for the comparative security it has enjoyed since the outbreak of war between England and Spain in 1739. The northern provinces insulate them from the French and the southern provinces from the Spanish, while "our People have, till lately, slept securely in their Habitations" (*Papers*, 3:191). Indeed, Philadelphia, unlike Boston, emerges from this first period of midcentury imperial conflict more affluent than when the war began, partly because of geographic location and partly because Philadelphia merchants were able to profit from high wartime prices and privateering.[8] William Lawrence, a merchant and member of the Pennsylvania Provincial Council who became a lieutenant colonel in the Association militia, outfitted his own privateer during the war, which he generously offered to put at the public's disposal during the period of the Association's existence.[9] Philadelphia's shipping was apparently not so defenseless as contemporary Council documents sometimes suggest, nor were Pennsylvanians as a whole quite so careless and sleepy as the unfortunate people of Laish in the Book of Judges, who were put to the sword by six hundred Danite warriors. The swift response to Franklin's pamphlet is not so much a tribute to his rhetorical powers as it is an indication of a degree of readiness to fight that makes Franklin's elaborate evocation of a cautionary biblical tale seem beside the point.

His aims, however, are much broader than simply filling the ranks of the Association militia with able volunteers. The Association would address a particular and immediate need of the city, but it was also a great occasion for addressing larger principles of mutual interest and the collective good, which were central to Franklin's view of the historical process. Invoking the experience of Rome and Israel at the outset of *Plain Truth* situates Franklin's reader at the intersection of several stories capable of exposing a range of challenges and opportunities inherent in the local crisis.

Before undertaking its main arguments, *Plain Truth* summarizes nearly verse by verse a detailed passage from Judges 18 as scriptural "Reproof, Instruction, and Warning" to the careless people of Pennsylvania. Franklin recognizes and appreciates the influential role of pulpit rhetoric in mobilizing the public will. His old friend Gilbert Tennent, among other Philadelphia ministers, preached sermons in support of the Association. But the passage from Judges that Franklin chooses to incorporate in the pamphlet's text is surprisingly involved and confusing for an exhortation to arms. The people of Laish with whose plight he apparently asks his readers to sympathize are part of a northern Canaanite tribe whom the migratory Danites of Israel expel. The Danites are especially unsympathetic in Franklin's account, despite their admirable military discipline and their membership among the Chosen People. They were "at this time," Franklin observes, "not very orthodox in their religion." Indeed, they have scarcely any religion at all, beyond a desire to learn from God whether their material designs on Laish will succeed. In their conquering progress northward, they rob the household of Micah, who sheltered their spies, of a silver idol, an ephod, and Teraphim–"Plenty of superstitious Trinkets," Franklin calls them–and take along as well Micah's mysterious household priest, who assured them that their "Way" was "before the Lord" (*Papers*, 3:192).

Franklin's scriptural reproof is immediately complicated by its inversion of customary cultural practice. Rather than identify the Anglo-European colonization of North America with the movement of Israel into Canaan, Franklin asks his readers instead to identify with the victimized people of Canaan. The opportunities suggested by the absence of kings in the Book of Judges are partly canceled by the chaos that prevails when people consult their personal well-being, rather than a vision of collective good, and when the restraining power of religion over human behavior is compromised by its vulnerability to idolatrous greed. Wherever Franklin's reader turns in this biblical passage to locate its instructive application to Pennsylvania in 1747, the results are more disquieting than reassuring. Are we Danites or Canaanites? peaceful or predatory? a material or a spiritual people? In the midst of these disorienting events and troubling questions, Franklin places the enigmatic figure of Micah's priest, "his Heart, as the Text assures us, being glad, perhaps for reasons more than one" (*Papers,* 3:193).

More than one reason accounts for Franklin's interest in this particular illustrative text over any number of more straightforward biblical appeals to righteous militance in the cause of self-defense. In the paragraphs from *Plain Truth* that follow the allusion to Judges, he points out that the fate of Pennsylvania's border settlers depends largely on the ability of the English colonies to retain the active support—or at least the neutrality—of the formidable Iroquois Confederation to the north. If the Six Nations were to join the French cause, "what may we expect to be the Consequence, but deserting of Plantations, Ruin, Bloodshed and Confusion!" (*Papers,* 3:194). Franklin's alarm appears genuine, in contrast to the peculiar note of equivocation that he strikes later, when he envisions the menace posed by marauding crews of foreign privateers: "the wanton and unbridled Rage, Rapine and Lust, of *Negroes, Molattoes,* and others, the vilest and most abandoned of Mankind. A dreadful Scene! which some may represent as exaggerated. I think it my duty to warn you: Judge for yourselves" (*Papers,* 3:198).

Franklin clearly distinguishes between sensationalized, racist fears and the realistic expectation of Indian warfare. One is a hysterical nightmare, the other a grim possibility. Two weeks after the publication of *Plain Truth,* Franklin ran a description in the *Pennsylvania Gazette* of the horrors experienced by the Spanish population of Portobello when the town was sacked by English privateers.[10] The wanton and unbridled appetites of humankind are clearly not associated, in Franklin's mind, with a particular race or nation.

In conjunction with the passage from Judges, however, *Plain Truth* does make clear that the "Canaanite" people of North America are invaluable allies rather than easy victims of the emigrant English of Pennsylvania. Franklin's opening allusion to Sallust implies the same conclusion. At the beginning of *Catiline's Conspiracy*, Sallust observes that the early Romans were a mixed people, a blend of colonizing Trojan exiles and the indigenous people of Italy, whom Sallust complacently pictures as "a race of men who ran wild in the woods." It is "wonderful," the Roman historian concludes, "how soon they became one undistinguished people."[11] Franklin's pamphlet is careful to maintain cultural distinctions between colonists and indigenous peoples, but he also points out that the vacillation of the crown has put the Iroquois nations in a diplomatic predicament in which their own interests may eventually alienate them from their English neighbors.

This breakdown in the alliance between Pennsylvania and the Six Nations may, Franklin fears, trigger a breakdown in the relationship between urban and rural residents in the colony:

> Perhaps some in the City, Towns and Plantations near the River, may say to themselves, *An Indian War on the Frontiers will not affect us; the Enemy will never come near our Habitations; let those concern'd take Care of themselves.* And others who live in the Country, when they are told of the Danger the City is in from Attempts by Sea, may say, *What is that to us? The Enemy will be satisfied with the Plunder of the Town, and never think it worth his while to visit our Plantations; Let the Town take care of itself.* These are not mere Suppositions, for I have heard some Talk in this strange Manner. But are these the Sentiments of true Pennsylvanians, of Fellow-Countrymen, or even of Men that have common Sense or Goodness? (*Papers*, 3:194–95)

When the union between the colony and its Indian allies breaks down, *Plain Truth* argues, the union between country and city is shaken. In Franklin's scenario, the mutual interests and obligations uniting the different classes of people and the different religions in Pennsylvania shortly experience the same infectious division.

The result is social and material ruin, which the colony's enemies can accomplish even without the risks of a direct invasion. Once the business of the city is brought to a standstill, trade will turn to other ports, debt will build up, and buyers for the colony's skills and goods will diminish. Labor will grow too cheap to attract inhabitants, the population will shrink, and the value of land will collapse. *Plain Truth* sketches a chain of economic consequences that is every bit as ruinous–though much less sensational—as a pirate raid or an Indian war. Franklin does not neglect the value of sensationalism in moving public opinion, but the great weight of his argument rests upon these relentlessly "plain" predictions. One of the homilies with which Sallust introduces his history of Catiline's conspiracy is the observation that "the head, and not the sword, is the great engine of war."[12] Similarly, Franklin's appeal on behalf of the Association is grounded not in bodily fear but in rational foresight.

The majority of the population of Pennsylvania has "no Confidence that God will protect those that neglect the Use of rational Means for their Security; nor have any Reason to hope that our Losses, if we should suffer any, may be made up by Collections in our Favour at Home" (*Papers*, 3:200). If we conduct ourselves with reasonable prudence, then God will not desert us. But however we choose to conduct ourselves, we can count on little or no help from England. Under these circumstances, Franklin concludes, the self-interested quarrel between prominent Quakers and their equally prominent opponents in the colonial Assembly is especially misguided. "Thro' the Dissensions of our Leaders," the lives, families, and fortunes of "the middling People" of the colony are exposed to destruction:

> It seems as if Heaven, justly displeas'd at our growing Wickedness, and determin'd to punish this once favour'd Land, had suffered our Chiefs to engage in these foolish and mischievous Contentions, for *little Posts* and *paltrey Distinctions,* that our Hands might be bound up, our Understandings darkned and misled, and every Means of our Security neglected. It seems as if our greatest Men, our *Cives nobilissimi* of both Parties, had *sworn the Ruin of the Country, and invited the French, our most inveterate Enemy, to destroy it.* Where then shall we seek for Succour and Protection? The Government we are immediately under denies it to us; and if the Enemy comes, we are *far from* ZIDON, *and there is no Deliverer near.* Our Case indeed is dangerously bad; but perhaps there is yet a Remedy, if we have but the Prudence and the Spirit to apply it. (*Papers*, 3:202)

American interests, as Franklin construes them in this wonderfully concentrated passage, appear to entail the peculiar blend of identities reflected in the shifting terms for colonial leadership that he invokes: tribal "Chiefs," the *Cives nobilissimi* of republican Rome, and the helpless victims of Laish who lament the absence of their great deliverer. At this rhetorically strategic point, near the conclusion of *Plain Truth,* Franklin introduces the outlines of his Association plan, drawing once again on language from Sallust and the Book of Judges, as if to emphasize the conceptual unity of his text at the same instant that he calls for unity among his readers.

Franklin openly identifies the voice of his pamphlet both with the republican Cato in Sallust's narrative and with the enigmatic Levite in Judges, who points out the path to the spies of Dan without sharing entirely their material and imperial goals. The household of Micah in which the priest resided is organized around an idol made from two hundred pieces of cast silver, which the Danite invaders steal in their march north toward Laish. The priest is not associated with the idol directly; he is a wanderer from Bethlehem in Judah who came to Micah's house in search of a place "to carry on his work." The nature of that work is never clear in the biblical text, but as Franklin's paraphrase reminds us, the priest from Bethlehem accompanies the mercenary invaders on their journey, "*being glad,* perhaps for reasons more than one." Franklin's emphasis on the hidden motives of an elusive religious figure, entangled in a clash of worldly appetites, corresponds to his linking of transcendent goals with worldly ones in his appeal to the people of Pennsylvania.

In effect, Franklin asks his neighbors to transcend, as well as to protect, themselves: to recognize their common interests with Indians as well as their natural indebtedness to the other colonies that help secure their borders, to overcome barriers of class and religious principle, to relish the assistance and the character of Irish Protestant immigrants as well as the "brave and steady Germans" of the colony, whose history is distinguished by their obstinate resistance to imperial Rome (*Papers,* 3:203). Once again, Franklin implies, historical circumstances appear to favor the formation of "one body of people" in North America, marked by the spirit of peace, friendship, faith, and equal justice, which Locke celebrates in his *Letters concerning Toleration.*

This new inclusive spirit, as Franklin practices it, is not without its limits. Whereas Locke (like William Petty) excludes atheists from his tolerant commonwealth, Franklin—in *Plain Truth* at least—is uncompromisingly anti-Catholic, accusing the French of being instruments of a "bigotted Popish King," whose missionaries were largely responsible for inciting the Canadian tribes to raid the English frontier. But within the English colonies Franklin envisions a pluralistic community consistent with the principles of William Petty's political economy, secure in its industry, charity, and tolerance rather than its military prowess. If, Sallust argues, the "powers of Genius" would only display themselves with equal vigor in "the calm seasons of peace" as they do during war, then armed conflict might grow much less frequent in human history.[13] *Plain Truth* is Franklin's effort to promote just such a seasonable exertion of those civic powers.

The most direct expression of this effort in Franklin's pamphlet is yet another proverbial saying: "One Sword often keeps another in the Scabbard." But Sallust's point is more complex than simply an endorsement of security through warlike vigilance. Franklin acknowledges these more profound sources of communal well-being in the prayer with which he closes his appeal:

> May the God of WISDOM, STRENGTH and POWER, the Lord of the Armies of Israel, inspire us with Prudence in this Time of DANGER; take away from us all the Seeds of Contention and Division, and unite the Hearts and Counsels of all of us, of whatever SECT or NATION, in one Bond of Peace, Brotherly Love, and generous Publick Spirit; May he give us Strength and Resolution to amend our Lives, and remove from among us every Thing that is displeasing to him; afford us his most gracious Protection, confound the Designs of our Enemies, and give PEACE in all our Borders, is the sincere Prayer of
>
> A TRADESMAN of Philadelphia (*Papers*, 3:204)

In the *Autobiography*, Franklin reports that his New England background led the Pennsylvania Provincial Council to ask him, early in December 1747, to draft their proclamation of a public fast requesting divine guidance and assistance for the beleaguered colony. The same skills at integrating piety with public policy are on display in the tradesman's prayer at the conclusion of *Plain Truth*. But Franklin does not have to summon up his Boston years to recall such language. The sentiments in the prayer that closes his 1747 call for union are identical to those with which he closes his arguments for an end to sectarian hostility in the "Dialogue Between Two Presbyterians" of 1735. They echo the relationship he describes between the good actions of men and the favor of the Deity in his 1730 Junto paper on the providence of God, as well as the petitions and prayers that he weaves into the text of his "Articles of Belief and Acts of Religion" at the beginning of his Philadelphia years.

Franklin's interest in Cato as a source for *Plain Truth*'s epigraph reflects a similarly long-standing fascination, which may well have begun at a performance of Addison's popular play on the London stage in 1725. Certainly by the time Franklin wrote his third Busy-Body paper in 1728 he had come to associate the figure of Cato with the same complex of religious and civic values that *Plain Truth* expresses. Franklin's Cato in the Busy-Body, like the Levite from Bethlehem in Judges, represents a fusion of wisdom and innocence, the serpent and the dove. He is a "judge" and not a king among his people, whose "Consummate Virtue" secures his extraordinary civic and spiritual influence. That virtue includes the chivalric attributes of fidelity and courage, but "generous Hospitality," charity, humility, piety, temperance, magnanimity, "Love to Mankind," and "Public-spiritedness" overwhelm the militant virtues in Franklin's portrait of a character that is "the Glory of his Country" (*Writings*, 97).

The Busy-Body paper envisions a civic saint, while the goal of *Plain Truth* twenty years later is to address the defensive necessities of what Franklin increasingly views as the de facto republic of Pennsylvania. But both texts invoke biblical and classical models of virtue in the service of Franklin's complex sense of vocation, the containment of the terrible confusions that spring from human division. In the case of *Plain Truth*, in particular, Franklin's use of the almanacs to serve these larger social ends is especially clear. Just as the *Autobiography* implies, Franklin uses the pages of *Poor Richard* for 1748 to extend and develop the implications of his pamphlet, to identify anniversaries that underscore the lessons of *Plain Truth*, and to suggest other models for republican heroism in addition to the ubiquitous figure of Cato.

Advertised for sale just three weeks before the publication of *Plain Truth*, *Poor Richard* for 1748 is the first of the "Improved" almanac series, 50 percent longer than its predecessors, with two pages, rather than one, devoted to each month and with correspondingly more room for written material. The expansion coincides with Franklin's anticipated retirement from his printing business and with his burgeoning interest in scientific experiments, but the additional space available in this particular year offers a tempting forum to address the political and military circumstances that would shortly prompt the publication of *Plain Truth*.

The almanac's 1748 commentary is particularly critical of the cult of military heroism and the ambitions of the French monarchy. In February, Franklin notes the birthday of Louis XV, "his *most christian* majesty," who is in reality "as great a mischief-maker as his grandfather; or, in the language of poets and orators, a *Hero*" (*Papers*, 3:249). The three great destroyers of mankind, Franklin observes, are "*Plague, Famine,* and *Hero*," but of the three the hero is surely the worst, for the hero destroys property as well as persons. The almanac prints six lines of verse on the terrors of war that make the lapses of *Plain Truth* into sensational journalism seem mild:

> In horrid grandeur haughty *Hero* reigns,
> And thrives on Mankind's miseries and pains.
> What slaughter'd hosts! What cities in a blaze!
> What wasted countries! and what crimson seas!
> With orphans tears his impious bowl o'erflows;
> And cries of kingdoms lull him to repose.

Franklin repeats virtually the same points in four lines of verse accompanying the calendar for June 1748, a comparatively rare instance of *Poor Richard's* aphoristic wisdom duplicating itself in the same almanac. In July, Franklin commemorates the Battle of Boyne in 1690 with a long passage in praise of William of Orange, "one of the right sort of *Heroes,*" who struggles "to *preserve,* and not to *destroy,* the lives, liberties, and estates, of his people." The Duke of Cumberland's victory at Culloden is another example of such "true" heroism, while the assault of the Spanish Armada in July 1588 (like the Jacobite invasion of 1746) further exemplifies the kind of heroic hypocrisy that the 1748 almanac sets out to expose.

Franklin punctuates the calendar for 1748 with the anniversaries of a number of English maritime victories, as if to stir up in his readers a determination to clear the infested waters of Delaware Bay. At the same time, he summarizes much of the forthcoming argument of *Plain Truth* in an aphorism for August—"He that's secure is not safe"—and reminds his readers of their vulnerability to a few privateers with torches by recalling in the almanac columns for September the great fire of 1666: "On the 2d of this month, *Anno* 1666, began the fire of London, which reduc'd to ashes 13,200 houses and 89 churches: Near ten times as much building as Philadelphia!"

The purpose of such direct and indirect incitements to "true heroism," however, is not to summon a great deliverer to Philadelphia's aid. The almanac pages for April 1748 contrast Oliver and Richard Cromwell in such a way that the drift of *Poor Richard's* sympathies is clearly in the direction of the more "peaceable" Richard Cromwell over the formidable conqueror and protector. Unlike his father, Richard "soon descended" from public prominence and "became a private man, living, unmolested, to a good old age; for he died not till about the latter end of queen Anne's reign, at his lodgings in Lombard-street, where he had lived many years unknown, and seen great changes in government, and violent struggles for that, which, by experience, he knew could afford no solid happiness" (*Papers,* 3:252).

The almanac returns to the subject of the Great Rebellion in its November pages, where Franklin uses the anniversary of the beginning of the Long Parliament to chastise the spirit of "party" in general as "the madness of many, for the gain of a few." This is precisely the sort of lesson with which Franklin associates Richard Cromwell's philosophic retirement. In the almanac's general skepticism concerning the nature of merely military accomplishments, it anticipates the most eloquent of the Quaker replies to *Plain Truth.* Samuel Smith's pamphlet, *Necessary Truth,* takes Franklin to task for showing an undue reliance upon "arms and ammunition" in securing the community's peace. Indeed, Smith argues, military vanity was probably the original source of the fatal complacency of Laish. In the end, the pomp of a militia such as the one *Plain Truth* advocates resembles its drums: "they make a great Noise," Smith observes, "but look into them and behold *what is there!"*[14]

The 1748 almanac's admiration for the peaceful example of Richard Cromwell suggests the extent of Franklin's attraction to the appeal of the kind of Quaker idealism that Smith represents. The calendar for March 1748 includes James Thomson's verses on Isaac Newton, glorifying the philosophic hero over the military triumphs of "old Greece and Rome," while poetic epigraphs to the months of February, May, June, July, and August celebrate the virtues of a simple, private life, which is closely associated with the almanac's emerging portrait of female character as a counterweight to the destructive example of the conventional "Hero."

A degree of public militance is the price for private security, in Franklin's view. Or, as James Logan observes in a letter to Franklin encouraging the activities of the Association, government without arms is a contradiction (*Papers,* 3:219). But Franklin's dilemma is in some respects as acute as that of the pacifist Quakers in the Pennsylvania Assembly. To be effective, the measures that the public takes in its own defense must be vigorous and, ideally at least, unified. The largest possible proportion of the community must participate in the collective military response, but the result must not produce the same imperial cult of heroes and kings against which the colonies were in effect defending themselves.

In this respect at least, Pennsylvania was indeed repeating the experience of late republican Rome, in which Caesar, Catiline, Pompey, and Crassus competed over a period of years to assume the role of "Deliverer," which Cicero and Cato recognized as fatal to the city's republican tradition. Deliverers have a historic tendency to become destroyers, as the 1748 almanac points out in June when it commemorates the Russians' 1709 defeat of Charles XII of Sweden, a man who "had a great mind to be a *Hero*" but whose ambitions "brought his own country to the brink of ruin."[15] The *Form of Association,* which Franklin drafted shortly after the publication of *Plain Truth,* is careful to provide for the annual election and the rotation of military "offices" (not "ranks") in order to reduce the fear of military oppression and to emulate the virtue of the "Old Romans"—not their imperial successors—in their willingness "to serve as private soldiers, where they had been formerly Generals" (*Papers,* 3:209).

The 1748 almanac contributes to the efforts of the *Form of Association* by glorifying domestic heroism over the achievements of the citizen-soldier. The months of August, September, and October begin with verse epigraphs celebrating the managing and healing skills of women. The June epigraph coyly hints that it would disclose, at long last, the chief female "Charm," which proves to be virtue:

This Men and Angels prize,
Above the finest Shape and brightest Eyes.

The ladies of the French court, Poor Richard claims, volunteer their services in hospitals:

T' attend the Crouds that hopeless Pangs endure,
And soothe the Anguish which they cannot cure;
To clothe the Bare, and give the Empty Food;
As bright as Guardian Angels, and as good.

But more affecting than this angelic condescension of noblewomen is the example that the almanac presents in its last pages of the middling wives of Wansburg in Bavaria, whose city is beseiged by the German emperor. The emperor consents to a petition from these women to leave their homes "only with so much as they could carry on their backs." When the women emerge from the town, each carrying her husband, the emperor is moved to tears, pardons the men, and extols their wives "with deserved praises" (*Papers,* 3:262).

Richard and Bridget Saunders apparently disagree over whether the Wansburg story more honors the wives or the husbands, but Franklin's point is that it clearly prizes the bond of marital comradeship over that of the camp and the battlefield. The women of Wansburg emulate Aeneas's flight from a burning Troy with the aged Anchises on his shoulders. This is the sort of heroism, the almanac implies, upon which great cities may be built. It could not have hurt Franklin's cause with his audience that this last instance of self-sacrificing virtue in the 1748 almanac reaches out to the large German population of Pennsylvania.

In part 3 of the *Autobiography*, written more than forty years after the events of 1747 and 1748, Franklin recalls that he refused a high commission in the Association militia because he thought himself unfit for military command. Instead, he drafted mottoes and insignia for the city's women to sew onto flags and banners for the various Association companies. Later, he served a "Turn of Duty" as a common soldier on watch at the city's battery. This retrospective claim of unfitness corresponds quite closely to the Old Roman virtue of service in humble offices as well as in glorious ones that Franklin identifies at the time as an inspiration for the *Form of Association*. Though the gesture seems on the surface to be self-effacing, Franklin is in fact modeling what he hopes will become the practice of republican Pennsylvania, or republican America, in its efforts to avert the grim fate of republican Rome.

Some pages later, when Franklin is discussing Edward Braddock's 1755 expedition to Fort Duquesne, he deliberately omits any mention of George Washington, whose poise and courage during the chaos of the British retreat saved the expedition from even greater disasters and brought Washington to prominence as a potential colonial military leader.[16] The omission would have seemed particularly glaring to Franklin's colleagues and contemporaries in 1788, who had just drafted the Constitution under Washington's presiding eye and who were determined that only George Washington could serve as the first president under the new form of government. But where Franklin seems deficient as a historian, he is consistent as an advocate of the collective civic virtues over individualistic military ones. The people are inevitably least secure when they conceive themselves to be dependent upon the singular exertions of their deliverers.

In Washington's place, the *Autobiography* offers Franklin himself, not as the moving spirit behind Pennsylvania's irregular militia but as an informal quartermaster to Braddock's small army. In 1755, the Pennsylvania Assembly sent Franklin to the British encampment at Frederick, Maryland, ostensibly in his capacity as postmaster but actually as an envoy to try to remove the "violent Prejudices" against their government that they feared Braddock had acquired. Franklin is successful in the mission and concludes his visit by offering to serve as Braddock's intermediary in securing badly needed transport wagons from the civilian population of Pennsylvania. He reprints in the *Autobiography*, as a "Piece of some Curiosity," the lengthy "Advertisement" he employed to secure those wagons. It is by far the longest extract from his papers incorporated into his memoir and the only one of his previously published writings that he indicates any previous intention of including in the *Autobiography*, an especially curious fact since Franklin claims to have lost many of his personal papers in the war.

However suspicious the survival of this ephemeral advertisement may seem, Franklin uses it to dramatize his paradoxical role as both a benevolent "Well-wisher" of peaceful citizenry and an agent of Braddock's troops, who are fully prepared to seize what the people of Lancaster, York, and Cumberland counties do not voluntarily provide. In his supplement to the terms by which Braddock proposes to engage wagons, teams, and drivers, Franklin identifies his readers by the sonorous names of their counties, evoking great English ducal houses whose titled representatives distinguished themselves in their country's military history. "Friends and Countrymen," Franklin begins, not unwilling to echo Mark Antony's address to the Roman people in Shakespeare's *Julius Caesar*, provided he is permitted to cast Braddock alone in the role of military adventurer and potential tyrant, while he adopts a much more pacific or avuncular tone. Braddock's agents are the officers and troops who might easily seize the supplies that the expedition needs. Franklin's sole representative to this audience of embattled farmers, other than his words, is his son.

The appeal that the 1755 "Advertisement" makes is addressed to the enlightened self-interest of this audience. The liberties of Pennsylvania are directly threatened not only by the French garrison at Fort Duquesne but also by the British deliverer sent to dislodge them, with two regiments of regular troops and a reputation for violent prejudices. Franklin's address deliberately minimizes or distorts Braddock's temperamental reputation in a manner that must have struck many of his readers at the time as at best whimsical and at worst mocking. The general and his officers are, in Franklin's words, "extremely exasperated" at the lack of horses and wagons in Maryland and northern Virginia, through which their march had taken them. "It was proposed" to resort immediately to confiscation and armed compulsion. The mild-mannered Franklin, however, being "occasionally at the Camp," concludes that "many and great Inconveniences to the Inhabitants" might result from such an expedient and expresses his determination to take the "Trouble of trying first what might be done by fair and equitable Means" (*Writings,* 1437).

Franklin does not account for his evident success at postponing Braddock's crude measures for fourteen days, but the implication is that he soothed the general's pique as one might the tantrums of an angry child. Though Braddock's mission is indeed in the larger interests of colonial security, it is Franklin himself who is "fair and equitable" at the same time that he is alert to commercial opportunity. The expedition's expenses may be the means of increasing the colony's money supply by "upwards of Thirty thousand Pounds . . . in Silver and Gold of the King's money," provided that the citizens of Pennsylvania have the sense to accept the general's terms for hiring civilian auxiliaries. Individuals might pool their resources and divide the king's pay among themselves, as they see fit. Military service is hazardous, Franklin acknowledges, but the baggage train is generally well secured because it is in the army's interest to do so, just as it is in the interests of the larger empire to keep its colonies secure from the military threats of their neighbors.

Moreover, Franklin observes, "your Loyalty will be strongly suspected" if you fail to contribute to "the King's Business . . . what may be reasonably expected from you" (*Writings,* 1438). Loyalty obtained by such generous dispersals of gold and silver, however, is suspect to begin with. "So many brave Troops, come so far for your Defense, must not stand idle," Franklin scolds his readers, but the admonition—like so much of Franklin's writing in these volatile years—has a complex rhetorical life that its superficially parental tone just barely conceals. So many brave troops have, apparently, already come quite far on an errand of dubious urgency to a community whose sense of peril is markedly less acute than that of their deliverers. "I have no particular Interest in this Affair," Franklin concludes, beyond the desire "to do Good and prevent Mischief," but if the necessity for Braddock's presence in America was indeed pressing, surely Franklin's interests too would be involved. As he argues in *Plain Truth* seven years earlier, in the face of a similar military predicament, "When the Feet are wounded, shall the Head say, *It is not me* . . . Or if the Head is in Danger, shall the Hands say, *We are not affected, and therefore will lend no Assistance*" (*Papers,* 3:195).

Instead of such appeals to Pauline rhetoric on behalf of the civil body, Franklin's 1755 "Advertisement" seeks to minimize both the immediate peril of the colony and the damage that Braddock might inflict through Sir John St. Clair's predatory hussars, whom the general shortly proposes to send on a foraging expedition into southern Pennsylvania. More than "mischief" would be involved in such an incursion; more direct interests than furthering "the King's business" tie the farmers of western Pennsylvania, as well as the citizens of Philadelphia, to the orderly execution and successful outcome of Braddock's march.

The emphasis of Franklin's address, however, is on the ephemeral impact that Braddock's presence—or that of any deliverer from distant lands—is likely to make on colonial life. This immediate military service will be light, easy, and brief, Franklin assures his fellow citizens, and in the end you will have increased your circulating currency. But the deeper implication of Franklin's carefully weighted prose is that no thoughtful colonial reader must expect to resolve the dilemma posed by the competition among European and Native American interests through triumphal military display. The true avenue to coexistence and increase in the western regions of North America would require a union much more extensive and durable than the 120-day partnerships among a few farmers that the advertisement seeks. Franklin outlined and defended his conception of just such a union in the months preceding Braddock's arrival in America.

In 1754 the British Board of Trade requested Governor De Lancey of New York to convene at Albany a "congress" of commissioners from all the colonies for the purpose of renewing good relations between the Iroquois Confederation and English colonial governments. The commissioners did meet with delegations from the Iroquois tribes through late June and early July of that year, but at the instigation largely of Franklin and a handful of other representatives, the congress also decided to exceed its mandate and offer a long-term proposal for addressing the problems of future colonial growth and security. The Plan of Union that emerged from these deliberations in early July 1754 was based upon Franklin's draft and was sustained by the arguments Franklin made in its behalf and recorded for Thomas Pownall's use when Pownall, an agent of the British government, submitted the document to Lord Halifax and the Board of Trade for approval.[17]

Neither the Board of Trade nor the various colonial assemblies accepted the Albany proposals. Indeed, the Pennsylvania Assembly (in Franklin's absence) rejected the plan barely a month after the congress adjourned. By December 1754, when Franklin was still arguing over the necessity and the terms of an equitable colonial union with Governor Shirley of Massachusetts, Braddock's troops had already embarked for Virginia. By the spring of 1755, when Franklin made his pacific visit to

Braddock's Maryland camp, events as well as the reluctance of the parties had eliminated any hope that the work of the Albany congress could be salvaged.

Some of the studied detachment with which Franklin proposed to mediate between Braddock and the citizens of Pennsylvania might well derive from Franklin's impatience with this failure of the colonial legislatures to endorse his earlier efforts on behalf of their security. In his 1754 discussion of one of the Albany Plan's proposals, he had in fact forecast with considerable accuracy Braddock's later difficulties in securing wagons and teams to aid in his campaign. Military officers for service in the colonies, Franklin argued at the Albany congress, should be nominated by the president general of the proposed union but subject to the "approbation" of the Grand Council of colonial representatives. Americans would serve willingly in the kind of brief campaign projected by Braddock only "under officers they know," whose integrity they trusted, and "for whom they had an esteem and affection" (*Papers*, 5:415). Military appointments that reflected only royal prerogative or partisan interest would prove to be "very prejudicial to the service." Had the Albany Plan been accepted with this provision in place, the predicament of Braddock's regulars one year later might never have arisen and their suicidal march, under a leader so ill equipped to conduct it, might never have taken place.

The sensible management of military commissions, however, was a subordinate element of the Albany Plan. The primary purpose of Franklin's proposed design—and of the final version of the plan adopted by the Albany Congress—was to manage colonial growth in such a way that the occasion for military conflict would not occur in the first place. If the colonies would pool their strength in this permanent institutional fashion, Franklin reasoned, they would be sufficiently formidable to deter attacks before they were mounted. If the colonies would agree to delegate to a single authority the power of negotiating with the Indian tribes on all issues of territory, trade, war, and peace, then quarrels or misunderstandings arising from intercolonial competition, the venality of traders, or the greed of private parties seeking to purchase new land could all be controlled or eliminated (*Papers*, 5:410). New settlements in the west could be quickly and equitably established, by the collective efforts of the eastern colonies, to serve as barriers to French expansion and as a line of defense against possible Indian attack. The united colonies would bear the costs of constructing frontier forts or maintaining small warships to protect commerce. Once the new western settlements had grown sufficiently popu-

The *Pennsylvania Gazette* of May 9, 1754, illustrated an account of recent border hostilities with the French with this cartoon, attributed to Franklin and closely associated with the arguments he would shortly advance for a larger colonial union at the Albany Congress later that summer. Exactly three years earlier, on May 9, 1751, Franklin had printed in the *Gazette* his proposal to return rattlesnakes to England in return for shiploads of transported felons, despite the fact that the more honorable rattlesnake (unlike English criminals) "gives Warning before he attempts his Mischief." This figurative association, along with the biblical emblem of the brazen Serpent in the Wilderness from Numbers 21.8–9 and John 3.14, may have shaped Franklin's choice of images.

lous, the president general and Grand Council of the United Colonies would assist them in forming "compleat and distinct governments" and in joining the union (*Papers,* 5:411–12).

Franklin's object in urging the Albany Congress to make its ambitious proposal was not primarily defense but growth, managed in such a way as to preserve good relations with the Indian tribes and to prevent "monopolies of vast tracts" of land falling under the control of "particular persons" (*Papers,* 5:411). Small land grants to actual settlers, Franklin believed, would develop the frontier population more rapidly and generate more revenue from quitrents to help meet the expenses of the general government. In support of this vision of colonial expansion sustained largely by small farmers, Franklin devotes his 1755 almanac to a series of pastoral celebrations of bucolic virtue: the "happy Swain" who "Far from the venal

World can live secure, / Be moral, honest, virtuous–tho' but Poor"
(*Papers,* 5:469). The monthly epigraphs in *Poor Richard* for 1755 are all
drawn from a single poem that glorifies the figure of the farmer, in Shaftesburean terms, as a meditative natural philosopher who learns "Beneath
the Covert of embow'ring Shades" to pity the futile grandeur of kings.

In Franklin's practical vision for a general colonial government, however, the king is somewhat more useful than these disparaging lines imply.
The framers of the Albany Plan agreed that the union could come into
being only through an act of Parliament. In effect, the king would help
neutralize colonial jealousies by imposing upon them a union in which
the chief executive officer would be a royal appointee. The broad nature
of the union would be another check upon local jealousy, since the selfish
rivalries of separate colonial governments would be (as Franklin puts it)
"swallowed up in the general union" (*Papers,* 5:401). Moreover, the necessity for "frequent meetings-together of commissioners or representatives
from all the colonies" to conduct the business of the general union would
gradually educate the colonies in their common interests. They would, in
his view, "learn to consider themselves, not as so many independent
states, but as members of the same body," bound together by ties of cordiality as well as policy.

Royal prerogative would mingle, in the Albany Plan, with colonial self-
determination. The interests of large colonies would combine equitably
with those of smaller ones in the scheme of proportional representation
that the plan envisioned. Taxes would, in principle, strive to discourage
luxury and encourage industry. Small landholders, and not great land-
lords, would be the intended result of a westward growth that sought to
make a fair accommodation with Indian owners. In every feature of its
compound design and idealistic purposes, the Albany Plan reflects Franklin's personal fusion of the workable with the visionary. Indeed, the plan
failed to secure the support of the colonial assemblies in large part because
of the reluctance of individual colonies to surrender their local prejudices
and "selfish views" to the restraints imposed by a general union built upon
a conception of the general well-being. It was not that the plan favored
the king that made it unappealing; it was the proposed creation of a totally new authority derived from the collective interest that sealed its fate
with colonial legislators.[18]

Franklin hoped that, in time, practical experience in accommodating
the particular and the local to the general good might eventually swallow
up differences. At the very least, the different colonies might fall into

habits of collective cordiality that would make mutually beneficial policies easier to effect. The plan, in other words, was instrumental to the formation of a collective character, much as Franklin's private ethical and religious discipline had been. Its larger end was the substitution of constructive social habits for destructive ones. Cordiality would restrain suspicious self-interest; the amiable excellences would supersede private partiality on a scale much greater than the Junto, the Philosophical Society, or Franklin's didactic journalism ever realized. Meetings of the colonial congress, in time, might even come to resemble Franklin's vision of an uncommon union of virtuous representatives, disciplined in their obedience to uncommon laws.

This close identification between the Albany Plan and Franklin's redemptive idealism made the plan's ultimate rejection especially frustrating to him. He suggests late in his life that the adoption of the recommendations of the Albany congress might well have prevented or postponed the American Revolution (*Papers*, 5:417). Even at the time, however, he points directly to the issues that would ultimately lead to war between Great Britain and America and ties them to the financial implications of rejecting the Albany Plan. In two extensive letters to William Shirley written in December 1754, Franklin seeks to argue before the British Board of Trade that only the colonies could tax their citizens directly and that they already enriched the "home" island through a host of indirect taxes, through the incentives they offered to the growth of English shipping, and through the variety of their produce and the numbers of their inhabitants:

> Could the Goodwin Sands be laid dry by banks, and land equal to a large country thereby gain'd to England, and presently filled with English Inhabitants, would it be right to deprive such Inhabitants of the common privileges enjoyed by other Englishmen . . . . Would this be right, even if the land were gained at the expense of the state? And would it not seem less right, if the charge and labour of gaining the additional territory to Britain had been borne by the settlers themselves? . . . In fine, why should the countenance of a state be *partially* afforded to its people, unless it be most in favour of those, who have most merit? and if there be any difference, those, who have most contributed to enlarge Britain's empire and commerce, encrease her strength, her wealth, and the numbers of her people, at the risque of their own lives and private fortunes in new and strange countries, methinks ought rather to expect some preference. (*Papers*, 5:450–51)

The analysis of the implications of colonial growth that Franklin offered barely three years earlier in "Observations Concerning the Increase of Mankind" take on, in this complaint to Shirley, the first signs of the adversarial posture of revolution.

Franklin's personal response to the failure of the colonies to embrace the Albany Plan is much more chastened. A year after Braddock's defeat, as he prepares the text of *Poor Richard Improved* for 1757, he looks back over his entire colonial career in a reflective mood, returning to the lessons he had learned and tested over thirty years of experience in the management of human nature. In the context of the time, this retrospective self-examination seems intended as a means both of acknowledging the recent frustration of Franklin's hopes for colonial union and of confirming the spiritual ends and the tactical means that would guide him in the diplomatic career he was about to begin.[19]

The verse epigraphs for each of the months in 1757 are taken from Benjamin Stillingfleet's *An Essay on Conversation* (1737), a typical didactic meditation of the day, instructing the reader on the importance of good nature, humility, and sincerity in the conduct of social relations. The lines amount to a versification of Franklin's principles of spiritual self-government from the 1728 "Articles of Belief" or the youthful project for achieving moral perfection:

> Would you both please, and be instructed too,
> The Pride of shewing forth yourself subdue.
> Hear ev'ry Man upon his fav'rite Theme,
> And ever be more knowing than you seem.
> The lowest Genius will afford some Light,
> Or give a Hint that had escap'd your Sight.
> Doubt, till he thinks you on Conviction yield,
> And with fit Questions let each Pause be fill'd.
> And the most knowing will with Pleasure grant,
> You're rather much reserv'd than ignorant.
> (*Papers*, 7:77–78)

In the ethical vision that Franklin and Stillingfleet share, pride's favorite themes are incidental to the general human pleasure of being heard. The tactics of personal advancement diminish in significance in the face of the rewards of a mutual pleasure to which the lowest as well as the most knowing may contribute.[20] Poor Richard's 1757 aphorisms extend the atmosphere of self-assessment that the epigraphs invoke but at the same time compress their Augustan couplets into the facetious epigrams of a coffeehouse wit. They resemble in many respects the best sayings from earlier almanacs in their subversive brevity: "He that would rise at Court, must begin by Creeping"; "Men take more pains to mask than mend." The effect is much as if Franklin seeks within the format of this late almanac to evoke the competing voices of his youth, deflating the Shaftesburean resonance of Stillingfleet's lines with the reductive vigor of Mandeville's acerbic intelligence.

At the same time, Franklin incorporates into the text of the 1757 almanac two lengthy passages from *A Collection of Select Aphorisms* by Charles Palmer, which he modifies in ways that enrich their application to his mature convictions. The most openly retrospective of these passages is the first, printed in the almanac's pages for January, with an allusion to Matthew 25—which Franklin adds. The Parable of the Talents is the biblical source he invokes all his life in defense of his personal faith in a religion of works. It is to Matthew 25 that Franklin appeals in the 1738 letter to his parents defending his religious integrity and assuring them that, in the midst of his opposition to the Presbyterian Synod, he has not abandoned a genuinely "vital" faith. The close identification that Franklin feels with this portion of the New Testament suggests that the aphorism to which he adds it has a particular significance to his own evaluation of the recent past:

> When a Man looks back upon his day, Week or Year spent, and finds his Business has been worthy the Dignity of human Nature, it exhilerates and revives him, enables him to pass his own Approbation on himself, and, as it were, to anticipate the *Euge,* the *Well done, good and faithful Servant,* he shall one Day receive from his great Master. But he that gives himself only the idle Divertisements of a Child, cannot reflect on Time past without Confusion; and is forced to take Sanctuary in a total Inconsideration, or run from one Amusement to another, to avoid Thinking, or answering to himself the Question, *What have I done?* Idleness, and its Amusements are in the End more tiresome than Labour itself. (*Papers, 7:77*)

Franklin's sense of restored purpose is implicit in the conviction that even abortive labor, like that represented by the deliberations of the Albany Congress, is not fruitless as long as it is consistent with the dignity of human nature.

A second aphorism from Palmer's collection that Franklin reprints, again with his own variations, emphasizes the duty (and the utility) of submission to the will of God, but after this second passage Franklin appears to have adopted the model but not the actual language of Palmer's collection. The moral instruction in the 1757 almanac is largely contained in six substantial paragraphs for which no source has been found. They may well be Franklin's own work, drawing heavily on his reading, and they form a collective portrait of his moral nature that could not be more different from Father Abraham's celebrated performance of the following year. These meditative paragraphs remind the reader that jests can be destructive of friendship; that selfish ambition is "the secret Maker of most Mischiefs" in human life, while an ambition to serve others is quiet, orderly, and resigned; that man's individual powers of accomplishment are limited, whereas his powers of action in society are great.[21] Franklin is reasserting in the pages of this next-to-last almanac the vital intersection between private piety and public works that guided his entire life.

As if to invest this affirmation of joint secular and sacred purposes with an apocalyptic significance, Franklin closes *Poor Richard* for 1757 with an account of the anticipated appearance of Halley's comet sometime between July of that year and October 1758. The vast orbit of the comet, and the peculiarly "unequal" nature of its "Periods," made the precise time of its reappearance difficult to fix. "As these huge tremendous Bodies travel thro' our System," Franklin observes, "they seem fitted to produce great Changes in it" (*Papers*, 7:90). Indeed, William Whiston believes he could associate the biblical Deluge with an earlier, catastrophic visitation of the comet of 1668. Noting the size, the properties, and the proximity of some celebrated comets in the past, Franklin concurs that a comet may one day be the chosen vehicle for the fulfillment of biblical revelation: "Should a Comet in its Course strike the Earth, it might instantly beat it to Pieces, or carry it off out of the Planetary System. The great Conflagration may also, by Means of a Comet, be easily brought about; for as some of them are supposed to be much bigger than this Globe we live on, if one should meet with us in its Return from the Sun, all the Disputes between the Powers of Europe would be settled in a Moment; the World, to such a Fire, being no more than a Wasp's Nest thrown into an Oven" (*Papers*, 7:91).

Perhaps unintentionally, at this climactic moment in his career, Franklin transforms Bernard Mandeville's grumbling hive of human vice and human empire into the brittle paper architecture of a wasp's nest, instantly consumed in a judgmental fire.[22] But it is a vision that he immediately tempers with some lines from Pope's *Essay on Man* describing the "equal

Eye" of God calmly viewing universal ruin. "There are an infinite Number of Worlds under the divine Government," Franklin warns his reader. "We must not presume too much upon our own Importance."

Disputatious human powers, European or colonial, cannot hope to build a community that can survive such a decisive and inevitable catastrophe. Franklin's title for these celestial reflections at the close of his almanac, "Of the expected Comet," is meant to be ominous as well as informative. The refuge he offers is not in the frame of physical nature but in the ethical conduct of life:

> At the Day of Judgment, we shall not be asked, what Proficiency we have made in Languages or Philosophy; but whether we have liv'd virtuously and piously as Men endued with Reason, guided by the Dictates of Religion. In that Hour it will more avail us, that we have thrown a Handful of Flour or Chaff in Charity to a Nest of contemptible Pismires, than that we could muster all the Hosts of Heaven, and call every Star by its proper Name. For then the Constellations themselves shall disappear, the Sun and Moon shall give no more Light, and all the Frame of Nature shall vanish. But our good or bad Works shall remain forever, recorded in the Archives of Eternity.

As he did in his earliest, enthusiastic responses to Shaftesbury, Milton, Addison, and Thomson, Franklin, on the threshold of his second ocean voyage, turns once again to the language of the moral sublime.

CONCLUSION

Late in January 1757—the month that Poor Richard cautions his reader on the necessity of creeping at court—Franklin was appointed to represent the Pennsylvania Assembly in London "to solicit the removal of our Grievances" in the Assembly's long-standing quarrel with the Penns (*Papers,* 7:110). The language of the Assembly resolution is at once an assertive and a wistful request that its agent "go Home to England." Franklin considered some time before formally accepting the commission, but within two days of the Assembly's action he wrote his old friend William Strahan (whom Franklin had never actually seen) cautioning him to "look out sharp" for the unexpected arrival of "a fat old fellow" in search of a little "Smouting" work at Strahan's printing house. The impending journey had a personal significance to Franklin that went far beyond its public occasion and the Assembly's formulaic nostalgia for "home."

He would be able to greet in person old correspondents like Strahan and Peter Collinson, who had for decades been Franklin's intellectual agents and friends in the English capital. James Ralph was still active as a political journalist and historian. He and Franklin would be able to reminisce over the events of their first months in the city thirty-three years earlier and to measure the visible changes that time had made in each of them. Hans Sloane was dead, but the old bookseller, John Wilcox, was still alive, and the bookstores of Little Britain would again be available to answer Franklin's undiminished appetite for reading. Pope and Thomson were dead, but Johnson and Young still represented the living traditions of literary taste that Franklin had frequently incorporated into the pages of the almanac. The appealing prospect of living the rest of his life abroad—as well as the uncertainties of an Atlantic voyage—clearly influenced Franklin in the preparations that he made for his embarkation in early June.

Sometime in these first months of 1757, Franklin wrote the epitaph and commissioned the monument for his parents' grave in Boston, celebrating their personal qualities as well as the general principles of human union, virtue, and increase that had come to play such an influential role in Franklin's mature political and religious convictions. These two people—of decidedly middling status in life, with no estate, and without a lucrative trade—were the progenitors of thirteen children and seven grandchildren, the epitaph declared, raised comfortably and reputably "By *constant Labour*, and *honest Industry*." "Be encouraged to Diligence in thy Calling," Franklin advises the reader of the epitaph, paraphrasing one of his father's favorite proverbs, "And distrust not Providence" (*Papers*, 7:230).

Human trust, however, even in combination with a long and virtuous life does not constrain the disinterested esteem of Franklin's God. The apparently simple details of the epitaph suggest the mixed nature of experience: fulfillment and frustration, increase and diminishment are all part of the story. How is it that these thirteen reputable children dwindled to seven in the third generation? Why were two aging grandparents so closely involved in the rearing of their grandchildren? Why does it fall to the duty and "filial Regard" of the youngest son to place their stone? A degree of resignation consistent with the implications of this complex family narrative is captured in Franklin's closing admonishment to "distrust not Providence." Piety and prudence, virtue and discretion—the traits of character the epitaph associates with Josiah and Abiah Franklin—are marks of human reserve as much as human confidence, testaments of a faith that does not presume too much.

Indeed, in key respects the epitaph that Franklin wrote for his parents echoes the stark contingencies with which Samuel Johnson closes "The Vanity of Human Wishes" (1749), a poem that appeared in the pages of Franklin's almanac almost as soon as it was published in London:

Enquirer, cease, petitions yet remain,
Which heav'n may hear, nor deem religion vain.
Still raise for good the supplicating voice,
But leave to heav'n the measure and the choice

. . . .

Pour forth thy fervours for a healthful mind,
Obedient passions, and a will resign'd;
For love, which scarce collective man can fill;
For patience sov'reign o'er transmuted ill;
For faith, that panting for a happier seat,
Counts death kind Nature's signal of retreat:
These goods for man the laws of heav'n ordain,
These goods he grants, who grants the pow'r to gain'
With these celestial wisdom calms the mind,
And makes the happiness she does not find.

Franklin's personal sense of the distribution of Heaven's "goods," however, led him to a degree of trust in providence that Johnson's anguished experience, finally, could not grant. In the closing passages of the "Last Will and Testament" which he revised during the spring of 1757, Franklin itemizes the elements of his good fortune: financial "competency," moderate passions, long residence "in a Land of Liberty, with a People that I love," good friends, "a loving and prudent Wife and dutiful Children" (*Papers,* 7:205). Such benefits had prepared him to accept death "chearfully," the will concludes,"reposing my self securely in the Lap of God and Nature, as a child in the Arms of an affectionate Parent."

These are the elements of a transcendental confidence in moral design that would mark the sensibilities of many of Franklin's successors who, like him, were shaped by Francis Hutcheson's ethical and religious vision. Like the optative mood of Ralph Waldo Emerson a century later, however, Franklin's spiritual resources would be tested by the unfolding confusions of a war that his private loyalties and affections would immediately recognize as an acutely "civil" conflict, waged within the boundaries of a common culture and a common history.

Sometime, too, in these first months of 1757 Franklin collected his old almanacs and began culling from them the material for the 1758 preface, the aphorisms that he would use to assemble Father Abraham's speech. The final text was dated in early July, when Franklin was again at sea—the birthplace of Silence Dogood and the scene of his youthful voyage journal, which holds the first indications of his lifelong plan of conduct. Father Abraham's speech—which was not entitled "The Way to Wealth" until 1773—has so effectively eclipsed the almanac in which it appears that few students of Franklin have troubled to read the unattributed poem

"On Ambition," which forms the verse epigraphs for the months of Franklin's last issue of *Poor Richard.*

Like the prose meditations in the almanac from the previous year, "On Ambition" is a retrospective summary of the moral lessons of life, delivered in the voice of a wise preceptor addressing a "young Friend." The fiction is similar in structure to Father Abraham's vernacular address, but its poetic form and its high seriousness call attention to its origins in less democratic literary appetites. The struggle with individual passions, Franklin's speaker notes, is in some respects analogous to the political struggle in which Pennsylvania's emissary will shortly be embroiled: "In Passion's Strife, no Medium you can have; / You rule a Master, or submit a Slave." If the choices were not quite so stark in Anglo-American politics, at least for the time being, it was primarily because people in society could seek support and assistance, in the pursuit of virtue, from friends. Many of the lines from "On Ambition" suggest Franklin's fond reminiscences of the Junto, the affectionate circle for whom he thanked his Maker in his will:

> Be yours, my Son, a nobler, higher Aim,
> Your Pride to burn with Friendship's sacred Flame;
> By Virtue kindled, by like Manners fed,
> By mutual Wishes, mutual Favours spread,
> Increas'd with Years, by candid Truth refin'd,
> Pour all its boundless Ardours thro' your Mind.
> Be yours the Care a chosen Band to gain;
> With them to Glory's radiant Summit strain,
> Aiding and aided each, while all contend,
> Who best, who bravest, shall assist his Friend.
> (*Papers,* 7:353)

"Pour forth thy fervours for a healthful mind," Johnson counsels in his great poem; in Franklin's suggestive revision, the mind is its own restorative agent through the "boundless Ardours" of friendship. If these lines look back to the chosen band of Franklin's youth—the young moralists with whom he undertook a competition to versify the Eighteenth Psalm as well as those who joined him in the disinterested pursuit of truth to which the Junto members pledged themselves—then the final lines of "On Ambition" extend these personal reflections on Franklin's past to his personal hopes for the future of the Anglo-American community.

A just ambition, the poetic speaker argues, fills the mind with charity toward all the inhabitants of the "common Earth," defeats the designs of envy and the "Knave-led, one-eyed Monster, Party Rage":

> Ambition jostles with her Friends no more;
> Nor thirsts Revenge to drink a Brother's Gore;
> Fiery Remorse no stinging Scorpions rears:
> O'er trembling Guilt no falling Sword appears.
> Hence Conscience, void of Blame, her Front erects,
> Her God she fears, all other Fear rejects.
> Hence just Ambition boundless Splendors crown,
> And hence she calls Eternity her own.

This calm repudiation of civil violence in favor of a prospect of boundless splendors is the immaterial wealth to which Franklin's final almanac points the way.

LIBRARIES, CATALOGS, AND BOOKLISTS

The "Republic of Letters," to the imagination of the late seventeenth and early eighteenth centuries, was both a disorderly and an exhilarating place—a setting for Swift's *Battle of the Books* and for Saavedra Fajardo's satiric dream visions as well as an indispensable repository of past wisdom. Reconstructing the physical form of this metaphysical republic, as Franklin knew it, in eighteenth-century libraries, bookstores, and periodicals was the lifework of Edwin Wolfe, beginning with "The Reconstruction of Benjamin Franklin's Library," through Wolfe's liberally annotated review of the subject, "Franklin's Library."[1]

Wolfe reports that the appraisers of Franklin's estate found 4,276 volumes in his library at his death, the titles of which their duties did not require them to record. During forty years of study, Wolfe was able to locate evidence of Franklin's ownership of 3,700 titles and to trace the locations of many books dispersed through gift or sale. But Wolfe's invaluable work does not give a clear, selective account of the range of Franklin's access to books in his earliest years, before the long residences in England and France, when he was able to add numerous titles to his personal collection.

In particular, it would be helpful if we could recover a detailed description of the library of Matthew Adams, the Boston tradesman who allowed Franklin access to his "pretty" collection of books, or a complete sale catalogue of John Wilcox's inventory from his secondhand bookshop in Little Britain, which Franklin made use of as a lending library for nearly a year in London when he lodged next door to Wilcox's shop. No record of Adams' collection has survived, however, and Wilcox was not as active as some of his contemporaries in printing sale catalogues. The British Museum lists a 1725 catalogue advertisement for a special library sale to be held by "J. Wilcox at Davis's Coffee-house," but library sales were special occasions, often conducted as auctions at public gathering places like coffeehouses and do not necessarily reflect the contents of a shop inventory.

Franklin did leave a reasonably detailed list of books that he offered for sale during his business years in Philadelphia. This inventory takes the form of purchasing orders scattered through his correspondence and occasional sale advertisements in the *Pennsylvania Gazette,* particularly the extensive booklist from the *Gazette* for May 25, 1738 (*Papers,* 2:211), supplemented by a large sale catalogue that Franklin printed in 1744, probably in anticipation of reducing his stock in preparation for turning over his business to David Hall. A selection from these titles indicates, to some degree, both what Franklin thought would sell and what he thought worth selling.

The most revealing record of Franklin's intellectual tastes during the first forty years of his life can be compiled from several sources, beginning with his direct testimony concerning his reading in these years. The *Autobiography* provides a familiar list of titles with which to begin—Bunyan's *Pilgrim's Progress,* Mather's *Bonifacius,* Shaftesbury's *Characteristics,* Defoe's *Essay on Projects,* Young's verse satires on fame—to which the early papers and correspondence make it possible to add other books and writers: James Thomson's poetry, Thomas à Kempis's *Imitatio Christi,* Jonathan Edwards' *Some Thoughts Concerning the Revival of Religion,* Trenchard and Gordon's *Cato's Letters,* Milton's *Paradise Lost,* William Petty's economic treatises. The almanacs confirm Franklin's early familiarity with the poetry of Herbert, Waller, Cowley, Pope, Swift, and Johnson, as well as his reading of less familiar contemporary poets: Richard Blackmore, Benjamin Stillingfleet, James Burgh, Moses Brown, Richard Savage.

In 1741, Franklin printed *A Catalogue of Books belonging to the Library Company of Philadelphia,* providing a complete account of a large collection that Franklin played a significant role in developing through the first ten years of its existence. In some instances, the 1741 *Catalogue* provides fairly complete bibliographic information; in other instances, it lists only titles, often informally condensed from the conventionally elaborate full titles of the time. The entries sometimes indicate individual book donors by name and informally indicate Franklin's own donations to the collection with his initials, a practice that suggests that Franklin was the cataloguer as well as the printer of the catalogue. The entries for many volumes include extensive summaries of their contents. The description of a three-volume imprint of *The Philosophical Works of Francis Bacon,* for example, consists of nearly a full column of itemized contents, including a translation of *De Sapientia Veterum* entitled "The Mythology or Concealed Knowledge of the Ancients, decypher'd and explain'd." The lifelong admirer of Joseph Addison could not resist adding to the catalogue entry on holdings from the *Spectator,* the *Tatler,* and the *Guardian,* that these were "Written by some of the most ingenious Men of the Age, for the Promotion of Virtue, Piety, and good Manners." The catalogue entry for Sidney's *Discourses Concerning Government* notes ominously that these are the papers "which, being found in his closet, cost him his life."

In 1757 the firm of Franklin and Hall printed *The Charter, Laws, and Catalogue of Books of the Library Company of Philadelphia* on the eve of Franklin's departure for England. This *Charter* replaced the Library Company's original draft of rules and procedures, which in 1731 Franklin had asked Charles Brockden to prepare from Franklin's suggestions. By 1739 the property of the company had grown so extensive that the directors solicited a formal charter from the proprietors. The names of the library subscribers who served on the committee to draft the *Charter* are not recorded, but Franklin was among the library's directors when the document was finally signed and formal thanks offered to the proprietors for granting it.

The conventions of eighteenth-century legal language reflected in the *Charter* sound strikingly political to a modern ear. In the document's formal prose, the Library Company is "one Body Politick and Corporate" claiming the right to "establish Laws, Statutes, Orders, and Constitutions [for] the Government of the Library Company." Officers are elected and their "Trust and Authority" carefully limited. Company members agree to tax themselves ten shillings a year "for the Increase and Preservation of the said Library." The decision to reprint this *Charter* in full, along with an updated catalogue of books, may reflect the growing political tensions of the time. In any event, Franklin's press not only documents the growing collection—more than doubled in the sixteen years since the 1741 catalogue—it also reminds company members that they too are a government among governments.

Franklin did serve on the committee of three that wrote the company's official letter of thanks to the Penns. The last paragraph of that acknowledgment indicates the company's hope that the presence of the library will help heal the "unhappy Divisions and Animosities" that had broken out in Pennsylvania, restore a spirit of "charitable and friendly Intercourse" among its citizens, and promote the "Peace and Welfare of the Province" (*Papers*, 2:348). Like the language of the *Charter*, this letter contributes to the systematic appropriation of governmental missions by extragovernmental bodies that had engaged Franklin throughout much of his colonial career.

The four book lists that follow are extracts from the 1738 *Gazette* advertisement, the 1744 sale catalogue, and the 1741 and 1757 catalogues of the Library Company of Philadelphia. The large catalogues, in particular, are full of contemporary reference texts, legal manuals, medical handbooks, and gardening, farming, and botanical books, most of which I omit in favor of literary, historical, philosophical, and scientific work. Edwin Wolfe presents a general description of the complete Library Company catalogues in "Franklin and His Friends Choose Their Books," a more accessible account than the microform images of the original documents but one that does not give the concentrated impression of a list.[2]

Altogether, Franklin's 1744 sale inventory lists 445 titles, a number that probably exceeds the holdings of the Library Company at the time. In 1741 the Library Company of Philadelphia owned 374 titles. By 1757 the Library collection had grown to 855, and the company also owned a selection of museum curiosities: a piece of marble "from the ruins of Herculaneum," a twelve-foot-long snakeskin, bottled specimens of snakes and scorpions, and "a 12 inch concave reflecting mirror" donated by Franklin.

The Library Company catalogues are unalphabetized lists organized by size of book. I have alphabetized them by author or title to conform with contemporary bibliographic practice; otherwise, the content of each entry reproduces the content of the original documents, though the complete text has been cut to keep the lists manageable. Supplementary information in brackets clarifies a few of the entries where Franklin's informal abbreviations for familiar books may no longer be recognizable to modern readers.

From the May 25, 1738, *Pennsylvania Gazette* (*Papers,* 2:211)

JUST IMPORTED, And to be Sold by B. Franklin, for Ready Money only; the lowest Price being marked in each Book.

Arabian Nights. 6 vols. *12mo.*
Atalantis. 4 vols. *12mo.* [Mary de la Riviere Manley. *Secret Memoirs and Manners . . . From the New Atalantis.* London, 1716, 1720, 1736]
Bacon's Essays.
Beveridge's Thoughts.
Bladen's Caesar.
Characteristicks. 3 vols. *8vo.* [Anthony Ashley Cooper, Third Earl of Shaftesbury. *Characteristics of Men, Manners, Opinions, Times.* London, 1711, 1714 and many editions thereafter]
Crusoe's Life. 2 vols. *12mo.*
Croxal's Esop.
Congreve's Works. 3 vols. *12mo.*
Collection of Novels. 6 vols.
Dryden's Virgil. 3 vols. *12mo.*
——— Fables.
Gay's Fables.
Gravesande's Elements. 2 vols. *8vo.*
Hive. 4 vols. *12mo.* [*The Hive; a collection of the most celebrated songs.* 4 vols. London, 1726-33]
Hudibras.
Lock of Human Understanding.

Milton's Paradise Lost.
Otway's Plays.
Ovid's Epistles.
Pembroke's Arcadia.
Pope's Homer. 11 vols. *12mo.*
Prior's Poems. 2 vols. *12mo.*
Stanhope's Epictetus.
Seneca's Morals.
Spectators. 8 vols.
Selden's Table-talk.
Tale of a Tub.
Telemachus. 2 vols. *12mo.* [Fenelon. *The Adventures of Telemachus.* London, many editions in English after 1699]
Watts's Psalms.
Eutropius. [*Breviarium historiae romanae ab urbe condita.* A chronicle history of Rome in 10 books. Many contemporary editions/translations]

From *A Catalogue of Choice and Valuable Books.* Philadelphia: B. Franklin, 1744 [Evans #5396]

Antoninus's Meditations.
Astel's Religion of a Church-of-England-Woman. [Mary Astell. *The Christian Religion, as professed by a Daughter of the Church of England.* London, 1705, 1717]
Lord Bacon's Letters and Memoirs.
Beverly's History of Virginia, with Cuts.
Boerhaave's Chemistry. 2 vols.
Brown's Vulgar Errors.
Bunyan's Works, 2 vols. *with fine Cuts.*
Burnet's History of his own Time. 6 vols.
Institution de la Religion Chrestienne, en 4 Livres, par Jean Calvin.
Clarendon's History of the Civil Wars. *6 vols.*
Coke's Institutes of the Civil Law.
Collection of Scarce Pamphlets about Plots, Popery, *etc.*
Common Sense. *2 vols.* [*Common Sense, or the Englishman's Journal, A collection of letters, political, humorous, and moral.* 2 vols. London, 1738]
The Common Prayer, *black letter.*
Cure of Diesm in Answer to Tindall and Shaftesbury. [Elisha Smith. *The Cure of Deism, or the Mediatorial scheme by Jesus Christ the only true religion.* 4 editions. London, 1736-40]
Defoe's Family Instructor. *2 vols.*
Don Quixote . . . *With Cutts, 4 vols.*

Dryden's Virgil. *3 vols.*

Some Thoughts concerning the Revival of Religion in New England, *by J. Edwards.*

English Liberties, or the Free-Born Subject's Inheritance.

Lemuel Gulliver's Travels.

Herodotus.

History of Edward III.

Hobbes's Leviathan, *very scarce.*

Hooker's Ecclesiastical Polity.

Hutcheson's Enquiry into the Ideas of Beauty and Virtue.

Hutcheson On the Passions.

Law's serious Call to a devout and holy Life.

Leeke and Serle's Euclid with Dee's preface.

Lock's Letters concerning Toleration.

Longinus on the Sublime, *translated by William Smit.*

Malebranche's Treatise of Morality.

Montaigne's Essays.

Enchiridion Ethicum, per Moore. [Henry More. *Enchiridion Ethicum]*

Ovid's Metamorphoses. 2 vols.

M. Paschal's Moral and Divine Thoughts, *with the Life of the Author.* [Blaise Pascal. *Pensees.* translated by Basil Kennet]

Pemberton's View of Sir Isaac Newton's Philosophy.

Polybius's History.

Pope's Iliad and Odyssey. *11 vols.*

Puffendorf's Introduction to the History of Europe.

Quarles's Emblems.

Rawlinson's Method of Studying History.

The Republic of Letters in a Vision, *by Saavedra.* [Diego de Saavedra Fajardo. *Republica literaria; or, The Republic of Letters; being a vision.* London, 1727, 1728]

Sprat's History of the Royal Society.

Shaftesbury's Characteristicks. *3 vols.*

Shakespeare's Plays . . . *with fine Cuts.*

Stillingfleet's Weapon-Salve for the Church's Wound.

Taylor's Holy Living and Dying.

Tillotsen's Sermons.

Voltaire's History of Charles XII of Sweden.

Watt's Psalms and Watt's Hymns.

Xenophon's Cyropaedia. *2 vols.*

Count Zinzendorff's 16 Sermons, *preached in Berlin.*

From *A Catalogue of Books belonging to the Library Company of Philadelphia*. Philadelphia: B. Franklin, 1741 [Evans #4787]

Athenian Sports. Lond. 1707.

Mr. *Bayle's Historical and Critical Dictionary* . . . the Author being, for his prodigious Learning and Industry, esteemed the Wonder of this latter Age. 6 vols. 1733.

A Natural History, in Ten Centuries; written by Sir *Francis Bacon.* Whereto is added, his History of Life and Death, and the new Atlantis.

The *Philosophical Works of Francis Bacon* . . . methodized, and made English from the Originals . . . By *Peter Shaw*, M.D.

Creation, a Philosophical Poem: Demonstrating the Existence of a GOD . . . By Sir *Richard Blackmore.*

The *Philosophical Works of* the Hon. *Robert Boyle*, Esq . . . Lond. 1738.

The History of the Buccaniers of America . . . 3d Edit. Lond. 1704.

Bishop Burnet's History of his own Time.

Burnet's Theory of the Earth.

Cato's Letters, 4 vols.

M. Tully Cicero's five Books of Tusculan Disputations.

The Complete Tradesman. 2 vols. . . . 1732. [Daniel Defoe. *The Complete English Tradesman*]

Physico-Theology . . . By *W. Derham*, F.R.S. 1732.

Astro-Theology . . . By *W. Derham* . . . 1731.

Epictetus's Morals, with *Simplicius* his Comment. Made English from the Greek, by George Stanhope.

Fox's Acts and Monuments of the Church.

A New Method of Studying History, Geography, and Chronology . . . By M. *Languet du Fresnoy.* 2 vols. 1730. (*Given by* B.F.).

The *Oceana, and other Works of James Harrington*, Esq . . . Lond. 1737.

Hudibras, in Three Parts . . . Adorned with a new Set of Cuts, by Mr. *Hogarth.* Lond. 1732.

A Practical Treatise upon Christian Perfection. By *William Law*, A.M. 4th Edit. Lond. 1737.

W. Law's Serious Call to a devout and holy Life.

The Works of John Locke, Esq; In 3 vols. . . . Lond. 1740.

Two Treatises of Government . . . By *J. Locke*, Esq; 1698. (*Given by* B.F.).

A Collection of several Pieces of Mr. John Locke . . . *viz.* 1 The fundamental Constitutions of Carolina . . . 5 Some Thoughts Concerning Reading and Study for a Gentleman . . . 7 Rules of a Society which met once a Week for the Improvement of useful Knowledge, and the Promoting of Truth and Charity. Lond. 1720.

An *Essay upon Education of Children*, by Mr. *Lock.*

The *Works of Nicholas Machiavel.*

The *Christian Philosopher* . . . By *Cotton Mather.*

Milton's Paradise Lost and Regained: To which is added *Samson Agonistes* . . . with a Tractate on Education.

A Complete Collection of the Historical, Political, and Miscellaneous Works of Mr. John Milton . . . Lond. 1738.

Essays of Michel de Montaigne . . . 2 vols. 1685. (*Given by B.F.*).

Sir Thomas More's Utopia.

A General History of Printing . . . By *S. Palmer,* Printer. London 1733.

Ten Epistles in Verse, by Mr. Pope; containing his Essay on Man . . . Lond. 1733.

Pope's and *Swift's Miscellanies.* 6 vols. Lond. 1736.

The History of Polybius, the Megalopolitan . . . Translated by Sir *H.S.* To which is added a Character of *Polybius* by Mr. *Dryden.*

Plutarch's Morals, in English.

The History of the World, by Sir *Walter Raleigh* . . . 1733.

Ray's Wisdom of GOD, manifested in the Works of the Creation. 1728.

Sallust the Historian, translated into English . . . By *J. Rowe,* Esq.

Seneca's Morals.

Sidney's Discourses on Government; which, being found in his Closet, cost him his Life.

The Works of Mr. Edmund Spenser, in 6 vols.

Steel's Dramatick Works. 1730.

The Annals and History of Tacitus, translated by Mr. *Gordon* . . . 2 vols. 1728.

All the Works, Moral, Political, Historical . . . of Sir *William Temple,* Bart. 2 vols.

The excellent Poems of Mr. Thomson, on the Four Seasons, with that on Sir Isaac Newton and his *Britannia.*

Liberty; a Poem. By Mr. *Thomson.* Lond. 1735.

The Revolutions of Portugal. by *Vertot.*

The *Works of Virgil* . . . Translated into English verse, by Mr. *Dryden.*

The *Religion of Nature Delineated.* By *William Wollaston* Lond. 1726.

Wood's Athenae Oxoniensis . . . Lond. 1721.

Love of Fame the Universal Passion; in 7 characteristical Satyres. By Mr. *Young.* 1730.

From *The Charter, Laws, and Catalogue of Books of the Library Company of Philadelphia.* Philadelphia: B. Franklin and D. Hall, 1757.

The History of Appian of Alexandria, in two Parts . . . The second containing five Books of the Civil Wars of Rome . . . London, 1679.

An Attempt towards a Natural History of the Polype . . . By *Henry Baker* . . . London, 1743.

Psyche: Or, Love's Mysterie, in 20 Canto's: Displaying the Intercourse between Christ and the Soule. By *Jos. Beaumont* . . . London, 1648.

Religio Medici. By Sir *Thomas Brown* . . . Also Sir *Kenhelm Digby's* Observations. London, 1736.

The Canterbury Tales of Chaucer. Modernized by several Hands Lond. 1741.

The History of the Five Indian Nations of Canada . . . By the Honorable *Cadwallader Colden* . . . London, 1747.

The Morals of Confucius . . . London, 1724.

The History of Tom Jones, a Foundling. By *Henry Fielding,* Esq . . . London, 1749.

The History of Cold Bathing, Antient and Modern . . . By Sir *John Floyer* . . . London, 1732.

The Harleian Miscellany; or, A Collection of scarce, curious, and entertaining Pamphlets and Tracts . . . London, 1744.

An Enquiry Concerning the Principles of Morals. By *David Hume.* London, 1751.

A Brief History of the War with the Indians of New England . . . By *Increase Mather.* London, 1676.

Koran, or Alcoran of Mohammed. translated from the original Arabick . . . By *George Sale.* London, 1734.

Modern Plays, 1750. viz. Coriolanus, A Tragedy. By *James Thompson* . . . Gustavus Vasa, A Tragedy. By *Henry Brooke.*

The Spirit of Laws. Translated from the French of M. *De Secondat,* Baron of Montesquieu . . . London, 1752.

The Pennsylvania Gazette; from its first Publication in the Year 1728, to 1747, 5 vols.

A Relation, or Journal of the Beginning and Proceedings of the English Plantation settled at Plimouth. London, 1622.

The Political Anatomy of Ireland. By Sir *William Petty.* London, 1691.

Of the Use and Abuse of Parliaments: In two historical Discourses . . . London, 1744.

The Rambler. 6 vols. London, 1752.

Letters Concerning the English Nation. By M. de *Voltaire.* London, 1

Notes

Preface

1. John Locke, *Some Thoughts concerning Education* (1693), in *The Works of John Locke* (London, 1823), 9:11–12. Franklin cites Locke's advice on swimming in his *Proposals Relating to the Education of Youth in Pensilvania* (1749). See *Writings*, 328.

2. Norman Fiering, *Jonathan Edwards's Moral Thought and Its British Context* (Chapel Hill: University of North Carolina Press, 1981), 4–5.

3. Jürgen Habermas emphasizes the pioneering role of English "moral weeklies" like the *Spectator* in the formation of the idea of public reason in the late seventeenth and early eighteenth centuries. See Habermas, *The Structural Transformation of the Public Sphere* (1962), trans. Thomas Burger (Cambridge: MIT Press, 1989), 39–59.

4. J. G. A. Pocock, "Radical Criticisms of the Whig Order" in *The Origins of Anglo-American Radicalism,* ed. Margaret Jacob and James Jacob (London: Allen and Unwin, 1984), 34.

5. It was, in fact, in the workplace where Franklin found his leisure. The *Autobiography* records that, though he avoided "Places of idle Diversion" and fishing trips during his first years in business, he was on occasion "debauch'd . . . from my work" by a book. The daily schedule that Franklin reproduces in part 2 of the *Autobiography* limits the workday to eight hours, allows a two-hour lunch to "read, or overlook my Accounts, and dine," and provides for morning and evening periods of study, music, and conversation (*Writings*, 1369). James T. Kloppenburg's dismissal of Franklin as "the notoriously calculating embodiment of the spirit of

capitalism" is representative of the durable, modern stereotype. See Kloppenburg, "The Virtues of Liberalism: Christianity, Republicanism, and Ethics in Early American Political Discourse," *Journal of American History* 74 (1987): 23.

6. Kammen draws this suggestive phrase from Ortega y Gasset. See Michael Kammen, *People of Paradox: An Inquiry Concerning the Origins of American Civilization* (New York: Knopf, 1972), 57–85.

7. Gordon Wood, *The Radicalism of the American Revolution* (New York: Knopf, 1992), 95–99.

8. Pocock, "Radical Criticisms," 36.

9. John Trenchard and Thomas Gordon, *Cato's Letters; or, Essays on Liberty, Civil and Religious* (London, 1733), 1:81, 96.

10. Franklin may have drawn his confidence in this curious proverb partly from Thomas Gordon's tribute to John Trenchard in *Cato's Letters,* 1:xlvii. "He was very knowing," Gordon writes, "but not learned; that is, he had not read many Books." Gordon follows Locke in distinguishing between a reader who is "knowing" rather than merely "learned." See Locke, "Some Thoughts concerning Reading and Study for a Gentleman," in *Works,* 3:293–95.

11. D. H. Lawrence inaugurated this iconoclastic tradition but it has proven to be quite durable, particularly in literary criticism. See, for instance, Cynthia S. Jordan's recent account of what she considers the *Autobiography*'s pattern of suppression and artful contrivance in her *Second Stories: The Politics of Language, Form, and Gender in Early American Fictions* (Chapel Hill: University of North Carolina Press, 1989), 27–57. Jordan's example is especially revealing because she is, through much of her chapter on Franklin, an astute and appreciative reader who nevertheless insists that the *Autobiography* is fundamentally deceitful, a position that her own critical intelligence will not sustain.

12. Mitchell R. Breitwieser, *Cotton Mather and Benjamin Franklin: The Price of Representative Personality* (Cambridge: Cambridge University Press, 1984), 178–79. Breitwieser goes on to attribute this lack of complexity to the fact that Franklin's work displays "no interiority" only an "obstinate blankness," language that eloquently expresses Breitwieser's frustrations but that does not disclose much about Franklin.

13. Alvin Kernan, *Samuel Johnson and the Impact of Print* (Princeton: Princeton University Press, 1987).

14. Robert A. Ferguson, "'We Hold These Truths': Strategies of Control in the Literature of the Founders," in *Reconstructing American Literary History,* ed. Sacvan Bercovitch (Cambridge: Harvard University Press, 1986), 1–28. Steven Shapin's recent work establishes the historical context for Franklin's interest in the maintenance of communities of trust that could tolerate disagreement. See Shapin, *A Social History of Truth: Civility and Science in Seventeenth-Century England* (Chicago: University of Chicago Press, 1994), 3–125.

15. Henry F. May, *The Enlightenment in America* (New York: Oxford University Press, 1976), 126–32.

16. Michael Warner, "Savage Franklin," in *Benjamin Franklin: An American Genius,* ed. Gianfranca Balestra and Luigi Sammpietro (Rome: Bulzoni Editore, 1993).

INTRODUCTION

1. Mary Lynn Johnson and John E. Grant, eds., *Blake's Poetry and Designs* (New York: Norton, 1979), iii.

2. Ibid., 102. The emblematic beasts may derive from the 1726 version of James Thomson's "Winter":

> while, thro' the Gloom,
> Far, from the dire, unhospitable Shore,
> The Lyon's Rage, the Wolf's sad Howl is heard,
> And all the fell Society of Night.
> (*The Seasons,* ed. James Sambrook [Oxford: Clarendon, 1981], l:351–54)

But both poets draw on Isaiah 65.25:

> The wolf and the lamb shall feed together,
> the lion shall eat straw like the ox;
> but the serpent—its food shall be dust!

See William Spengemann's discussion of the relationship between Franklin's *Autobiography* and Blake's *The Marriage of Heaven and Hell* in *A New World of Words: Redefining Early American Literature* (New Haven: Yale University Press, 1994), 178–207.

3. Johnson and Grant, *Blake's Poetry and Designs,* 113.

4. Between the Treaty of Utrecht (1713) and the so-called War of Jenkins's Ear (1739), England was officially at peace, though habitually anxious about Jacobite military ambitions. After the outbreak of war with Spain in 1739, conflict was more or less uninterrupted until the first Peace of Paris in 1763. See Donald Greene, *The Age of Exuberance* (New York: Random House, 1970), for a summary of background knowledge to the English eighteenth century. Franklin's early career in Philadelphia coincides pefectly with the extraordinary period of peace and expansion in the colonies that Jack P. Greene describes in *The Intellectual Construction of America* (Chapel Hill: University of North Carolina Press, 1993).

5. Johnson and Grant, *Blake's Poetry and Designs,* 87.

6. Franklin's account in the *Autobiography,* including the suggestive hints from his fragmentary outline, is the only direct source for the events of his first London residence, supplemented by Bernard Fay's recreation of London life in the months of Franklin's stay. See *Writings,* 1342–53; and Fay, *Franklin: The Apos-*

tle of Modern Times (Boston: Little, Brown, 1929), 83–108. In the nearly seventy years since Fay's book was published, no biographer has devoted a comparable degree of attention to Franklin's extraordinary experience in Europe's largest city.

7. Thomson's poem went through two editions before Franklin left the city in late July 1726.

8. This is probably the same bookselling Wilcox who greeted Samuel Johnson on his arrival in London in 1737 with the advice that a man of his build ought to become a porter rather than a writer. See the editor's note in James Boswell, *Life of Johnson,* ed. George B. Hill and L. F. Powell (Oxford: Clarendon, 1934), 1:102–3. The anecdote has become a favorite of biographical critics. See Paul Fussell, *Samuel Johnson and the Life of Writing* (New York: Norton, 1971), 184.

9. The title page of the first issue of the first edition of Francis Hutcheson, *An Inquiry into the Original of our Ideas of Beauty and Virtue in Two Treatises* (London, 1725), identifies the book as a defense of Shaftesbury against Mandeville, but Thomas Mautner is clearly correct in suggesting that Hutcheson's goals were much broader than simply replying to *The Fable of the Bees.* See Mautner's introduction to his edition of Hutcheson's letters from the November 1724 *London Journal:* Frances Hutcheson, *On Human Nature,* ed. Thomas Mautner (Cambridge: Cambridge University Press, 1993). Shaftesbury and Mandeville are the subjects of Martin Price's paired chapters in *To the Palace of Wisdom: Studies in Order and Energy from Dryden to Blake* (Garden City, N.Y.: Doubleday, 1964), 79–128. Norman Fiering affirms Hutcheson's influence throughout the eighteenth century in *Jonathan Edwards's Moral Thought and Its British Context* (Chapel Hill: University of North Carolina Press, 1981), 132–49. See also James Sambrook, *The Eighteenth Century: The Intellectual and Cultural Context of English Literature, 1700–1789* (London: Longman, 1986).

10. The most detailed account of the experience of reading the *Spectator* is in Michael G. Ketcham, *Transparent Designs: Reading, Performance, and Form in the "Spectator" Papers* (Athens: University of Georgia Press, 1985), 82–104. See also Charles A. Knight, "*The Spectator's* Moral Economy," *Modern Philology* 91 (1993): 161–79. Knight suggests that the essays embody what Addison calls in *Spectator* #251 the "cries of London," a manifestation of the varied and vital economy of the city, to which the *Spectator's* odd correspondent, Ralph Crotchett, foolishly objects. See Habermas's account of the role played by the "moral weeklies" in the development of the complex political self-consciousness of the early eighteenth century in *Structural Transformation of the Public Sphere,* 42–43.

11. Religious zeal is a kind of "form," in Addison's judgment, disguising "Pride, Interest, or Ill-nature." See *Spectator,* 3:63. Franklin quotes from this number in the last of Silence Dogood's letters.

12. F. B. Kaye cites *The Dunciad* passage in the appendix to his splendid edition of *The Fable of the Bees* (Oxford: Clarendon, 1924), 2:429.

13. Bernard Mandeville, *An Inquiry into the Causes of the Frequent Executions at*

Tyburn (1725), Reprint 105, Augustan Reprint Society (Los Angeles: University of California Press, 1964). Martin Price astutely observes that "conservatism is the other side of Mandeville's mocking reductivism." See Price, *To the Palace of Wisdom,* 119.

14. For Hutcheson's experiments with moral equations, see *Inquiry into the Original of our Ideas of Beauty and Virtue,* 177–78.

15. A. O. Lovejoy, Reflections on Human Nature (Baltimore: Johns Hopkins University Press, 1961), 129–215.

16. See Mather's account of his acquaintance with inoculation in Cotton Mather, *The Angel of Bethesda,* ed. Gordon W. Jones (Barre, Mass.: American Antiquarian Society and Barre Publishers, 1972), 107–16. Kenneth Silverman summarizes the complete controversy in *The Life and Times of Cotton Mather* (New York: Columbia University Press, 1985), 336–63.

17. Shapin, *Social History of Truth,* 126–92. In Daniel Defoe, *The Complete English Tradesman* (1726; Gloucester, England: Alan Sutton, 1987), 231, character produces credit, which is in turn the foundation of personal gentility and national security: "Credit makes war, and makes peace; raises armies, fits out navies, fights battles, besieges towns; and, in a word, it is more justly called the sinews of war than the money itself. . . . The force of credit is not to be described by words; it is an impregnable fortification, either for a nation, or for a single man in business."

18. Silence Dogood's second letter to the *Courant,* printed in the week of April 9–16, 1722, is accompanied by reports on the progress of the plague in southern France and on English attempts to prevent the spread of the disease to English ports. Subsequent issues through the spring of 1722 continue to note the status of the epidemic.

19. In the months before the publication of the *Journal,* Defoe wrote in support of Walpole's proposed Act of Quarantine, which aimed at containing the Marseilles plague. See David Roberts, introduction to *A Journal of the Plague Year,* ed. Louis Landa (Oxford: Oxford University Press, 1990), vii–ix.

20. Locke, *Works,* 10:312–14.

21. Cotton Mather's description of the organization and purpose of private religious associations also anticipates Franklin's Free and Easy fraternity. Mather, however, never countenanced the exclusion of women from such societies, but like Franklin, he did envision that an original group might "*swarm into more*" once it had reached a "fit number" of members. See Cotton Mather, *Bonifacius: An Essay Upon the Good,* ed. David Levin (Cambridge: Belknap, 1966), 63–68. English freemasonry was well established during the time of Franklin's first visit to London. He may have modeled some elements of his society on Masonic practice as well. See Margaret C. Jacob, *The Radical Enlightenment: Pantheists, Freemasons, and Republicans* (London: Allen and Unwin, 1981), 107–81; and Margaret C. Jacob, *Living the Enlightenment: Freemasonry and Politics in Eighteenth-Century Europe* (Oxford: Oxford University Press, 1991).

CHAPTER ONE: ARTICLES OF BELIEF

1. The pulpit that the younger Mr. Cotton lost "for his Notorious Breaches of the Seventh Commandment" was that of Plymouth Church, from which he was dismissed in 1697. See Samuel Sewall's account of the event in *The Diary of Samuel Sewall,* ed. M. Halsey Thomas (New York: Farrar, Straus, and Giroux, 1973), 1:378. Thirty years earlier, this same Cotton had been excommunicated from his father's church for "lascivious unclean practices with three women and his horrid lying to hide his sinne." In the early phases of his own ministerial career, Cotton Mather had presided over the judgment of another adulterous clergyman, Thomas Cheever, in 1686. See David Levin, *Cotton Mather: The Young Life of the Lord's Remembrancer* (Cambridge: Harvard University Press, 1978), 128.

2. This complex of qualities vividly illustrates Bruce Granger's distinction between the impassioned voice of Silence Dogood and the comparatively dispassionate observation of Addison's *Spectator.* See Granger, *Benjamin Franklin: An American Man of Letters* (Ithaca: Cornell University Press, 1964), 22–38. Franklin's creation, in fact, has a great deal in common with the spiritual ambitions and fervor of Cotton Mather, who exhorts himself in his diary "To *love* that which *God* Loves, and *hate* that which *God* hates; to be *holy as God is holy,* and like Him, a *great forgiver.*" Cited in Levin, *Cotton Mather,* 99.

3. James Sappenfield, *A Sweet Instruction: Franklin's Journalism as Literary Apprenticeship* (Carbondale: Southern Illinois University Press, 1973), 38, cites Mrs. Dogood's determination to exercise her talents as a seminal moment in Franklin's development and associates this passage with a "tone of bellicosity" in the Dogood letters. Ormond Seavey's identification of a pattern of "withdrawal from hostilities" in Franklin's early work more accurately captures the amiability of Franklin's complex narrative voices. See Seavey, *Becoming Benjamin Franklin: The Autobiography and the Life* (University Park: Pennsylvania State University Press, 1988), 128.

4. The youngest of James Franklin's associates on the *Courant,* John Eyre, was twenty-one during the inoculation controversy, five years older than Benjamin Franklin and a graduate of Harvard. William Douglass and John Checkley, key members of James's circle, were much older than Eyre and both were much more widely traveled and better educated than most citizens of Boston. Douglass, at thirty-one, had the only medical degree in America at the time and knew French, Dutch, Latin, and Greek. Any one of these three would have been a more conventional choice to oversee the publication of the newspaper than a sixteen-year-old apprentice. See the account of the *Courant* circle in Arthur Bernon Tourtellot, *Benjamin Franklin: The Shaping of Genius—The Boston Years* (Garden City, N.Y.: Doubleday, 1977), 248–51, 275–310.

5. Robert Arner, though, points out Franklin's participation in the rich tradi-

tion of "temperance" literature. See Arner, "Politics and Temperance in Boston and Philadelphia," in *Reappraising Benjamin Franklin: A Bicentennial Perspective,* ed. J. A. Leo Lemay (Newark: University of Delaware Press, 1993), 52–77.

6. Part of the *Spectator*'s complex treatment of love includes a passage describing the kind of bond between father and son that Franklin may have hoped to renew with his son William through the medium of the *Autobiography:* "It is the most beautiful Object the Eyes of Man can behold, to see a Man of Worth and His Son live in an entire unreserved Correspondence . . . . It is a sublime Pleasure which encreases by the Participation. It is as sacred as Friendship, as pleasurable as Love, and as joyful as Religion" (*Spectator,* 3:90). On the significance of human affections in the overall structure of the *Spectator,* see Ketcham, *Transparent Designs,* 105–23.

7. The *New England Courant* printed articles on some of the more prominent houses of prostitution in Boston in the early spring of 1722, just before the first letters of Silence Dogood appear. See Carl Bridenbaugh, *Cities in the Wilderness* (1938; New York: Knopf, 1955); and Tourtellot, *Benjamin Franklin,* 386– 90.

8. Michael Warner's suggestion that Mrs. Dogood's first name is representative of her "abnegation of the personal" springs from his determination to see the Dogood letters as "purely socializing texts" in a public "regime of supervision." She is "silent," he argues, because she disappears into the "civic vision of print." In Franklin's contemporary ethical context, however, the silence is meaningless unless it is in fact "personal." See Warner, *The Letters of the Republic: Publication and the Public Sphere in Eighteenth-Century America* (Cambridge: Harvard University Press, 1990), 82–87.

9. Mather, *Bonifacius,* 62.

10. See, for additional background, Steven Shapin's summary of the ethical and performative assumptions that shaped the tradition of "reluctant" authorship in Shapin, *Social History of Truth,* 175–84.

11. Arthur Tourtellot provides the most thorough treatment of William Douglass's pugnacious character in Tourtellot, *Benjamin Franklin,* 233–74; but see also Silverman, *Life and Times of Cotton Mather,* 344–45; and Robert Middlekauff's brief discussion in *The Mathers: Three Generations of Puritan Intellectuals, 1596–1728* (New York: Oxford University Press, 1971), 354–59.

12. See Lovejoy, *Reflections on Human Nature,* 217–45.

13. The passage is quoted from Shepard's *Parable of the Ten Virgins* in Norman Fiering, *Jonathan Edwards's Moral Thought and Its British Context* (Chapel Hill: University of North Carolina Press, 1981), 178n.

14. Alexander Pope, "Epistle II," *An Essay on Man,* l:101–10.

15. Locke, *Some Thoughts concerning Education,* 119.

16. Frank E. Manuel, *The Changing of the Gods* (Hanover, N.H.: University Press of New England, 1983), 77–78.

17. Nicholas Malebranche, *Recherche de la verite,* quoted in Lovejoy, *Reflections on Human Nature,* 133.

18. The surviving records suggest that Abiah Folger Franklin was a forceful intellectual presence in Franklin's life: scrutinizing her son's religious opinions, following Franklin's early diplomatic ventures, seeking reports on the growth and education of her grandchildren. She appears to have objected to Franklin's involvement with Freemasonry at least partly on the grounds that the Masons excluded women, and she took a sufficiently deep interest in colonial politics to prompt her son to send her a copy of an Indian treaty that he had helped to negotiate. Late in his life, Franklin attempted to keep in contact with his Folger relatives, noting in a letter to his sister, Jane Mecom, his admiration for their "honest plainness" of speech and formidable tempers—attributes that these siblings seem to have associated with their spirited mother. Like Silence Dogood, Abiah Folger seems never to have hidden her talents. See Franklin's 1738 letter to his parents in *Writings,* 426, as well as the notes on a draft of that letter in *Papers,* 2:202–3. Later letters to Jane Mecom in *Writings,* 870, 1170–71, illuminate Franklin's interest in his Folger heritage, and letters to his mother in *Papers,* 3:179–80, 388–89, 474–75, suggest the range of their relationship.

19. See, too, Albert Furtwangler's suggestion that "Janus" may be a joke on the *New England Courant*'s double-faced editorship (James and Benjamin Franklin); see Furtwangler, *American Silhouettes: Rhetorical Identities of the Founders* (New Haven: Yale University Press, 1987), 15–34.

20. The account of the *Dissertation* that follows makes claims for its spiritual and rhetorical ambition that differ considerably from the influential assessments of Alfred Owen Aldridge in *Benjamin Franklin: Philosopher and Man* (Philadelphia: Lippincott, 1965), 18–19; and Aldridge, *Benjamin Franklin and Nature's God* (Durham: Duke University Press, 1967), 12–24. Donald Meyer's more recent account indicates the extent to which Aldridge's views continue to shape discussion of Franklin's complex personal faith. See Meyer, "Franklin's Religion," in *Critical Essays on Benjamin Franklin,* ed. Melvin Buxbaum (Boston: Hall, 1987), 147–67.

21. William Wollaston, *The Religion of Nature Delineated* (1724; Delmar, N.Y.: Scholars Facsimiles and Reprints, 1974), 36, 119.

22. Hutcheson, *An Inquiry into the Original of our Ideas of Beauty and Virtue,* 121.

23. James Sambrook summarizes the nature of this ongoing intellectual conversation in *Eighteenth Century,* 67–71. F. B. Kaye observes that Mandeville may not have read Shaftesbury's work before the 1723 edition of *The Fable,* when he first explicitly contrasts his own thinking with the ethical position of the *Characteristics.* In a little over a year, Francis Hutcheson took up Shaftesbury's defense, replacing William Law as Mandeville's primary antagonist. Martin Price accurately and suggestively casts Shaftesbury and Mandeville as representative of William James's contrast between the tender-minded and the tough-minded thinker.

See Price, *To the Palace of Wisdom: Studies in Order and Energy from Dryden to Blake* (Garden City, N.Y.: Doubleday, 1964), 79–128.

24. Edward Young, *The Poetical Works of Edward Young* (Boston: Houghton Mifflin, 1880), 2:66–67.

25. Mandeville, *Inquiry into the Causes of the Frequent Executions at Tyburn*, 24. Mandeville's account of the hellish discord of public executions precedes by nearly thirty years that of Henry Fielding (1751), which Michel Foucault cites in his discussion of the subversive solidarity that began to develop between the lower classes and the condemned criminal on the scaffold. See Foucault, *Discipline and Punish: The Birth of the Prison* (1975), trans. Alan Sheridan (New York: Vintage, 1995), 57–69.

26. Dryden, *Oedipus*, act 3, scene 1, lines 244–48, quoted in *Papers*, 1:58n.

27. A key ingredient to the exercise of true charity, in Mather's view, was the abandonment of all pretense to merit as a result of one's good works. His disparagement of "merit-mongers" is in Mather, *Bonifacius*, 31.

28. Hutcheson, *An Inquiry into the Original of our Ideas of Beauty and Virtue*, 245. This broad suspicion of the powers of reason is a common feature of Augustan humanism. See Paul Fussell, *The Rhetorical World of Augustan Humanism* (Oxford: Clarendon, 1965), 15–21. Fussell, though, excludes Hutcheson from the humanist camp as a spokesman of what he derisively terms the "new sentimentalism." Ernest Tuveson observes that "the 'Age of Reason' distrusted Reason—as it had been understood for many centuries—far more deeply than did any preceding period." See Tuveson, *The Imagination as a Means of Grace: Locke and the Aesthetics of Romanticism* (1960; New York: Gordian, 1974), 24.

29. This passage from Hutcheson, *Inquiry*, 63–64, forms the basis of his conviction that human beings experience a general aesthetic "relish" from the perception of uniformity amid diversity, the theoretical position that Martin Battestin identifies as "the most substantial and carefully reasoned statement of aesthetic principles before Hume and Burke." See Battestin, *The Providence of Wit: Aspects of Form in Augustan Literature and the Arts* (Oxford: Clarendon, 1974), 30–32. Tuveson, *Imagination as a Means of Grace*, 133–37, treats Hutcheson's work in the context of the development of romantic aesthetics, with the ideal of harmonious form at its center.

30. Wollaston, *Religion of Nature Delineated*, 208.

31. Locke, *Some Thoughts Concerning Education*, 157–58.

32. Gerald Stourzh, *Benjamin Franklin and American Foreign Policy* (Chicago: University of Chicago Press, 1954), 22–30.

33. Bernard Fay reports that *Macbeth, Hamlet,* and *The Tempest* were all staged in the London theaters during 1725 and 1726, though they were all produced from texts that differ significantly from modern editions of Shakespeare's plays. Franklin could also have seen operettas at Lincoln's Inn Field such as *Oroonoko*

(drawn from Aphra Behn's 1688 novella) and *The Fair Quaker,* a title likely to at-tract the attention of a citizen of Philadelphia. See Fay, *Franklin: The Apostle of Modern Times* (Boston: Little, Brown, 1929), 96.

34. Locke, *Works,* 10:313.

Chapter Two: Acts of Religion

1. On the status of Hutcheson's work as an "anatomy" of the early eighteenth-century's ideal of moral order, see Battestin, *Providence of Wit,* 16–17, 30–32.

2. The richly theatrical nature of the "Articles of Belief," as well as portions of the *Autobiography,* make Franklin one of the most complex examples of the cul-tural phenomenon that Jeffrey H. Richards describes in *Theater Enough: Ameri-can Culture and the Metaphor of the World Stage, 1607–1789* (Durham: Duke Uni-versity Press, 1991).

3. See Steven Shapin's discussion of this phenomenon in *Social History of Truth,* 65–125.

4. John Ray, *The Wisdom of God Manifested in the Works of the Creation,* 2d ed. (London, 1692), 2:156.

5. Line numbers refer to the April 1726 edition of James Thomson, "Winter," in Geoffrey Tillotsen, Paul Fussell, and Marshall Waingrow, eds., *Eighteenth-Cen-tury English Literature* (New York: Harcourt Brace, 1969), 706–11.

6. Tuveson, in fact, associates Shaftesbury with the tradition of the eigh-teenth-century sublime poem that Thomson's work exemplifies. See Tuveson, *Imagination as a Means of Grace,* 71; and R. L. Brett, *The Third Earl of Shaftes-bury: A Study in Eighteenth-Century Literary Theory* (London: Hutchinson House, 1951), 123–64.

7. Marjorie Nicolson traces the paths of influence, in some detail, from Shaf-tesbury, through Addison's essays on "The Pleasures of the Imagination" (an in-fluential source for Hutcheson, as well), to Thomson and his contemporaries. See her *Mountain Gloom and Mountain Glory* (1959; New York: Norton, 1963), 289–354.

8. A glance at Xenophon's text makes clear one formal consequence of the dif-ference between his portrait of Socrates and that of Plato: Xenophon's units of composition are far briefer, emphasizing not the extended process of the dialogue but the concise delivery of some specific judgment or opinion. See Hugh Treden-nick's general introduction to Xenophon, *Conversations of Socrates* (New York: Viking-Penguin, 1990).

9. Alfred O. Aldridge, *Benjamin Franklin and Nature's God* (Durham: Duke University Press, 1967), 25–33. The idea of an inhabited universe played a critical role in a number of late seventeenth-century and early eighteenth-century literary movements. Nicolson, *Mountain Gloom and Mountain Glory,* 130–40, notes that Henry More's poetic celebration of the aesthetics of the infinite in *Democritus*

Platonissans (1646) springs from his perception of the "Infinity of Worlds." Joseph M. Levine traces the conflict between the ancients and the moderns to the appendixes that Fontanelle attached to his 1686 discussion of the plurality of worlds, as well as to Thomas Burnet's *Sacred Theory of the Earth.* See Levine, *The Battle of the Books: History and Literature in the Augustan Age* (Ithaca: Cornell University Press, 1991), 13–26. See Frank Manuel's discussion of Bayle, Fontanelle, and the growth of comparative mythology in *The Eighteenth Century Confronts the Gods* (Cambridge: Harvard University Press, 1959), 24–53.

10. William Wollaston, *The Religion of Nature Delineated* (1724; Delmar, N.Y.: Scholars Facsimiles and Reprints, 1974), 80.

11. Cotton Mather, *The Christian Philosopher* (London, 1721), 18.

12. Hutcheson, *Inquiry into the Original of our Ideas of Beauty and Virtue,* 147.

13. Franklin does, however, suggest the enthusiasms of the "Articles of Belief," even in the more restrained presentation of the project for achieving perfection in the *Autobiography.* The epigraph from his "little Book" of virtues and lapses begins with a portion of the hero's soliloquy from act 5 of Addison's *Cato:*

> It must be so—Plato, thou reasonest well—
> Else whence this pleasing hope, this fond desire,
> This longing after immortality?
> Or whence this secret dread, and inward horror
> Of falling into naught?
>
> . . . .
>
> The soul, secured in her existence, smiles
> At the drawn dagger, and defies its point.
> The stars shall fade away, the sun himself
> Grow dim with age, and nature sink in years,
> But thou shalt flourish in immortal youth,
> Unhurt amidst the wars of elements,
> The wreck of matter, and the crush of worlds.

Franklin's citation in the *Autobiography* selects the least enthusiastic moments in Cato's speech, but Addison's play was so popular throughout the eighteenth century that any contemporary would have detected the association with the moral sublime in Franklin's choice. See the text of Addison's play in John Hampden, ed., *Eighteenth-Century Plays* (1928; New York: Dutton, 1954), 5–51. On the popularity of *Cato* among eighteenth-century Americans, see Richards, *Theater Enough,* 182–84.

14. Perhaps because of this complex delight and meaningful disorder in Franklin's "Articles of Belief," they are easy to misread as insincere. See, for instance, Elizabeth E. Dunn, "From a Bold Youth to a Reflective Sage: A Revaluation of Benjamin Franklin's Religion," *Pennsylvania Magazine of History and Biography*

III (1987): 501–24. Even given the peculiar nature of the "Articles," however, it is difficult to see how Dunn could position Franklin's invocations to the Deity "on a thin line separating serious imitation from cleverly disguised irreverence."

15. Newton is careful to distinguish these divine "similitudes" from actual knowledge of the Deity's "Being." The central (and traditional) position of the "General Scholium" is that God has nothing in common with "corporeal" existence. See Isaac Newton, *Mathematical Principles of Natural Philosophy,* trans. Andrew Motte (Berkeley: University of California Press, 1934), 543–47. Franklin knew the "General Scholium" well enough to parody Newton's affirmation of the inexplicable nature of gravity: "to us it is enough that gravity does really exist." In an aside in *Experiments and Observations on Electricity,* Franklin consoles the reader by observing that we can preserve our china intact without being able to explain precisely why it falls. See *Benjamin Franklin's Experiments: A New Edition of Franklin's Experiments and Observations on Electricity,* ed. I Bernard Cohen (Cambridge: Harvard University Press, 1941), 219.

16. See the full account of the Hemphill controversy in Melvin H. Buxbaum, *Benjamin Franklin and the Zealous Presbyterians* (University Park: Pennsylvania State University Press, 1975), 76–115.

17. Alan Heimert makes the case for a relationship between the eighteenth-century religious revival and contemporary politics in *Religion and the American Mind: From the Great Awakening to the Revolution* (Cambridge: Harvard University Press, 1966). Heimert's argument for the politically and spiritually "preparational" nature of Calvinist rhetoric, particularly between 1765 and 1775, has drawn criticism for some excesses but remains quite convincing. David S. Lovejoy confirms many of Heimert's essential observations in *Religious Enthusiasm in the New World: Heresy to Revolution* (Cambridge: Harvard University Press, 1985), 195–230.

18. Franklin in fact adapted the analogy between individually unique beliefs and the features of the human face from Locke in *Some Thoughts concerning Education,* a gesture that confirms the impression of great care in composition, which the letter to his parents suggests.

19. See the textual and translation history sketched out by William C. Creasy in his introduction to an edition of the *Imitatio* (Macon: Mercer University Press, 1989).

20. Thomas à Kempis, *The Imitation of Christ,* ed. Harold C. Gardiner (New York: Doubleday, 1989), 35.

21. Ibid., 36.

CHAPTER THREE: HUMANITY'S POCKET MIRROR

1. Bernard Capp, *English Almanacs 1500–1800: Astrology and the Popular Press* (Ithaca: Cornell University Press, 1979). I am indebted throughout this chapter to Capp's learned book, particularly to his biographical and bibliographic appendixes.

2. Walter Benjamin, *Illuminations* (1955), ed. Hannah Arendt, trans. Harry Zohn (New York: Harcourt, Brace and World, 1968), 108.

3. Claude-Anne Lopez and Eugenia Herbert, otherwise astute and sympathetic interpreters of Franklin's domestic experience, overlook this dimension of Franklin's almanacs when they conclude that "there is little joy in *Poor Richard.*" See Lopez and Herbert, *The Private Franklin* (New York: Knopf, 1975), 39.

4. Capp, *English Almanacs,* 223.

5. See the publication history of the papers in Jonathan Swift, *Bickerstaff Papers and Pamphlets on the Church,* ed. Herbert Davis (Oxford: Basil Blackwell, 1957), 275–88. Swift's *Miscellanies* were in the collection of the Library Company of Philadelphia.

6. Capp's bibliography of English almanacs and their compilers documents this transformation and exchange of titles across the seventeenth century.

7. Capp, *English Almanacs,* 258.

8. Cameron C. Nickles argues that "Richard Saunders" is purely an "ironic persona" standing in for his enlightened and satirical creator, but such a reading effectively superimposes Swift upon Franklin, whose relationship to the nominal superstitions of Saunders is far more tolerant and complex than the concept of ironic detachment would allow. See Nickles, *"Poor Richard's* Almanacs," in *The Oldest Revolutionary: Essays on Benjamin Franklin,* ed. J. A. Leo Lemay (Philadelphia: University of Pennsylvania Press, 1976), 77–89.

9. For a history of the almanac in America, see Marion B. Stowell, *Early American Almanacs* (New York: Burt Franklin, 1977).

10. *William Lilly's History of His Life and Times, From the Year 1602 to 1681, Written by Himself* (1715; London, 1822), 7–25. Lilly's parents (like Franklin's) educated him to rise above his station—"my mother intending I should be a scholar"—but family debts forced him to seek his fortune as a servant and a secretary in London.

11. Capp, *English Almanacs,* 124.

12. Ibid., 117.

13. Ibid., 162.

14. Ibid., 249. Irvin Ehrenpreis describes Partridge's widespread notoriety in the first decade of the eighteenth century and points out that Swift's attack on Partridge as the era's chief charlatan was only one of many, from a variety of sources. See Ehrenpreis, *Dr. Swift,* vol. 2 of his *Swift: The Man, His Works, and the Age* (Cambridge: Harvard University Press, 1967), 197–200.

15. Swift, *Bickerstaff Papers,* 145.

16. Ibid. The extent of the hoax occupies Swift for a little over a year, from late February 1708 to April 1709. See Ehrenpreis's dating of the Bickerstaff pamphlets in *Dr. Swift,* 200–205.

17. This ghostly visit may partly reflect the curious account, probably by Elias Ashmole, of William Lilly's death, which concludes Lilly's autobiography. After a

meticulous list of the various ailments—bloody fluxes and "ripe" abscesses— from which Lilly suffered at the end of his life, the memoirist solemnly notes that "Immediately before his breath went from him, he sneezed three times," a detail that could suggest the ticklish passage of Leeds's spirit through Saunders's nostril. See *William Lilly's History of His Life and Times*, 244–45.

18. Titan Leeds has, in fact, a great deal more in common with Franklin than with Swift's dubious target, John Partridge. Leeds' Philadelphia almanacs share Franklin's moral earnestness, citing passages from Bacon's *Essays* at the head of the calendar pages. Daniel Leeds, Titan's father and the originator of the family almanac business, quoted a couplet in one of his own almanacs that is quite Franklinian in character:

Created Forms, Diffinitions, Orders, Rules
Bones of Religion make us fit for Fools.

This is a sentiment that the defender of Samuel Hemphill might heartily endorse. See Stowell, *Early American Almanacs*, 5–66. 140–58.

19. Swift, *Bickerstaff Papers*, 28.

20. Ibid., 43–63.

21. Ibid., 57.

22. Though he disparages "A Project for the Advancement of Religion" as the "flattest" of Swift's essays and admires "An Argument" as one of Swift's finest, Ehrenpreis acknowledges that Swift's advocacy of forced hypocrisy is the inescapable basis of both pieces. "From this blind alley," Ehrenpreis reluctantly concludes, "there is no exit." See *Dr. Swift*, 279–94. Claude Rawson confirms this account of Swift's entangled position in *Order from Confusion Sprung: Studies in Eighteenth-Century Literature from Swift to Cowper* (London: Allen and Unwin, 1985), 49–58.

23. Ehrenpreis, *Dr. Swift*, notes that Swift quickly disavowed the attribution.

24. Swift, *Bickerstaff Papers*, 11.

25. Ibid., 57.

26. Ibid.

27. Locke, *Some Thoughts Concerning Education*, 52.

28. The aphorism could also rely on a community of readers instructed in the pleasures of *sententiae*. Alfred O. Aldridge describes the extraordinary prestige of *Poor Richard*'s aphorisms with French readers, responding to work in the traditions of Pascal and La Rochefoucauld. See Aldridge, *Franklin and His French Contemporaries* (New York: New York University Press, 1957), 38–59.

29. See Terry Castle's account in *Masquerade and Civilization: The Carnivalesque in Eighteenth-Century English Culture and Fiction* (Stanford: Stanford University Press, 1986), 1–51.

30. The first volume of the Yale edition of the *Papers* prints a facsimile of *Poor*

Richard for 1733, which makes these particular relationships between aphorisms and dates evident.

31. Ehrenpreis, *Dr. Swift,* suspects that Swift timed the publication of his second burlesque of John Partridge—the anonymous letter describing Partridge's "death"—to occur on April 1, 1708, a gesture that conforms to almanac tradition.

32. William Law, *A Serious Call to a Devout and Holy Life* (1728; London: Dent, 1906), 134.

33. Stowell, *Early American Almanacs,* 54.

34. James A. Sappenfield, *A Sweet Instruction: Franklin's Journalism as Literary Apprenticeship* (Carbondale: Southern Illinois University Press, 1973), 153–58.

35. Diogenes Laertius, *Lives of the Eminent Philosophers,* trans. R. D. Hicks (Cambridge: Harvard University Press, 1925), 167. English translations first appeared in London in 1688 and 1696.

36. Sappenfield first suggested the conjunction of the almanacs with the Hemphill controversy. See *Sweet Instruction,* 139.

37. Law, *Serious Call to a Devout and Holy Life.* The idea is present throughout Law's text, but see especially 5–6, 52, 105–12.

38. Ibid., 54.

39. Ibid., 74.

Chapter Four: The Theater of Science

1. Ernst H. Kantorowicz, *The King's Two Bodies: A Study in Medieval Political Theology* (Princeton: Princeton University Press, 1957).

2. See Louis Marin's treatment of absolutist "iconography" in *Portrait of the King* (1981), trans. Martha M. Houle (Minneapolis: University of Minnesota Press, 1988). Marin's study begins with a consideration of the discussion of symbolic "signs" in *The Art of Thinking* by the Port-Royal theologians, a book that Franklin names among his intellectual influences in the *Autobiography.*

3. I. Bernard Cohen underscores the persistence of this division of scholarly attention in *Science and the Founding Fathers: Science in the Political Thought of Jefferson, Franklin, Adams, and Madison* (New York: Norton, 1995).

4. Alfred O. Aldridge, "Benjamin Franklin: The Fusion of Science and Letters," in *American Literature and Science,* ed. Robert J. Scholnick (Lexington: University Press of Kentucky, 1992), 39–57. The conduct of early scientific discourse through personal correspondence illustrates Shapin's thesis that gentlemanly conventions of conduct were systematically adapted to the problems of dealing with scientific testimony in a way that could avoid the "scandalously divisive" habits of traditional scholarly debate. See Shapin, *Social History of Truth,* 120–22.

5. On the contemporary prestige of the orrery, see Garry Wills, *Inventing America: Jefferson's Declaration of Independence* (Garden City, N.Y.: Doubleday,

1978), 100–104; and Sambrook, *Eighteenth Century,* 1–30. Brooke Hindle's account in his biography of Rittenhouse suggests that the orrery was as much a work of conceptual art as a useful scientific instrument. An empirically accurate orrery was impossible to construct, and the most ambitious mechanical approximations—like those of Rittenhouse—were continually breaking down. See Hindle, *David Rittenhouse* (Princeton: Princeton University Press, 1964), 27–40. *Poor Richard Improved* for 1753 employs the idea of the orrery to illustrate the natural consequences of earth's inclination from the plane of its rotation.

6. Willard Sterne Randall cites the origin of the proverb in *A Little Revenge: Benjamin Franklin and His Son* (Boston: Little, Brown, 1984), 48.

7. Ernst Cassirer surveys the phenomenon of physicotheology in "Nature and Natural Science," in his *The Philosophy of the Enlightenment* (1932), trans. Fritz Koelln and James Pettegrove (Princeton: Princeton University Press, 1951). In *Mountain Gloom and Mountain Glory,* 253–70, Nicolson establishes Ray's preeminence in English physicotheology, as well as his dependence on Henry More and his response to Thomas Burnet.

8. Ishmael enumerates a few of the men, "small and great," who have written on the whale, beginning with "The Authors of the Bible," through Pliny, Ray, and Linnaeus, to the Rev. Henry T. Cheever. See Herman Melville, *Moby-Dick* (1851; New York: Viking- Penguin, 1992), 146.

9. *The Philosophical Works of Francis Bacon* (1905), ed. John M. Robertson (Freeport, N.Y.: Books for Libraries Press, 1970), 101.

10. Bacon places Psalm 104 at the center of his *Translation of Certain Psalms into English Verse,* dedicated to George Herbert (London, 1625). See *The Works of Francis Bacon* (1872), ed. James Spedding, Robert Ellis, Douglas Heath (New York: Garrett, 1968), 7:281–84.

11. Cotton Mather, *The Christian Philosopher: A Collection of the Best Discoveries in Nature with Religious Improvements* (London, 1721), 68, 99, 131, 142–46, 176. Winton U. Solberg discusses Mather's extensive indebtedness to Ray in the introduction to his edition of *The Christian Philosopher* (Urbana: University of Illinois Press, 1994), l–lx.

12. John Ray, *The Wisdom of God Manifested in the Works of the Creation,* 2d ed. (London, 1692). The comments are from Ray's brief, unpaginated preface.

13. Francis Bacon, "Religious Meditations," quoted in *Works,* 7:252. Bacon made clear, too, in *Novum Organum* (1620) that, next to scripture, natural philosophy is "at once the surest medicine against superstition and the most approved nourishment for faith," a position with which the nonjuring Ray was likely to agree. See "Aphorism LXXXIX," in *The New Organon,* ed. Fulton Anderson (Indianapolis: Bobbs-Merrill, 1960), 88.

14. Ray, *Wisdom of God,* 1:168–69.

15. Ibid., 2:176. See Francis Bacon's influential diagnosis of the anxieties of atheism in *Works,* 7:251–52.

16. Margaret C. Jacob, *The Cultural Meaning of the Scientific Revolution* (Philadelphia: Temple University Press, 1988).

17. Ray, *Wisdom of God*, 1:155.

18. See the textual background on the voyage journal in *Papers*, 1:72.

19. Mitchell Breitwieser confirms the figurative richness of the voyage journal, though he treats it as an allegory of the dark *aporiae* in Franklin's consciousness. See Breitwieser, *Cotton Mather and Benjamin Franklin: The Price of Representative Personality* (London: Cambridge University Press, 1984), 302–5.

20. *Diary of Samuel Sewall*, 2:960.

21. Daniel Defoe, *A Tour through the Whole Island of England and Scotland* (1724–26), abridged and edited by Pat Rogers (New York: Viking-Penguin, 1971), 1:52–53.

22. *Poor Robin*, July 1691.

23. Ray, *Wisdom of God*, 2:84.

24. Marcus Rediker observes that the years between 1725 and 1737 appear to have been one of the most repressive periods of nautical discipline in the history of the British merchant fleet, a fact that Franklin's voyage seems partly to reflect. See Rediker, *Between the Devil and the Deep Blue Sea* (Cambridge: Cambridge University Press, 1987), 205–14.

25. Keimer's original announcement of the *Gazette*'s purposes (October 1, 1728) is a study in presumption, promising to print "the most compleat Body of History and Philosophy ever yet published since the Creation." Franklin's aims seem modest by comparison.

26. See the account of the Royal Society's early history in Marie Boas Hall, *Promoting Experimental Learning: Experiment and the Royal Society, 1660–1727* (Cambridge: Cambridge University Press, 1991).

27. Cohen, *Benjamin Franklin's Experiments*, 166. I cite this invaluable edition hereafter in the body of the chapter. I. Bernard Cohen treats Franklin's science more fully in *Franklin and Newton* (Philadelphia: American Philosophical Society, 1956).

28. J. L. Heilbron notes the analogy between Franklin's principle of conservation of charge in electricity and the reciprocal relationship of pleasure and pain in Franklin's *Dissertation on Liberty and Necessity* (1725), but he does not extend what Franklin calls the electrical plenum to the metaphysical one. See Heilbron, *Elements of Early Modern Physics* (Berkeley: University of California Press, 1982), 187–95. Heilbron develops some of Franklin's analogical habits of thought further in "Franklin as an Enlightened Natural Philosopher," in Lemay, *Reappraising Benjamin Franklin*, 196–220.

29. Eighteenth-century audiences particularly enjoyed seeing versions of this demonstration performed by traveling exhibitors. See Cohen, *Franklin and Newton*, 462n.

30. Jonathan Edwards, *Some Thoughts Concerning the Present Revival of Relig-*

ion in New England (1742), in *The Great Awakening,* vol. 4 of *The Works of Jonathan Edwards,* ed. C. C. Goen (New Haven: Yale University Press, 1972), 298–301.

31. Jonathan Edwards, "Sinners in the Hands of an Angry God," in *The Norton Anthology of American Literature,* 4th ed. (New York: Norton, 1994), 1:417–18.

32. In Cohen, *Experiments and Observations,* 406, an advertising bill for one of Ebenezer Kinnersley's electricity lectures is reproduced. It indicates that Kinnersley took the artificial spider on tour, much like an itinerant revivalist.

33. Franklin discerns the operations of electricity throughout the "whole economy of nature." See Cohen, *Franklin and Newton,* 287.

34. For a summary of what we know of the beginnings of Franklin's experimental work, including the nature of his first laboratory apparatus, see I. Bernard Cohen, *Benjamin Franklin's Science* (Cambridge: Harvard University Press, 1990), 40–60.

CHAPTER FIVE: A VAST DEMAND, A GLORIOUS MARKET

1. The textual history of "Observations Concerning the Increase of Mankind" is summarized in the introductory note prepared by the editors of the *Papers* 4:225–26.

2. On Collinson's advocacy for the rights of Indians, see Fothergill's early memoir of Collinson's life in *The Works of John Fothergill* (London, 1784), 415–23. The texts Fothergill cites are letters from Collinson to John Bartram, a member of the American Philosophical Society and a contributor to *Poor Richard's Almanac,* that take issue with Bartram's antagonistic attitude toward Indians. Late in his life, Collinson drafted "A Plan for a Lasting Peace with the Indians," conciliatory proposals for adjusting the relations between the colonies and the native tribes, which he published in the September 1763 *Gentleman's Magazine.* These aspects of Collinson's career are summarized in the only modern biography of Collinson: Norman G. Brett-James, *The Life of Peter Collinson* (London: Dunstan, 1925).

3. Paul W. Connor discerns the revolutionary implications of the "Observations" in his thoughtful discussion of the text, but he persists in associating Franklin's position with a policy of racist exclusion. See Connor, *Poor Richard's Politicks: Benjamin Franklin and His New American Order* (New York: Oxford University Press, 1965), 69–87.

4. The editors of the *Papers* identify Carl Van Doren as the source of the connection between Franklin's 1751 "Observations" and the Iron Act of 1750. See Van Doren, *Benjamin Franklin* (New York: Viking, 1937), 216–18.

5. Abraham Trembley, a French naturalist, published a celebrated account of the regenerative powers of the polyp in 1744, arguing that the organism was a biological bridge between animals and plants. Franklin's allusion in the almanac a few years later exploits this contemporary interest. On the vogue of "Trembley's

polyp," see Cohen, *Science and the Founding Fathers,* 49–53; and Sambrook, *Eighteenth Century,* 24.

6. *Selected Poetry and Prose of Daniel Defoe,* ed. Michael F. Shugrue (New York: Holt, Rinehart, Winston, 1968), 52–53.

7. John Milton, *Paradise Lost,* ed. Merritt Y. Hughes (Indianapolis: Bobbs-Merrill, 1962), bk. 9, 568–83.

8. Ibid., bk. 12, 87–88.

9. Polly Baker's wonderful combination of physical vigor and metaphysical confidence makes her the perfect tutelary spirit for Franklin's prolific garden, but for an account of what LeMay considers the pessimism and despair in Polly Baker's speech, see *Oldest Revolutionary,* 91–120. In addition to its associations with human jealousy, fennel was also the tinder that Prometheus used to steal fire from the gods. See Francis Bacon's well-known interpretation of the Prometheus story in *De Sapientia Veterum* (1609), translated and reprinted many times throughout the seventeenth and eighteenth centuries. Franklin clearly hopes his reader will share his appreciation for the volatile subject matter.

10. Connor, *Poor Richard's Politicks,* 75–77, is representative of the scholars who find Franklin committed to cultural homogeneity.

11. On the prestige of the Dutch as an example of successful economic policy, see Joyce O. Appleby, *Economic Thought and Ideology in Seventeenth-Century England* (Princeton: Princeton University Press, 1978), 73–98.

12. Trenchard and Gordon, *Cato's Letters,* 4:3–12.

13. Appleby, *Economic Thought and Ideology,* 248.

14. In their review of Franklin's economic thought, Tracy Mott and George W. Zinke name Petty among Franklin's influences but devote most of their attention to Franklin's impact on Marx—who observed that Franklin built directly on Petty's treatises. See Mott and Zinke, "Benjamin Franklin's Economic Thought: A 20th-Century Appraisal," in Buxbaum, *Critical Essays on Benjamin Franklin,* 111–27.

15. *The Economic Writings of Sir William Petty,* ed. Charles Henry Hull (1899; New York: Augustus M. Kelley Reprints of Economic Classics, 1963), 1:285.

16. Ibid., 1:201–3.

17. Ibid., 1:113.

18. Ibid., 1:119.

19. Appleby notes that Francis Bacon preceded Petty in the desire to restrict the numbers of "unproductive" workers: clergy, lawyers, and beggars. See Appleby, *Economic Thought and Ideology,* 133. For Petty's disparaging account of the clergy, see his *Economic Writings,* 1:72–73.

20. Petty, *Economic Writings,* 1:28–29.

21. Anthony A. Wood, *Athenae Oxonienses: An Exact History of All The Writers and Bishops who have had their Education in the University of Oxford,* reprinted from the 1721 edition (New York: Johnson Reprint Corporation, 1967), 4:214–20.

The 1721 edition was in the collection of the Library Company of Philadelphia by 1741 (see appendix). The best modern biography of Petty is E. Strauss, *Sir William Petty, Portrait of a Genius* (London: Bodley Head, 1954).

22. These features of Petty's remarkable life—his familiarity with the harsh existence of the common sailor in particular—can be used to temper Rediker's view of Petty as a cold, aristocratic foil to Edward Barlow, Rediker's representative of exploited seamen. Petty understood their plight, a fact that Rediker misses in his otherwise fine book, *Between the Devil and the Deep Blue Sea,* 10–76.

23. Wills, *Inventing America,* 132–48.

24. In Jefferson's "Query XIV" on "Laws," he speculates that an inclusive system of public education through the most basic levels of instruction might be the best means of raking "twenty of the best geniuses . . . from the rubbish annually," an idea similar to—but much less charitable than—Petty's speculation that one in twenty of the state's publicly educated orphans might prove exemplary servants of the king.

25. Franklin's key sources—Milton, Locke, Fordyce, Walker, Rollin, and Turnbull—are identified in *Papers* 3:397–98. James Axtell provides a thorough account of seventeenth-century English writing on education in his introduction to *The Educational Writings of John Locke* (Cambridge: Cambridge University Press, 1968). In Axtell's account, Locke supplants Walker as the most popular educational guide in the early decades of the eighteenth century. William Petty left manuscript instructions for the education of his children, which (Axtell speculates) may have had some indirect influence on Locke.

26. Franklin's "Observations Relative to the Intentions of the Original Founders of the Academy in Philadelphia" (June 1789) indicates this tuition fee. See *The Complete Works of Benjamin Franklin,* ed. John Bigelow (New York, 1888), 10:86–115.

27. Charles Rollin, *The Method of Studying and Teaching the Belles Lettres* (London, 1758), 4:234.

28. See "Observations Relative to the Intentions" for Franklin's complaint about the growing partiality of the Academy's trustees for the Latin course of instruction rather than for Franklin's preference, the English school.

29. Algernon Sidney, *Discourses Concerning Government,* 2 vols. (Philadelphia, 1805). Bernard Bailyn, Henry F. May, and Edmund Morgan all confirm the pervasive influence of Sidney's work on the revolutionary politics of eighteenth-century America. See, for example, Bernard Bailyn, *The Ideological Origins of the American Revolution* (Cambridge: Belknap, 1967), 34–35.

30. See the letter for June 15, 1723, which appeared several weeks after Mandeville published the 1723 edition of *The Fable,* in Trenchard and Gordon, *Cato's Letters,* 4:236–46.

31. Jonathan Scott, *Algernon Sidney and the English Republic, 1623–1677* (Cambridge: Cambridge University Press, 1988), 13.

32. Sidney, *Discourses Concerning Government,* 2:319.

33. [James Ralph], *Of the Use and Abuse of Parliaments in Two Historical Discourses* (London, 1744), 1:18. Sidney's "General View" is at 1:1–78.

34. The engraving of the "Magic Circle of Circles" that Franklin sent to Collinson appears in the 1769 edition of Franklin, *Experiments and Observations on Electricity.* Along with Franklin's whimsical title for his puzzle, the drawing itself suggests his awareness of the long tradition of hermetic iconography associated with Masonic practice and astrology. A number of Giordano Bruno's magic circles from the late sixteenth century are strikingly similar to Franklin's drawing. The *Monas Hieroglyphica* of John Dee is sometimes reproduced as a fusion of the astrological sign for Mercury with a diagram of concentric circles representing the solar system. See, for example, the illustrations reproduced by Frances Yates, *Giordano Bruno and the Hermetic Tradition* (Chicago: University of Chicago Press, 1964), 306–10, 339. Almanacs routinely dealt in simple versions of astronomical iconography. Franklin was clearly aware of all these dimensions of meaning when he sent his sketch to Collinson.

CHAPTER SIX: PLANS OF UNION

1. In Franklin's sale catalogue, Locke's *Letters Concerning Toleration* is item 107. See Benjamin Franklin, *A Catalogue of Choice and Valuable Books* (Philadelphia, 1744).

2. Locke, *Works,*, 6:35.

3. This linking of Rome and Israel in *Plain Truth* is Franklin's rhetorical variation on a pervasive contrast in eighteenth-century historiography, the distinction between "Hebrews and Hellenes" that Peter Gay describes in *The Rise of Modern Paganism,* vol. 1 of *The Enlightenment: An Interpretation,* (1966; New York: Norton, 1977), 31–71.

4. See the editor's introduction to *Plain Truth* in *Papers,* 3:180–88, as well as the account of Franklin's role in the Association in Sally F. Griffith, "Order, Discipline, and a few Cannon: Benjamin Franklin, the Association, and the Rhetoric and Practice of Boosterism," *Pennsylvania Magazine of History and Biography* 116 (1992): 131–55.

5. Gary B. Nash, *The Urban Crucible: Social Change, Political Consciousness, and the Origins of the American Revolution* (Cambridge: Harvard University Press, 1979), 229–32.

6. Sallust, *Catiline's Conspiracy,* in *The Works of Sallust* trans. Arthur Murphy (London, 1807), 84–92. Murphy was an actor, playwright, and man-of-letters in eighteenth-century London, an early editor and biographer of Henry Fielding, and an associate of Samuel Johnson. His translation—though it appears nearly twenty years after Franklin's death—is in the idiom that characterizes translations of Franklin's day.

7. Thomas Gordon praises Sidney's heroism and quotes extensively from his

book ("It makes us some Amends for the Loss of *Cicero's* Books *de Republica*") in letter 26, published on April 22, 1721, but by July 15, in letter 37, he seeks to dissociate himself from the label "Republican." See Trenchard and Gordon, *Cato's Letters,* 1:195–96 and 2:28.

8. See Nash, *Urban Crucible,* 229–32.

9. Robert L. D. Davidson, *War Comes to Quaker Pennsylvania, 1682–1756* (New York: Columbia University Press, 1957), 62.

10. The article in the *Gazette* appeared on December 3, 1747.

11. Sallust, *Catiline's Conspiracy,* 8–9.

12. Ibid., 3.

13. Ibid., 3–4.

14. Samuel Smith, *Necessary Truth or Seasonable Considerations* (Philadelphia, 1748), 10.

15. The most familiar use of Charles's career as moral exemplum is from Samuel Johnson, *The Vanity of Human Wishes,* ll. 191–222:

On what foundation stands the warrior's pride,
How just his hopes let Swedish Charles decide.

But Franklin knew, as well, Voltaire's *History of Charles XII, King of Sweden* (1731; trans. 1734) and may have read Defoe's account of the Swedish wars upon which Voltaire partly bases his book.

16. Garry Wills' account of Washington's pattern of strategic resignation—securing power by resigning it—suggests that Franklin's omission of his role in Braddock's expedition is curiously consistent with Washington's tactically self-effacing practice. See Wills, *Cincinnatus: George Washington and the Enlightenment* (New York: Doubleday, 1984). George Bancroft's *History of the United States of America,* which began appearing in 1834, suggests the light in which Washington's heroic conduct and "providential" survival at Braddock's defeat came to be viewed. See Bancroft, *History of the United States of America* (1885; Port Washington, N.Y.: Kennikat, 1967), 2:423–24.

17. Esmond Wright observes that the secondary literature on the Albany Plan is voluminous, but I have not found it to be so, at least in the forty years since the publication of Robert Newbold, *The Albany Congress and Plan of Union of 1754* (New York: Vantage, 1955). Lawrence H. Gipson touched off a scholarly controversy on the authorship of the plan, which does not bear directly on the design and significance of the plan itself. A number of historians of eighteenth-century Anglo-American politics (Jack P. Greene, Michael Kammen, Patricia Bonomi, Edmund Morgan, Alison Olson) touch on the plan briefly in various books but devote very little attention to specific features of its text. Even a recent, richly detailed account of Euro-Indian relations during this period, Richard White, *The Middle Ground: Indians, Empires, and Republics in the Great Lakes Region, 1650–1815* (Cambridge: Cambridge University Press, 1991), mentions the plan only in

passing. The reason that some of the most active and fertile historical minds in recent years have not given much thought to the plan may be that it was never accepted by the colonies or by the English government. From a historical point of view, it seems a dead letter.

18. Paul Connor's dismissive account of the Albany Plan as a "blueprint for a cultural invasion" does not take into account the implications of this remarkably swift repudiation of Franklin's design by the colonies. Presumably, if the plan were indeed such a blueprint, the colonial assemblies at least would have embraced it. See Connor, *Poor Richard's Politicks,* 88–95. A number of factors other than direct disapproval played roles in the plan's repudiation. Alison G. Olson points out in *Making the Empire Work: London and American Interest Groups, 1690–1790* (Cambridge: Harvard University Press, 1992) that 1754 marks the end of a thirty-year period of influence enjoyed by "American" interests in the British government. Henry Pelham's death in that year brought to a close the Walpole-Pelham-Newcastle "triumverate," which lent stability to the conduct of colonial policy for over three decades. Pelham and Walpole headed the English ministry for all but a handful of those years. In the eight years following 1754, four different ministries held power in London. The proposals of the Albany congress came before the Board of Trade during this period of comparative turmoil in English leadership. See also Alison G. Olson, "The British Government and Colonial Union, 1754," *William and Mary Quarterly* 17 (1960): 22–34. On the response of provincial assemblies to the plan, see John V. Jezierski, "*Imperii in Imperio:* The 1754 Albany Plan of Union and the Origins of the American Revolution," *NDQ: North Dakota Quarterly* 42 (1974): 18–35.

19. The actual request to serve as Pennsylvania's colonial commissioner and representative in London did not come until January 28, 1757.

20. As he does with much of the poetry that he quotes in the almanac, Franklin alters Stillingfleet's lines to minimize the presence of destructive passions. Stillingfleet's more ominous "Watch well the rage of shining to subdue" becomes "The Pride of shewing forth yourself subdue." See J. Dodsley, *A Collection of Poems in Six Volumes by Several Hands* (London, 1766), 1.298–321.

21. This skepticism about the efficacy of individual human action is part of Franklin's wider participation in the humanist ethos of the early eighteenth century. See Fussell, *Rhetorical World of Augustan Humanism.*

22. The image of the wasp's nest as a figure for the world may have come to Franklin from Francis Quarles's *Emblems,* an edition of which was included among the books that Franklin advertised for sale from his print shop in 1744. Quarles illustrates Proverbs 14:13 with a picture of two cherubic children surrounded by a cloud of insects, which have emerged from the emblematic "globe" that Quarles associates with the deceptions of earthly life. The verse accompanying the picture reads:

Alas fond Child
How are thy thoughts beguil'd
To hope for honey from a nest of wasps?

The world's a hive
From whence thou can'st derive
No good

Proverbs 14:13 reads: "Even in laughter the heart is sad, and the end of joy is grief." See Quarles, *Emblems* (London, 1696), bk. 1:12–13.

APPENDIX: LIBRARIES, CATALOGUES, AND BOOKLISTS

1. Edwin Wolfe, "The Reconstruction of Benjamin Franklin's Library," in *Papers of the Bibliographicv Society of America* 56 (1962): 1–16; Wolfe, "Franklin's Library," in Lemay, *Reappraising Benjamin Franklin: A Bicentennial Perspective.*

2. Edwin Wolfe, "Franklin and His Friends Choose Their Books," *Pennsylvania Magazine of History and Biography* 80 (1956): 11–36.

Index

BOOKS IN THE SERIES

LIBRARY OF CONGRESS CATALOGING-IN-PUBLICATION DATA

Anderson, Douglas, 1950–

The radical enlightenments of Benjamin Franklin / Douglas Anderson.

    p.   cm.— (New studies in American intellectual and cultural history)
Includes bibliographical references and index.

   ISBN 0-8018-5445-8 (alk. paper)

   1. Franklin, Benjamin, 1706–1790—Knowledge and learning.
I. Title.   II. Series.

E302.6.F8A57   1997   96-33236
973.3´092—dc20   CIP